MW01492670

# Speculative Grammatology

Deconstruction and the New Materialism

Deborah Goldgaber

EDINBURGH
University Press

Edinburgh University Press is one of the leading university presses in the UK. We publish academic books and journals in our selected subject areas across the humanities and social sciences, combining cutting-edge scholarship with high editorial and production values to produce academic works of lasting importance. For more information visit our website: edinburghuniversitypress. com

© Deborah Goldgaber, 2021

Edinburgh University Press Ltd
The Tun – Holyrood Road
12(2f) Jackson's Entry
Edinburgh EH8 8PJ

Typeset in 11/13 Adobe Sabon by
Servis Filmsetting Ltd, Stockport, Cheshire

A CIP record for this book is available from the British Library

ISBN 978 1 4744 3833 9 (hardback)
ISBN 978 1 4744 3835 3 (webready PDF)
ISBN 978 1 4744 3834 6 (paperback)
ISBN 978 1 4744 3836 0 (epub)

# Contents

# Series Editor's Preface

Deborah Goldgaber's reputation as an original interpreter of Derrida far predates the publication of this book. What makes *Speculative Grammatology* different from other existing works on Derrida is its portrayal of that polarising Frenchman as a speculative philosopher who dances secretly to a realist tune. While it is true that other commentators have tried to depict Derrida as a realist, this has usually amounted to little more than a 'realism of the residue' in which every act of speech or writing is haunted by a trace of irrecuperable otherness. Goldgaber goes much further, pushing her treatment of textuality towards the realm of lower animals and even the inorganic. From this alone, the reason for including Goldgaber's book in a series on Speculative Realism (SR) should be clear.

As a committed though unorthodox Derridean, Goldgaber offers an olive branch to the original Speculative Realists, none of whom were ever great fans of Derrida. The Derridean critique of presence, she argues, covers much the same ground as the SR critique of correlationism. For both, the purported coincidence of thought and being is an illusion or fetish, so that SR should seek alliance with such Derridean terms as 'text', 'trace', 'spacing' and 'arche-writing', which Goldgaber frames in ways that make an alliance seem strangely inviting. She also concedes that there are very good reasons why both friends and opponents of Derrida have always found him to be *obviously* anti-realist and anti-materialist in spirit. Even so, Goldgaber is more aware than most of the difference between Speculative Realism and New Materialism: a difference often suppressed even by critics as keen-eyed as Slavoj Žižek and his circle.[1]

---

[1] See Russell Sbriglia and Slavoj Žižek (eds), *Subject Lessons: Hegel, Lacan, and the*

Chapter 1, 'Materialism and Realism in Contemporary Continental Philosophy', introduces a number of contemporary authors with whom Goldgaber is engaged in serious internal dialogue, especially Karen Barad, Claire Colebrook and Cary Wolfe. There is a separate dialogue here with me and Levi R. Bryant. Goldgaber expresses agreement with us that twentieth-century critiques of the 'Cartesian subject' – by the likes of Michel Foucault – failed to get to the root of the problem, since the ostensibly post-Cartesian landscape still left human beings at the centre of the picture. Stated differently, Goldgaber is not playing the tired old game of critiquing 'humanism' while doing nothing to displace humans from their philosophical throne. Derrida, she assures us, is a critic of *correlationism* rather than realism, and thus deserves to be counted as a Speculative Realist *avant la lettre*. She builds a basis for this case with several crucial citations from Derrida in which he overtly opposes the idea of the 'linguistic turn'.

In Chapter 2, we are first treated to a new approach to Quentin Meillassoux's problem of the arche-fossil.[2] While it is often wrongly assumed that Meillassoux thinks that he *refutes* correlationism by appeal to the 'ancestrality' of the universe prior to the existence of all consciousness, Goldgaber notes the explicit similarities between Meillassoux and the correlationist. Above all, they assume that *direct* evidence is the only kind there is, despite the crucial difference that Meillassoux is troubled by the consequences for science. What Goldgaber seeks instead is *absolute* rather than direct evidence, meaning a kind of evidence independent of all transcendental activity: this, she holds, is exactly what Derrida provides. Written texts cannot be correlated with a subject, and are 'structurally readable' apart from humans. This leads her to an original account of Derridean 'iterability' as referring not just to repeatability, but to a heterogeneity implicit in all repetition. This heterogeneity is interpreted further as a form of parasitism, in which the mark is not identical with itself because it always hosts another mark that structures it. While some of the Derridean terminology will seem familiar, the realist uses to which Goldgaber puts it are not.

*Future of Materialism* (Evanston: Northwestern University Press, 2020). Although most of the chapters in this collection exaggerate the similarities between Speculative Realism and New Materialism, it is still an invaluable resource.

2  Quentin Meillassoux, *After Finitude: Essay on the Necessity of Contingency*, trans. R. Brassier (London: Continuum, 2008).

In Chapter 3, Goldgaber argues that Derrida is an eliminativist with respect to meaning, which he replaces with the notion of translatability. In this he is influenced by Walter Benjamin's idea of 'translation beyond the human'. While Derrida wants to preserve both signifier and signified as two separate terms, they are not taxonomical opposites, as if one thing were merely a sign and that at which it pointed were a pure terminus of self-evident meaning. Instead, translatability means that any supposed meaning is itself just another text, with one text always modifiable by another in what Goldgaber calls an 'exchange of form'. Thought itself is just another form of translation; nothing survives without mutating.

Chapter 4 turns to Derrida's enigmatic concept of 'arche-writing', as defined in *Of Grammatology*'s second chapter.[3] Despite more than fifty years of scholarly attention, there is no consensus interpretation of this term, nor even of 'trace', as J. Hillis Miller observes.[4] Goldgaber reads arche-writing as concerning the ubiquitous entanglement of inside and outside for Derrida, and links this with Karen Barad's important book *Meeting the Universe Halfway*.[5] This reader wonders, however, whether Goldgaber and Barad are really natural allies on the question of entanglement; much like Niels Bohr, Barad holds that entanglement requires the mind as one of its terms, which is precisely what Goldgaber rejects in her efforts to help Derrida escape the transcendental thought–world relation. This is also the chapter where Goldgaber gives us a close reading of the linguistics of Ferdinand de Saussure, with further attention to the theories of Roman Jakobson and Wilhelm von Humboldt.

But the real fireworks are reserved for Chapter 5, which concludes the book. Referring to the Derridean trace as 'ultra-transcendental', Goldgaber soon makes clear that by 'ultra-' she does not mean *very much* transcendental, but *beyond* transcendental. Far from claiming all the credit for this insight, she salutes allies on all sides: just as Barad carries the Derridean trace structure down to the quantum level, as does Wolfe for systems theory, so too does Martin Hägglund account for evolu-

---

[3] Jacques Derrida, *Of Grammatology*, trans. G. Spivak (Baltimore: Johns Hopkins University Press, 1997).

[4] J. Hillis Miller, *Reading Derrida's* Of Grammatology (London: Continuum, 2011), pp. 47–51.

[5] Karen Barad, *Meeting the Universe Halfway: Quantum Physics and the Entanglement of Matter and Meaning* (Durham, NC: Duke University Press, 2007).

tionary processes in Derridean terms. But not everyone is an ally: Bernard Stiegler remains suspicious of any Derrida-of-the-outside-world, and Goldgaber specifically takes issue with his approach. Given the generality of the trace structure, absolutely *everything* can be considered as a form of memory. But here an important difference between Goldgaber and Object-Oriented Ontology (OOO) also comes to light. In agreement with Colebrook, she holds that deconstructive materialism can have nothing to do with substances or objects, since neither of these concepts rises to the challenge of the *plasticity* of the trace. And speaking of plasticity, who better to consult on this term than Catherine Malabou? The final pages of the book essentially give us Goldgaber's running inner debate with Malabou. While the two authors agree on philosophical essentials, Goldgaber generally defends Derrida on those points where Malabou thinks he falls short. More specifically, whereas Malabou thinks that 'writing' remains trapped in the old opposition of matter and form, Goldgaber argues the contrary. And while Malabou asserts that her idea of the 'plastic coding of experience' is non-grammatological because it is non-graphic, Goldgaber sees no graphic restriction in general grammatology.

Quite aside from the details of her argument, Goldgaber brings the interpretation of Derrida to a place that would have been unthinkable in the 1980s and 1990s, when the application of grammatology to the level of worms and stones could only have invited ridicule. She is also unique in the challenge she poses to Derrideans. In recent years, those who have claimed that 'Derrida was really a realist all along' have too often done so with the pretence that this had always been obvious, as if recent materialists and realists were Johnny-come-latelies and plagiarists in no position to ask questions of their elders. Goldgaber's take is more honest: while acknowledging the anti-realist baggage of Derrida scholarship, she offers a powerful demonstration of the possible realism lurking beneath the surface of his work. She has already changed my mind on a number of crucial points.

Graham Harman
Long Beach, California
March 2020

# Acknowledgements

This project received generous funding from ATLAS, a program of the Louisiana Board of Regents, and from LSU's Office of Research and Development (ORED). Without this material support, writing this book would have been a great deal more difficult than it was.

This book is the result of very many years of thinking about (and with) Derrida, about the philosophical significance of the grammatological project and the connection between the various accounts of the trace found in the three books published in 1967: *Speech and Phenomena*, *Writing and Difference* and *Of Grammatology*. This obsessive engagement with a few texts – and with a few of the readers of these same texts – cannot be justified by any utilitarian calculus. I cannot say whether the results of this reading constitute philosophical progress, but I do believe that the text 'reactivates' some neglected possibilities of these founding texts of deconstruction. It is my sincere hope that others will benefit from the arguments and perspective presented in this book and that it will contribute to the *sur-vival* of grammatology and Derrida's work, and the inexhaustible richness of French philosophy in the 1960s.

I would like to acknowledge the support of colleagues, friends and editors whose comments, advice and encouragement have substantially benefited this book. First, I would like to thank Carol Macdonald at Edinburgh University Press, for encouraging the project from the start and for her patience with me as I developed and revised it, and then revised it again; Graham Harman, editor of the Speculative Realism series at Edinburgh University Press, for his comments on the manuscript, support for the project and whose series provided the impetus for framing the story of speculative grammatology in terms of speculative realism; Jon Cogburn, my excellent philosophy comrade at LSU, for encouragement, for many hours of interesting philosophical discussion, and for suggesting I place the project in the Speculative Realism series. Many thanks to Virgil Brower for critically reading parts of the manuscript and responding with so much care and insight.

Finally, I am immensely grateful that Thomas Adams was *Speculative Grammatology*'s first reader and friend. Immeasurable gratitude is due for his intellectual fortitude, thoughtful comments, incisive questions and copious edits – including all those made over many days of what was supposed to be a vacation. Thanks to him, I have much greater confidence in the soundness and force of this book's arguments. Thanks to his companionship and support, I am much sounder of mind and body than I otherwise would have been.

I would like, finally, to remark my debt and gratitude to Penelope Deutscher and Samuel Weber who taught me so much about how to read Derrida. Any failures in this regard are entirely my own. This book is dedicated to my maternal grandparents, Robert and Larissa Reider, who first taught me about *sur-vival*.

# Preface:
# The (Un-)Timeliness of Grammatology

This is not a book about Jacques Derrida, the author of *Of Grammatology*. It *is* a book about *grammatology*, the proposed science of general writing, and about the productivity and prospects of doing grammatology today. Though grammatology is usually and even exclusively identified with Derrida, the latter kept his distance from the project and its fate. Despite some hedging, Derrida did, however, insist that the science of general writing had every right to exist; its status assured by the changing conceptions of writing ushered in by structuralism, genetics, computing and cybernetics.[1] Writing, no longer 'the substantial double of the signifier', no longer a 'technics in the service of language' comes even to '*comprehend* language' – and go beyond it.[2]

Writing now refers not only to representation and 'the system of notation secondarily connected with activities ['which give rise to an inscription'], but to the essence and the content of these activities themselves'. Not just cartog*raphy* and cinematog*raphy*, then, but genetic codes and 'the entire field covered by the cybernetic "program"' (OG, 10). As Jacques Lacan noted, cybernetics promised, for the first time, to give an account of the *autonomy* of

---

[1] It is, of course, true that Derrida insisted that, because of its absolute generality, arche-writing could not be situated as an *object* in a positive field. As the general condition (of everything?) and therefore of science, arche-writing could not itself be a science. It is worth noting, however, that this conception of arche-writing results from the deconstructive critique of an existing grammatological discourse that already treats writing as a scientific object. Therefore, while its limits as a science may be established speculatively, these limits do not forbid the development of grammatology. Indeed, Derrida suggests that the project ought to be pursued (perhaps under the auspices of 'cybernetics', whose notion of the 'program' is 'the field of writing', or through another such metatheoretic discourse) until *its* (metaphysical) limitations are revealed.

[2] Derrida (1997: 6–9). Subsequent references to *Of Grammatology* are cited parenthetically in the text as OG with page number.

symbolic processes, free from intentional, conscious control.[3] To justify this 'inflation' of writing, to give it a firm foundation, grammatology must first 'liberate' writing from its narrow, subordinate designations in the fields of general linguistics and semiology.

If grammatology – at least in this positive, if not positivist, conception – and deconstruction should not be conflated, what, then, is their relation? Grammatology is inherently deconstructive because it seeks to *generalise* writing. A concept of general (as opposed to narrow) writing cannot exist without first deconstructing the oppositions which prohibit its appearance. 'Writing' is derivative, secondary, technical prosthesis, representational, a sign of the sign; its essential secondariness is opposed to forms of 'presence' broadly construed (objects, speech, consciousness, world). To generalise and prioritise writing is to stand our traditional and folk metaphysics on its head. The difficulty of executing the grammatological project is commensurate with the speculative intuitions motivating it – namely that technology and biology, culture and nature, humans and machines 'run' on the same logic or 'program', share the same 'arche-' conditions.

Despite its apparent theoretical promise, and whatever impetus the appearance of *Of Grammatology* may have given it, grammatology, as Catherine Malabou notes, never saw the light of day.

> One must acknowledge that ... grammatology has never 'entered upon the assured path of a science.' It has in fact never been constituted as a 'discipline.' Neither in a general way – it has never become a region of full-fledged knowledge – nor in some particular manner in Derrida's oeuvre. In his lifework, in fact, the grammatological project is not found outside of *Of Grammatology*. Grammatology as a positive science is nowhere else a question in the writing of Derrida ... The word itself is no longer used by the later Derrida except to recall the work of 1967. Why, then, does grammatology disappear from the moment of its appearance?[4]

The failure of grammatology to develop as a metatheoretic, speculative project along the lines of cybernetics cannot be due to Derrida's failure to pursue it beyond 1967. But how then should we explain this failure, given deconstruction's relative success –

---

[3] Franklin (2015: 66).
[4] Malabou (2007a: 433).

and the relative popularity of *Of Grammatology*? Did grammatology fail for essential (philosophical) reasons? Did it yield, in the end, the wrong conception of general writing? Or, as Malabou argues, did it fail to produce a truly *general* concept of writing?

Malabou claims that Derrida's conception of general writing is a reduction of *différance*. The limits of grammatology correspond to the limits of the inscriptive metaphor. The 'image' of writing is too graphic to be of much use in accounting for material processes. General writing could not inform, illuminate or offer itself as a scientific programme because any conceptual work it could do had already been done. Writing could not really be generalised; what permitted its generalisation up to a certain point limited it to the idea of a linear, aplastic code or program. Grammatology was 'programmed' to fail by the inflexibility of its founding image – that of scriptural or inscriptive writing.

Insofar as *Of Grammatology* succeeded in justifying the expansion of 'writing' in the *air du temps*, Malabou argues, it added nothing new to the notion of writing – only making explicit what was implicit in a great many discourses of its day. Its *a priori* limits were evidenced by the subsequent developments of scientific discourses incorporating materialist and epigenetic principles of development, chief among them plasticity and self-modification. The owl of Minerva flies at dusk, but Derrida did not know it. The fecundity of writing and the metaphors of inscription had dried up. Derrida's retreat from and disavowal of some of his apparently audacious claims (in *Of Grammatology*) are, Malabou suggests, less from philosophical conviction than disappointment. *Of Grammatology* came too late; a text with no progeny and pregnant with no futures.

But perhaps *Of Grammatology* was untimely in another sense. While it is true that Derrida does not appear to pursue the project of grammatology after the publication of *Of Grammatology*, he does not relinquish key grammatological terms such as writing, trace and *différance*. In later works, Derrida rearticulates the structure of the trace in his account of sur-vival (*sur-vivance*), which he relates explicitly to texts, textuality and translation.[5] Malabou overstates the extent to which Derrida – and scientific

---

[5] For an account of grammatological textuality as translatability, see Goldgaber (2018). On the relations of writing, sur-vival and translation, see especially Derrida (1981: 20; 1985) and Derrida and Venuti (2001).

discourse – closed the book on writing. Technical, scientific discourses have certainly not abandoned scriptural 'metaphors' – if metaphors they are. For example, scientists describe gene-editing technologies (e.g. CRISPR) in the very same terms used to describe editing texts – 'cutting and pasting', 'looking for typos'. Moreover, the alliance between the cybernetic notion of the program and the most general notion of the gramme indicates that general writing, from the beginning, was no longer graphic. In the original 'cybernetic' sense, which *Of Grammatology* remarks, programs do not refer to a linear, deterministic or 'transcendental' code, but to the idea of 'retro-action' (feedback) and selection.[6] Grammatological programs rewrite themselves or are rewritten, initial conditions are displaced in what Derrida calls the 'prosthesis of origin'. Arche-writing, then, does not refer to the 'engraving', 'breaching' and 'inscription' of differential marks or a linear script – as Malabou's argument assumes – but to the conditions for textual adaptation, selection and reformation. Perhaps, then, the time for grammatology has not yet gone; after some fifty years of errance, perhaps it may still arrive.

*Of Grammatology* came too late to inform *the* prominent grammatological discourse of its day, cybernetics. It was interpreted – soon after and wrongly – as underwriting a peculiar sort of linguistic idealism, rather than defending the generality of writing. But today – when and because the generality of writing seems to go without saying – grammatology may yet yield its most productive insights.

The entanglement of biology and technology, human and machine – as envisioned by cyberneticists – is no longer speculative. Our technical prostheses (from synthetic sex hormones to targeted gene 'edits') effectively deconstruct the boundary between nature, culture and *techne*. But *philosophically*, our thinking has hardly managed to attain to the insights of cyberneticists such as Norbert Weiner or geneticists such as François Jacob. And *Of Grammatology* was, arguably, in advance of both. It was in advance because it recognised that the speculative discourses relying on the explanatory power of code, information or

---

[6] Therefore, when, in *Of Grammatology*, Derrida offers a grammatological redescription of palaeontologist's Leroi-Gourhan's anthropogenesis, he states that the sort of dynamic interaction between human form and technical objects that the latter describes must be understood as a program in the 'cybernetic sense' (Derrida 1997: 83–6).

program – all images of writing – to explain parts of an unknown or unseen reality would remain limited by the *image* of *narrow* writing. In 1970 Jacob reflected on the inherent limitations of the linguistic-scriptural metaphor. 'Today the world is messages, codes and information. Tomorrow what analysis will break down our objects to reconstitute them in a new space?'[7] But in 1967, Derrida's diagnosis of the limitations of writing was importantly different: the issue was not the metaphor per se but the image of inscription at the root of cybernetic analyses. Thus, tomorrow's analyses would not relinquish writing, but rather 'break down' and 'reconstitute' – *deconstruct* – our conception of 'messages', 'codes' and 'information' in order to more effectively 'break down our objects'. Grammatology will take longer, and arrive later, than we might think.

Grammatology is inherently speculative, but this speculation does not consist in asking what *would be* true of something (unknown or less well known) if it were *like* writing. It consists in clarifying what 'writing' would have to be like if writing pertained not only to secondary processes of notation but also to 'first-order' processes, such as 'life itself'. This task is imposed by the historical inflation of writing.

What makes this speculative project (of rewriting our conception of writing) inherently deconstructive? Deconstruction refers, principally, and particularly in Derrida's early work, to the 'metaphysics of presence', the highly imbricated set of inherited conceptual oppositions that presuppose and protect the value of 'presence' (that is, the unity of subject and object in a present perception, the presence of an object in the living present of consciousness). The meaning of 'presence', here, is identical to what speculative realists today call correlationism. Derrida discovered, however, that writing occupies a particularly important position in this conceptual system. Relative to the forms of presence that would make it possible, writing is inessential, reducible and radically dependent. Anything that disturbs or contests this inferior designation will disturb the conceptual system that 'represses' writing.

As a speculative project that seeks the most general concept of the gramme, grammatology is inherently deconstructive. However, grammatology is not defined by deconstructive aims, but rather by speculative ones: to understand what writing must be like if it is

---

[7] Jacob (1973: 324).

at the origin of things; how systems of writing are organised and evolve and interrelate. The deconstructive work or potential of this project lies in generating a general concept of writing, arche-writing. However, the speculative pay-off of arche-writing lies not in ousting the metaphysical oppositions that prevented its construction, but rather in putting arche-writing to work.

Recently, Cary Wolfe has called for a 'reconstruction of deconstruction', a new alliance between deconstruction and post-humanist, new materialist and systems-theoretic approaches that will keep the latter from falling into the same 'Cartesian' traps that sank the first generation of systems theory, cybernetics.[8] Arche-writing, *différance*, trace are indispensable for such a reconstruction of the notion of systems and their relations. The name I propose for such a reconstructive project is *speculative grammatology*.

[8] Wolfe (2010: 26).

# Speculative Realism

Series Editor: Graham Harman

Editorial Advisory Board

Jane Bennett, Levi Bryant, Patricia Clough, Iain Hamilton Grant, Myra Hird, Adrian Johnston, Eileen A. Joy.

## Books available

*Onto-Cartography: An Ontology of Machines and Media*, Levi R. Bryant
*Form and Object: A Treatise on Things*, Tristan Garcia, translated by Mark Allan Ohm and Jon Cogburn
*Adventures in Transcendental Materialism: Dialogues with Contemporary Thinkers*, Adrian Johnston
*The End of Phenomenology: Metaphysics and the New Realism*, Tom Sparrow
*Fields of Sense: A New Realist Ontology*, Markus Gabriel
*Quentin Meillassoux: Philosophy in the Making* Second Edition, Graham Harman
*Assemblage Theory*, Manuel DeLanda
*Romantic Realities: Speculative Realism and British Romanticism*, Evan Gottlieb
*Garcian Meditations: The Dialectics of Persistence in* Form and Object, Jon Cogburn
*Speculative Realism and Science Fiction*, Brian Willems
*Speculative Empiricism: Revisiting Whitehead*, Didier Debaise, translated by Tomas Weber
*Letting Be Volume I: The Life Intense: A Modern Obsession*, Tristan Garcia, translated by Abigail RayAlexander, Christopher RayAlexander and Jon Cogburn
*Against Continuity: Gilles Deleuze's Speculative Realism*, Arjen Kleinherenbrink
*Speculative Grammatology: Deconstruction and the New Materialism*, Deborah Goldgaber
*Letting Be Volume II: We Ourselves: The Politics of Us*, Tristan Garcia, translated by Abigail RayAlexander, Christopher RayAlexander and Jon Cogburn

## Forthcoming books

*Letting Be Volume III: Let Be and Make Powerful*, Tristan Garcia, translated by Christopher RayAlexander, Abigail RayAlexander and Jon Cogburn
*After Quietism: Analytic Philosophies of Immanence and the New Metaphysics*, Jon Cogburn
*Infrastructure*, Graham Harman
*The External World*, Maurizio Ferraris, translated by Sarah De Sanctis
*Indexicalism: The Metaphysics of Paradox,* Hilan Bensusan
*New Ecological Realisms: Post-Apocalyptic Fiction and Contemporary Theory*, Monika Kaup

Visit the Speculative Realism website at: edinburghuniversitypress.com/series-speculative-realism.html

# Introduction:
## To Speculate – with Derrida

In the space of these introductory pages, I want to reflect on the title of this book – to make explicit some of the resonances between speculation and grammatology on the one hand, and speculation and materialism on the other – in order to clarify what makes the approach of this book distinctive from other interpretations of early Derrida and from other approaches to materialism in contemporary continental philosophy.

To many of Derrida's readers, a *speculative* approach to grammatology will sound suspect because it entails 'ontologising' grammatological terms such as *arche-writing*, *trace* or *text* in order to speculate on grammatological *nature*, grammatological *matter*. For many, such speculation is contrary to the vigilant, critical spirit of deconstruction. Deconstruction does not propose *revisions* to metaphysics; it *forecloses* metaphysics. From this perspective, treating arche-writing or the trace as 'things of this world' – inscribing them in realist discourses – would restore the totalising, identitarian and 'presentist' categories that deconstruction works so hard to undo.

And yet Derrida, unmistakably, courts such a 'realist' reading.

> I have never ceased to be surprised by critics who see my work as a declaration that there is nothing beyond language, that we are imprisoned in language; *it is, in fact, saying the exact opposite*. The critique of logocentrism is above else the search for the 'other' and 'the other of language'.[1]

Despite Derrida's repeated affirmation – in *Of Grammatology*, 'Différance' and any number of other texts – that *différance* and arche-writing describe absolutely general relations, readers have resisted (or not known how to affirm) the ontological radicalisation of writing. Instead, as Francisco Vitale observes, Derrida's readers have affirmed the 'ontological radicalization of *hermeneutics*'.[2] The relation between mind and world is the same as the relation between reader and book. Instead of entertaining the properly grammatological thought that matter *writes and reads*, Vicki Kirby writes, we insist, instead, that matter appears or manifests by making a certain kind of 'sign'.[3] What has made it easier to accept that 'writing' gives an account of how *we* (human knowers) are lodged in the world, and more difficult to accept that 'writing' describes relations between non-human 'knowers' and 'agents'?

To answer this question, we have first to make explicit a number of assumptions that work to secure the epistemic-hermeneutic interpretation of writing against the speculative-materialist one. The first we might call the *critical* assumption. Writing refers to the conditions of knowing, specifically the formation of our concepts. Knowing and being do not share the same conditions. Yet materialist readings of deconstruction seem (unaccountably) to extend the account of concepts (and how they are structured) to the extra-discursive world. This sort of leap or jump, as Claire Colebrook notes, *is* philosophically illicit. To those who hazard such arguments, she asks 'is there not a sleight of hand in passing from "Deconstruction demonstrates that *concepts* of a stable self-present nature necessarily deconstruct themselves" to "Deconstruction is a theory of nature as instability"?'[4] To be sure, there is. If writing is 'general' – if it accounts for knowing *and* being – this must be carefully elucidated.

The second (related) assumption underwriting the epistemic-hermeneutic limitation of writing we can call the *meta-cognition* assumption. It states that while we *can* know about knowing, we cannot know about being. We have better access to our thinking (and how it functions) than to the extra-discursive world this thinking purports to be about. If deconstruction reveals how our concepts are organised – or 'discursively constructed' – this must be because the textual structure of cognition (and the nature of textual operations, such as reading and writing) are also knowable – in a way that extra-discursive reality is not. If both *meta-cognition* and *critical* are right, then deconstruction is essentially a transcendental discourse, even if 'arche-writing' designates a critique that displaces the transcendental subject.

Karen Barad, however, has very persuasively argued that deconstruction should have made us *more* sceptical of the possibility of meta-cognition than the epistemic-hermeneutic interpretation suggests. Why think that we face epistemically fair conditions with respect to meta-cognising our concepts, but epistemically poor conditions when it is a matter of non-cognitive processes?[5] Indeed, wasn't the point of Derrida's 'critique of presence' to show, *contra* Husserl (among others), that we have no better insight into our purportedly first-personal 'lived experience', and into 'the invariable structures of consciousness', than we have into the invariable structures of matter?[6]

Barad's critique of what I call the meta-cognition assumption makes explicit that many of Derrida's interpreters have been willing to speculate – apparently *with* Derrida – about concept production, about the *general* conditions of thought and the nature of language. These will all be the effects of *différance*. However, they have been unwilling to speculate – apparently *against* Derrida – about the nature of worldly processes and relations. But now it seems that the deconstruction of presence requires that we give up speculating about the discursive construction of our concepts for the same reasons that we had to relinquish speculating about an extra-discursive reality. While undermining the epistemic-hermeneutic interpretation of general writing, Barad's critique does not seem to get us any closer to justifying grammatological speculations about matter.

The prohibition on speculation that seems to result from Barad's critique, however, only obtains if we read Derrida's critique of presence as voiding phenomenological or introspective 'evidence' altogether. If this were the case, reflecting on consciousness or lived experience would tell us nothing about its structure. Derrida's critique, however, assumes that phenomenological reflection upon experience tells us quite a lot. Indeed, he argues that experience has a trace structure on the basis of how it is *given*! But how can Derrida both rely upon and impugn phenomenological evidence? This question has puzzled a number of Derrida's most careful readers.[7] Answering it requires recognising that Derrida's critique of presence entails a strongly revisionist account of evidence. Whereas phenomenology and meta-cognition require that first-personal experience yields *apodictic* evidence, Derrida argues that such evidence is *non-apodictic*.

In 'Apodicticity of Absence', Thomas Seebohm notes that Derrida rightly critiques the early Husserl for having an overly strenuous definition of phenomenological evidence or givenness. Derrida calls this evidentiary ideal the ideal of presence. The ideal form of givenness (or phenomenological evidence) is that of a present, self-transparent perception. Seebohm argues, however, that the mature Husserl had a much more pliable definition of apodicticity, which could easily accommodate the sort of 'absences' that Derrida's analyses revealed. Apodictic evidence (or givenness) is just that which reveals 'in its own underlying structure *what* is in question'.[8] Thus, for example, though the immediate past, as 'retained' in and constitutive of present perception, is not present in the old, full-blooded sense, phenomenological reflection on experience still reveals the structure in question. Derrida refers to this structure of non-presence as 'the trace' or *différance*, but seems to derive it from the same evidentiary grounds as those from which Husserl derived his account of inner time consciousness. Indeed, where else but from the structure of inner time consciousness as it appears to consciousness could Derrida have got it? Thus, Seebohm concludes, Derrida's critique of Husserl's account of evidence remains a phenomenological critique on phenomenological grounds.

Seebohm's reading, however, misses a crucial aspect of Derrida's critique of apodicticity or phenomenological givenness. Derrida argues that while careful phenomenological descriptions reveal the trace structure, experience does *not* reveal 'in its own underlying structure *what* is in question'. The structure in question does not explain or give an account of itself and, therefore, experience is not apodictic in the phenomenological sense. But if this were so, how could Derrida say, of experience, that it has (evidences) a trace structure? The answer, quite simply, is that experience is a non-apodictic form of evidence. Experience reveals a structure (the trace) that is recalcitrant to reflection.

Experience does not demonstrate anything like the kind of (transparent) self-relation that would make meta-cognition possible. The strong evidentiary warrant we were supposed to get from reflection on experience – from the form of its 'givenness' – does not obtain. The point is that neither transcendental reflection nor phenomenological analysis can tell us about the *a priori* or invariant structure of experience because the structures of experience are not transparent or apodictic, in the sense of having an immanent yardstick for their measure.[9] That is, *even* in the case of first-personal experience, we do not (always) know what is in question.

The apodicticity of experience assumes the *correlation* of the subject and object in a present experience. Phenomenology defines 'givenness' as this correlation. However, according to Derrida, phenomenological reflection reveals the non-apodicticity of experience, or the *non-identity* of subject and object. This non-identity or non-correlation – as phenomenologically revealed – is the ground for speculating about the *textual* structure of consciousness.

In 'To Speculate – on "Freud"', Derrida locates in Freud's work, particularly in the latter's speculations on the death drive and its relation to the pleasure principle, the notion of a 'speculative structure in general'.[10] 'Speculative structures' refer to what gives itself or evidences itself as excessive to presence. This phenomenological *excess* is equally deficiency – as lack of transparency or meaning. While for a critical philosophy, 'speculative' is reserved for those claims that cannot be grounded in a possible form of presence, Derrida reserves the term for that which evidences itself as *excessive* to any possible form of presence.[11] But what should we make of these speculative or textual structures? If introspection and (phenomenological) reflection will not give us the right sort of insight into their constitutive conditions, what philosophical tools, if any, might?

The philosophical novelty of Derrida's argument is that philosophy's incapacity to contend with these speculative structures is not due to the fact that these structures operate at a non-phenomenal level of cognition. The point is that phenomenological descriptions have failed to home in on what *is* given in experience. Phenomenological accounts reveal and conceal the textual structure of experience. It follows, then, that analysis of texts and their structure could tell us something about the speculative structure of experience. Reciprocally, insofar as non-phenomenological accounts of texts rely on assumptions about the non-textual nature of consciousness, these must be revised.

So, it seems that we can speculate about the textual nature of consciousness and experience only inasmuch as consciousness reveals or evidences its textual nature. But insofar as consciousness evidences its textual nature, it now appears as substantially like texts. From this will follow the conclusion that consciousness is textual, which means we are in some sense 'outside' it, or it is, in some sense, 'outside' itself. Interpretation is, indeed, irreducible.

The structure of non-correlational givenness is for Derrida the key to thinking of generalised textuality. Derrida's insistence that there is no 'outside-the-text' is not a claim about unlimited mediation. Textuality does not say that the conditions that make the world accessible make access to the world impossible. Instead, textuality names a speculative structure irreducible to the form of presence. Still, if textuality, in the first instance, describes something 'given' in experience – however 'darkly'[12] – what warrant do we have (to return to Colebrook's question) to generalise this structure to worldly processes that are apparently extra-textual? Why think that if experience is manifestly textual in structure that what it purports to be about is also textual – even if we admit that experience and texts are structurally or substantially similar and that they share the same conditions? Is this generalisation, from 'consciousness is textual' to 'everything is textual', not a bridge too far, speculatively speaking? This move from consciousness and experience to a cognition-transcendent world is warranted – *not* a 'sleight of hand' – if we understand textuality as said of evidence and if we understand evidence in non-correlational, non-cognitive terms.

If *all* evidence is necessarily textual – and if texts are not dependent upon, but rather the conditions for, consciousness – then there is no problem in principle in accounting for either the conditions of knowledge (they are textual) or for the objects of knowledge (also texts). If deconstructive terms are most often thought to pertain to questions related to language, meaning and experience, it is precisely to the extent that these are understood as phenomena. Whatever modification to phenomenological correlationism deconstruction achieves, it *begins* by assuming phenomenology's *epistemic* interpretation of phenomena, where the being of the phenomena is interpreted as the possibility of ideal self-evidence (apodicticity).

Deconstruction, I suggest, preserves phenomenology's evidentiary translation of the language of being but then translates phenomenology's account of evidence. It follows phenomenology in bracketing the natural attitude and in its reduction of objects to the mode and manner of their appearance. However, the deconstructive critique goes further by rejecting the correlationist view of evidence. Asserting that phenomenological givens are textual gives these a new, 'ultra-transcendental' meaning. This has the effect of translating evidence 'back' into the language of being or ontology. Texts are no more epistemic/ideal than ontological/real. This is the meaning of the substitution of text, spacing and archewriting for phenomena.

To be absolutely clear – to say of consciousness that it is textual precipitates a kind of crisis for the model of textuality. If we have speculative evidence in favour of thinking of experience as textual (as structured, let us say, *like* a text), at the same time it cannot be anything like a text – as traditionally construed – because philosophical accounts have traditionally defined texts as material marks *deprived* of Meaning. According to this model, texts are meaningful only insofar as a reduction to textually transcendent Meaning is possible. Derrida refers to such textually transcendent semantic items as 'transcendental signifieds', or what I will refer to throughout this book as 'Meaning'.[13] Thus, in order to make any sense of the proposed analogy or likeness, we have first to generate a more general conception of what the text is or could be if givenness is substantially like texts. Moreover, while we are perfectly free to speculate that what informs consciousness and what consciousness informs us about is also textual in nature, that is, that it has the same 'structure' as consciousness, our speculation is ungrounded – 'mere' speculation – until we have generated a general account of the text. The question of the generality of the text awaits an account of general or generalised writing.

Texts, in the narrow sense, are not models or schemas for a generalised textuality. They cannot tell us about non-textual stuff and processes, so long as texts are defined in opposition to the latter. We do not know what it means to say that something is textual, or like a text, so long as our understanding of texts relegates them to derivative and secondary processes opposed to the things they are about. Our account of texts is based upon their appearance in a highly determined and specific form. Quite simply, only texts narrowly construed appear to us as texts, while everything else looks or appears as something else – what Derrida calls a form of presence. General writing must account for the general non-appearance (or concealment) of the trace, but also the extent to which the text's appearance – particularly in the form of graphic writing – leads intuitions astray about what model of writing is in question when it is a question of general writing.

For Derrida, 'presence', construed as the coincidence of thought and being, is a philosophical illusion and fetish, unwarranted by any evidence. Therefore, on its own terms, critical philosophy has never escaped speculation. Presence is always already assumed to be the *form* of experience rather than interrogated. On the other hand, any attempt to challenge the value of presence, to go beyond experience, will appear to critical philosophy as unacceptably speculative. Yet if we are attentive enough to our evidence, to the manners and modes through which the world is given, we will discern 'speculative' structures that overflow the form of presence. These speculative structures, which Derrida names 'text', 'trace', 'spacing' and 'arche-writing', are the subject of this book.

\* \* \*

If there is a deconstructive materialism, its name is 'speculative grammatology'. Why should a deconstructive materialism require a detour through grammatology, the science of writing? *Of Grammatology* claims that writing is absolutely general. This obliges us not only to think the 'materiality' of arche-writing, but also the textuality of 'matter', where the latter has, until now, always designated non-textual exteriority in general. An adequate account of what it means to think of material processes as textual – what schema of textuality or textual form is implied – is the central interpretive task of any reading *Of Grammatology*. This book, therefore, has a triple aim: 1) to establish the meaning of a general writing that is no longer defined by the secondary and derivative status of writing 'in the narrow sense'; 2) to establish the grounds for the generality of general writing; and 3) to speculate on the materialist implications of generalised writing.

The plan for this book is as follows. In Chapter 1, I first consider how deconstruction has been read and interpreted by contemporary realists and materialists. I offer an account of some of the reasons why the anti-realist and anti-materialist readings of grammatology have seemed so intuitively obvious to Derrida's readers, including speculative realists, who have typically taken grammatology to name the sort of correlationist philosophical programme to be overcome. In resisting these anti-realist readings of Derrida and deconstruction, I am equally following and extending the work of important theorists working today on novel forms of philosophical materialism who do not necessarily identify as speculative realists.

Like speculative realists, new materialists such as Catherine Malabou, Karen Barad and Vicki Kirby critique correlationism – particularly in the form of linguistic 'enclosure' – with the aim of bringing the body, its substance and matter, powers and relations back into view. However, though they share with speculative realists the aim of recuperating matter in a philosophical discourse that has long neglected it in favour of issues 'closer to home', new materialists are decidedly less invested in the rhetoric of a rupture with correlationism than are speculative realists. Working with the various materialisms inherited from the continental tradition, in particular constructivist accounts of the body, new materialists radicalise the 'critique of Representationalism' undertaken by twentieth-century continental and feminist philosophy.[14]

The 'radicalisation' of the critique that new materialists propose would demonstrate that the sort of entanglement between representation and reality to which theorists of 'discursive construction' have attested is ontologically original and foundational. Representations will not simply be effective, morphogenetic in the case of social categories such as gender; nor is the entanglement of representation and reality to be understood in epistemic terms (as cognitive 'penetration'). It is ontological and general. New materialists find resources in the deconstructive project for this critical project, while suggesting that it has not always made explicit or followed through on its deepest insights. I suggest that grammatology offers an account of generalised entanglement in the figure of arche-writing that new materialists seek.

In the second chapter, turning to the speculative realist critique of correlationism, I argue that arche-writing and textuality are best understood as a critique of correlationism *avant la lettre*, and thus can be productively contrasted with Quentin Meillassoux's critique of correlationism and his notion of the ancestral. Derrida insists that the structure of the text can only be understood in the context of the radical absence of the human. Texts, he argues, remain structurally readable even in the case of the radical absence – death – of any and every possible reader.[15]

Derrida's readers, I show, tend to deflate this claim – assuming that what Derrida means is that a text necessarily transcends the context of its production. The correct reading, however, is that texts transcend any and all possible readers; they have an *extra-correlational* status. The structure of the text makes reading possible. The signified element is not transcendent to the text, a meaning correlated with a transcendental consciousness. It is embedded and entangled with the signifier.

Meillassoux's critique of correlationism (2008), and the significance of what he refers to as 'the ancestral', makes clear the stakes of Derrida's 'posthumous' texts. Meillassoux's ancestral events refer to events that are in principle unwitnessable. As with texts whose readability survives any and all readers, the ancestral by virtue of its stipulated position cannot be correlated to an intentional consciousness. However, the structure of Meillassoux's argument entails not affirming the necessity of non-correlated events, but rather affirming the necessity of non-correlated evidence or evidentiary traces. The structure of non-correlated evidentiary traces is just what Derrida calls textuality. Thus, not only is Derrida an anti-correlationist *avant la lettre*, his non-correlational account of evidence is arguably essential to the correlationist critique.

In the third chapter, I consider in more detail how Derrida's critique of the transcendental signified and his account of (non-correlational) textuality requires radically revising our understanding of both texts and Meaning. In particular, I consider the problem of what it means to think of reading other than as the (successful) reduction to meaning – to a transcendental signified. If textuality implies the impossibility of a reduction to meaning, it also implies the reduction of Meaning so construed (as an extra-textual, transcendental signified correlated to a transcendental consciousness).

Accounts that aim to reduce or eliminate Meanings seem to lead to absurdity. This absurdity, John Searle argued in his famous 'Chinese Room' thought-experiment, generalises to all accounts that would attempt to give a purely syntactical (that is, textual) account of linguistic function.[16] Searle's argument, however, is question-begging. Eliminating non-textual meanings does not require affirming that it is signifiers 'all the way down', as he assumes. Even if there are no transcendental signifieds, there may still be *textual* signifieds. The textuality of meaning implies that the difference between signifier and signified – without which no account of linguistic function is possible – is 'internal' to the structure of the text. The signifier and signified are entangled, mutually informing. This parasitic structure requires that we radically revise our account of textual objects, in the narrow sense, and of linguistic function and operations generally. Translation now becomes the privileged model for thinking through the latter.

In conclusion, I offer an account of cross-modal, perceptual translation to illustrate this grammatological account of textual meaning. If we take seriously that the signifier and the signified are entangled, and that textuality names this entanglement, then successful reading must involve something like a reverse translation, or decryption. This will not, admittedly, lead us to a non-textual meaning, but it does lead to a *heterogeneous* text. Reading means finding and restoring the 'parasitic' text encrypted or written in the 'host' text.[17]

In the fourth chapter, I track the generalisation of writing, from its narrow conception as graphic, phonetic writing to arche-writing in Derrida's reading of Saussure in *Of Grammatology*. My aim in this chapter is to specify what form or schema general writing entails – presuming it entails something different than the image of narrow, graphic writing – and why we should think, as grammatology claims, that this sort of structure is absolutely general.

Derrida describes the structure of the *gramme* in at least three ways in the chapter 'Grammatology and Linguistics': 1) as the object of a general science of writing; 2) as an essentially mnemonic or retentive form ('arche-phenomenon of memory'); and 3) as 'spacing' ('the becoming space of time and the becoming time of space'). Each of these descriptions is important for the generality claim, particularly spacing, since the latter decisively establishes the logical priority of the trace to the category of experience. I believe, however, that we lack any account that can make sense of the connection between general writing, the trace structure and spacing.

As is well known, Derrida questions Saussure's exclusion of writing from semiotics and general linguistics. However, less often remarked, he affirms the indissociability of signifier and signified that Saussure insists is the hallmark of the sign-form. The sign-form is radically constitutive of both sound and thought, and implies the original retention of sound and thought in the unity of the (articulated) phoné. However, Derrida argues that this retentive structure undermines Saussure's transcendental account of the sign and its function. The trace structure cannot be understood in terms of experience. Rather experience must be understood in terms of a movement of retention that is its ultra-transcendental condition. Arche-writing, therefore, will differ both from the model of writing that Saussure excludes and from the (transcendental) account of the linguistic sign he produces. Spacing elucidates the 'distance' of arche-writing from Saussure's transcendental semiotics.

Spacing allows Derrida to distinguish the space-time of the trace from the space-time of inner time consciousness, and establishes the former as grounding the latter. The space-time of the trace is not the accomplice of correlational or phenomenological consciousness. It allows us to see that phenomena do not have a correlational structure, as phenomenology argues, but a textual structure, as grammatology argues. As with all textual items, phenomena or experiential givens cannot be defined in terms of consciousness or the space-time of consciousness ('internal time consciousness') but rather in terms of the space-time of the trace (what Barad calls space-time mattering). Spacing allows Derrida to 'deconstruct' correlationism from within by specifying the ultra-transcendental status of the trace. 'The space-time of the trace' is no more ideal than real; it conditions phenomena on both sides and makes their entanglement thinkable.

The meaning of arche-writing, as Derrida emphasises, is not legible outside the 'transcendental text'. Taken out of this context, it will be given a naive realist interpretation incommensurate with spacing. Here then, in *Of Grammatology*'s chapter on Saussure, Derrida accomplishes what he refers to elsewhere as the rewriting of transcendental aesthetics. Space and time are not transcendental forms of experience but describe the constitutive 'movement' of the ultra-transcendental trace. Space-time mattering as general archivisation and memorialisation presuppose the retention of difference in heterogeneous differences.

In the fifth and final chapter, I consider the essential connection between generalised writing and plasticity qua modifiability and retention. The trace, I argued in the previous chapter, is defined by an origin-less and indefinite retention and modification. Speculative grammatology consists in the generalisation of memory or mnemonic form. The materiality of the trace, then, refers not to any substrate (of the graphic trace) but to the essential modifiability of textual structures. Modifiable texts retain heterogeneous texts. To demonstrate the productivity and pertinence of this account of arche-writing, I consider several grammatological descriptions of organic and material processes (including tree rings, organic recording devices more generally, and neurological memory trace).

In the second part of the chapter, I consider the extent to which plasticity may mark the speculative limits of grammatology. While plasticity is the condition of mnemonic form, it may not be exclusively mnemonic. Catherine Malabou argues that the mnemonic 'productivity' of the trace obscures the destructive powers of plasticity. While Malabou's critique is directed at neurological accounts of the 'non-graphic' trace, its force bears equally upon the grammatological account of arche-writing that I have reconstructed. The formation of form proceeds not only by retention but by what Malabou has called the 'sculpting' power of death. Does destructive plasticity point beyond speculative grammatology? Or does it rather indicate a necessary modification to the grammatological account of arche-writing? The answer, I suggest, hinges upon whether destructive plasticity can be thought in terms of an original modifiability *of* the trace. In this context, attention to descriptions of biological processes that involve degenerative regeneration – such as synaptic pruning, autophagy and apoptosis – may be indispensable.

In *Archive Fever* (1996), Derrida writes, enigmatically, of an anarchival, 'archiviolithic' principle that works against retention and memoralisation.[18] This anarchival principle, however, would not be the radical other of archivisation, as the death drive is the radical other to life in Freud's speculations. The two principles are originally entangled or bound together – writing with un-writing, bio-graphy with necro-graphy, memory with forgetting. This entanglement, I conclude, is the horizon of speculative grammatology.

## Notes

1. Derrida (1995: 123).
2. Francisco Vitale's *Biodeconstruction* (2018) appeared after *Speculative Grammatology* was already completed, and therefore too late for me to adequately engage with the text and its arguments. However, more than any other book recently published, it is, I believe, a companion text to *Speculative Grammatology*. At least on my reading, Vitale pursues the project of speculative grammatology under the name of 'biodeconstruction'. Departing from *Of Grammatology*, Vitale charts the development of arche-writing in Derrida's 1975–76 seminar at the École normale supérieure, *La vie la mort* (recently published in France by Seuil with an English translation forthcoming). In this seminar, Derrida established not only the biological provenance of arche-writing, but also the critical role of arche-writing vis-à-vis the linguistic-scriptural metaphors of 'code' and 'programme elaborated by cybernetics and implemented by biology' (Vitale 2018: 73).
3. See especially Kirby (2005b).
4. Colebrook (2011).
5. Barad (2003).

6. It seems to me that Richard Rorty (1977) has best articulated this impasse (as against the quasi-transcendental accounts of deconstruction). Rorty argues (correctly) that Derrida has shown that we have no better access to the conditions of our cognition than we have to the world. Rorty takes this sort of anti-transcendental position to be the aim and merit of Derrida's argument. The point is not to say how knowledge is possible, but to show that meta-cognition is *not* possible. As the remainder of this introduction aims to clarify, I do not agree with Rorty that the aim is exclusively 'negative'. On the contrary, I believe that demonstrating the 'textuality' of consciousness makes it possible to generate non-correlational accounts of texts, which in turn permits Derrida to generalise textuality. For an excellent discussion of Rorty's deflationary reading of Derrida, see Kates (2005: ch. 1).

7. In *Essential History* (Kates 2005: esp ch. 2), Joshua Kates offers an excellent account of a seemingly intractable epistemological problem that Derrida's critique of Husserl appears to entail. How can Derrida rely upon phenomenological evidence in order to radically impugn it? Is this not the phenomenological equivalent of the liar's paradox? However, while Kates motivates the problem well, he fails, at least on my reading, to (dis)solve it. As I will argue in the second chapter of this book, the paradox is dissolved as soon as we see that, for Derrida, the structure of lived experience reveals itself to be essentially uncorrelated with a transcendental consciousness.

8. Seebohm (1995: 199).

9. I have borrowed this formulation from David Roden (2013), whose notion of phenomenological darkness has most of the same features I attribute to 'non-apodictic' evidence.

10. Derrida (1987: 284). Here, Derrida argues that Freud's account of the relation between the (speculative) death drive and the pleasure principle will require recourse to the notion of 'a speculative structure in general'. In this context 'speculative' will refer 'simultaneously [to] the senses of specular *reflection*'; to speculative exchanges, for example 'the production of surplus value, of calculations and bets on the Exchange, that is, the emission of more or less fictive shares'; and finally '[to] *that which overflows the (given) presence of the present*' (emphasis mine). In the present context I focus specifically on the latter sense of speculative.

11. Derrida (1987: 285).

12. Roden (2013) introduces the idea of 'dark phenomenology'. Phenomenologically dark elements are those not transparent

to introspection, that are given without an 'internal' measure or yardstick for their interpretation. Negating Roden's definition of phenomenologically dark elements gives us, I think, an economical formulation of phenomenological evidence. All elements are given in such a way that their meaning is self-giving. Roden argues that dark phenomena cannot be accounted for *phenomenologically*. '[T]he domain of phenomenology is not the province of a self-standing, autonomous discipline but must be investigated with any empirically fruitful techniques that are open to us (e.g. computational neuroscience, artificial intelligence, etc.). Finally, it entails that while a naturalized phenomenology should be retained as a descriptive, empirical method, it should not be accorded transcendental authority' (2013: 169).

13. According to Derrida, theories of linguistic function have almost always involved the possibility of 'reducing' empirical language to meaning (Derrida 1982: 134). Philosophers and 'lay' speakers assume that words refer to and are underwritten by cognitive entities or items distinct from the language we use. It follows that to access these underlying meanings, we must, as it were, cash in the 'materiality of the signifier' – the material element of language exemplified by a written mark or spoken word – for the value it represents. Successful uses of language – reading, writing, translating – would each involve restoring to mind ('re-presenting') the underlying meanings that have been transferred through language. Philosophical accounts propose various theoretical entities that serve the required functional role of Meaning. Derrida refers to the theoretical entities that philosophers introduce as 'transcendental signifieds' (Derrida 1978: 279–80). This term captures the necessary condition for anything to serve the functional role of Meaning: ultimately, meaning must be transcendent to or outside language, and it must be correlated to a transcendental consciousness.

14. Barad (2003: 806–12).

15. 'A writing that is not structurally readable-iterable-beyond the death of the addressee would not be writing' (Derrida 1988: 7).

16. Searle (1980).

17. Derrida (1988: 88–90). 'Parasitism takes place when the parasite (called thus by the owner, jealously defending his own, his oikos) comes to live off the life of the body in which it resides – and when, reciprocally, the host incorporates the parasite to an extent, willy nilly offering it hospitality: providing it with a place' (1988: 90).

18. Derrida (1996: 14).

# Materialism and Realism in Contemporary Continental Philosophy

Language has been granted too much power. The linguistic turn, the semiotic turn, the interpretive turn, the cultural turn: it seems that at every turn every 'thing' – even materiality – is turning into a matter of language or some form of cultural representation . . . Language matters. Discourse matters. Culture matters. There is an important sense in which the only thing that does not seem to matter anymore is matter.

Karen Barad, *Meeting the Universe Halfway*

## Anti-(anti-)Realism and the New Materialism

For some time now, influential figures in contemporary continental philosophy have called for a materialist and realist turn, a decisive break from the insistent anti-realism that, Lee Braver argues, characterises the development of continental philosophy from Kant to Derrida. Continental anti-realism emphasises the activity of the knower in forming or constituting knowledge of the external world.[1] The world is *given* through an irreducible activity – even when this activity is characterised as the most 'passive' sort of 'synthesis'. It may be that in the passage from Kant to post-structuralism, the characteristic activity of the knower has been extended and offloaded to intersubjective linguistic or discursive structures. However, the displacement of the structuring activity leaves no space for thinking the autonomy of that which is disclosed. As Karen Barad argues, 'matter' and 'world' are defined *exclusively* in terms of the possibility of cognitive access.[2] The world that our cognitive and signifying activity reaches out to is limited to what we, knowers, make of it. What is more, we have no way of factoring or recognising any activity or agency on the part of what is disclosed.

Gayatri Spivak illustrates the sort of anti-realism that Barad is concerned about in the following quote: 'If one thinks of the body as such, there is no possible outline of the body as such. There are thinkings of the systematicity of the body, there are value codings of the body. The body, as such, cannot be thought, and I certainly cannot approach it.'[3] According to Spivak, positing the body *as such* negates the constitutive activity of the knower. By contrast, the approachable body is the one mediated by the 'thinkings' that code and systematise it, 'bringing it together' by producing an outline.

Heeding Spivak's warning seems to impose considerable – and arguably unacceptable – constraints on the sort of engagement that theorists can have with scientific discourses and practice. Her anti-realism entails a critique of any statements that make claims about the body and corporeal processes, rather than claims about how the body is 'known'. For example, when making statements characterising the mosaic structure of cells, biologists refer to morphogenetic processes immanent to matter – not to minds, knowers, or discourses. Claims about mosaic patterns are not equivalent to claims about the discursive production of 'outlines', which produce the cell's mosaic structure as if it were simply there. Perhaps, as Spivak suggests, the scientists' realism is hopelessly naive. Nonetheless, it does seem that making claims about *the body* requires rejecting Spivak's framing. The (appearing) body cannot be exclusively the effect of the acts that aim to grasp it, even if we cannot conceive its appearance without these acts.

Questioning anti-realism does not entail questioning 'discursive construction', if the latter is taken to refer to the material effects of representational practices. No doubt there is an important story to be told, as Judith Butler demonstrates, about how interpellative processes ('it is a girl') produce some of the very distinguishing features that they seem only to name. This type of denaturalising account will not necessarily support Spivakian anti-realism. Disciplinary practices, dietary regimes and differential social status more broadly have morphogenetic effects quite independent of the transcendental conditions of the body's appearance. Yet anti-realism cannot consistently account for these effects.

Such forms of anti-realism, Manuel DeLanda argues, must continually be surprised by the absolutely unsurprising observation that 'matter has morphogenetic capacities of its own and does not need to be commanded into generating form'.[4] Concurring with DeLanda, Catherine Malabou argues that any philosophical materialism worthy of the name must reject what Spivak's account of the body insists upon: namely, the principle that corporeal form is to be understood in terms of the activity of a transcendental subject or 'transcendental instance'.[5] To see form as calling for a transcendental explanation assumes that matter has no way of figuring or factoring in accounts of its appearance.

New or neo-materialism, as DeLanda calls it, may be distinguished theoretically by its claims that various forms of continental anti-realism have deprived matter of any life, vitality or autonomous activity. This is arguably most evident in the seemingly neutral decision to bracket the question of the ontological status of what appears or materialises to knowers, in order to focus on questions related to the mode and manner of an object's appearance, the conditions for its intelligibility, or its status within discourse. This bracketing, however, cannot remain entirely neutral, since the first thing it discloses is the dissimulative character of objective appearances. Bracketing the ontological 'claims' that objects make in their appearance transforms the object into an 'intentional' object – an object correlated to conscious awareness.

As Husserl argued, the 'natural attitude' – spontaneously and naively realist – characteristically effaces the activity of the transcendental subject in positing the object. It is the phenomenological mark of matter – the mode and manner of its *materialisation* – to appear as extra-discursive (as prior, original and indifferent to its materialisation). At the same time, traditional phenomenological descriptions of materialisation seem to leave room for realism inasmuch as they make explicit the layers of perceptual evidence that produce realist beliefs about objects. It is true that the phenomenological method prohibits going beyond the evidence of appearance to make a judgement about its existence; but the phenomenologist may affirm that the evidence is compatible with such judgements.

However, on the basis of the same phenomenological evidence, anti-realists, including Butler, argue that matter is produced or constructed as radical exteriority.[6] To be sure, matter materialises as if it were extra-discursive, but the dissimulative 'rhetoric' of perception must be thoroughly subjected to critique. Matter is anything but extra-discursive; it is the effect of a discursive process whose effect is to produce the very boundary between discourse and its others.

Phenomenology and related discourses, it seems, are unable to adequately grapple with the 'paradoxical fact', as Roy Bhaskar puts it, that the intransitive object of scientific statements is 'always already' transitive.[7] The scientist's naive realism reduces the object to its intransitive dimensions, while the anti-realist grasps the same object as essentially transitive. Phenomenologists' attempts to hold together both sides – accounting for the intransitive in terms of the transitive – are insufficient. They serve only to indefinitely defer the problem that Bhaskar locates in the equivocity of 'object'.

Bhaskar's 'intransitivity' paradox is rooted in the equivocal meaning of 'object of knowledge'. On the one hand, in scientific inquiry, the *object* of knowledge is typically defined as being independent of human activity: 'The specific gravity of mercury, the process of electrolysis, the mechanism of light propagation.' On the other hand, an object of *knowledge* is produced by human (social) activity, and 'is no more independent of this activity than the material apparatus' set up to measure the 'specific gravity of mercury'.[8] If the naive realist grasps one horn, the anti-realist grasps the other. The phenomenologists, for their part, attempt to dissolve the dilemma by affirming that the difference in question – between transitive and intransitive objects – is *internal* to perception and hence phenomenologically original and irreducible.[9] The phenomenologist might suggest that this difference reflects, in perception, the original correlation between subject and world.[10] But because this difference appears on this side of transitivity, it is equally susceptible to being explained by Butler's account of discursive construction. Bhaskar, by contrast, calls for a 'critical realism' – or an anti-anti-realism – that would resolve the paradox.

New materialists aim precisely at the sort of 'critique of the critique' that Bhaskar outlines. Barad and Kirby, for example, argue that accounts of discursive construction, in general, suffer from an incomplete critique of what Barad calls 'Representationalism'. By the latter, Barad refers to the metaphysical assumptions underwriting the opposition between representation and reality. An adequate critique would not account for the discursive construction of this opposition, nor demonstrate how, in exceptional cases, representations can produce the reality they describe: it would 'deconstruct' the opposition.[11]

Barad argues that a complete and thoroughgoing critique of Representationalism will generalise the *intra-activity* of representation and materiality beyond the human. The relation is *intra*-active (rather than inter-active) because it is constitutive, producing its relata as differences. Thus, according to Barad, what feminist theory has been describing under the name of 'construction', from a partial perspective, is the general material entanglement of representation and reality. She argues for a relational ontology, which, she suggests, resonates with Derridean *différance*.[12] Differences thought in terms of radical opposition (such as representation and reality) ought instead to be thought in terms of a generalised intra-activity or entanglement. An intra-active relation produces its relata as (entangled) differences.

On Barad's view, *contra* anti-realist accounts, material processes participate in their own intelligibility. Phenomena in quantum physics (for example, slit experiments) can be read as evidencing the sorts of relations that Derrida describes variously as trace, *différance*, writing and spacing. *Différance* refers to an original ontological entanglement which, for Barad, produces the ongoing differentiation of the world.

A number of new materialists have described their attempts to schematise the entanglements of nature/culture, mind/matter, representation/real in deconstructive terms. Despite prevalent views that Derrida's arguments amount to the sort of anti-realist position attributed to Butler and Spivak above, important features of Derrida's critique of metaphysical oppositions have been taken up by new materialists as a call to describe and schematise matter (and its relations) in terms of forms of non-presence. Matter is traced, differantial, heterogeneous and entangled. These materialist projects begin with a critique of the view that we are enclosed in a discursive web outside of which we cannot venture, which effectively crosses out matter in its difference from culture.

Elizabeth Wilson argues that feminist accounts of culture often proceed from outmoded ideas of science as always and everywhere imposing a reductionist programme that excludes and minimises the role of culture.[13] This is often reinforced by scientific accounts themselves. For example, she points to Simon le Vay's claim that 'homosexual and heterosexual identities have a neurobiological substrate'. This view is problematic, however, because it 'constitutes neurocognitive matter as self-present and originary' and forecloses the possibility of 'neurocognitive mobility' in response to and in relation to cultural processes. And yet, she demonstrates, such views can and ought to be criticised on the very grounds upon which they are made.

Wilson contends that connectionist accounts of neuronal activity present a critique of a self-present, originary, locatable psychical memory trace. Representations 'are stored in the spatial and temporal differences between connection weights . . . [t]hus there is a double displacement; from the locale of the unit or store to the connection, and then again from the connection to the spaces between connections'.[14] The structure of this material trace is 'nowhere locatable' or present. Wilson connects the structure of this material trace to Derridean and Freudian accounts of the trace. 'If it is through Derrida and Freud that we can formulate a cognitive trace that is not a present, fixed and locatable psychical entity, then it is in connections that we see an instantiation of these principles in a manner that is coherent to scientific psychology.'[15]

Our politics and our critical theory require an understanding of the complex relations of culture and nature, Wilson argues. However, scientific accounts often foreclose such an understanding with reductionist and determinist models of social identity. Yet the critical apparatus of feminist theory has been unable to diagnose the problems with these accounts, because of its resistance to engaging with scientific discourse despite the possibility of developing schemas that bring out the co-implication of nature and culture.

Attempts to ontologise the Derridean trace are in fact increasingly widespread, as Claire Colebrook observes. Yet, she argues, such accounts present us with distinctive interpretive challenges. To illustrate this challenge she considers several 'materialist reconstructions of deconstruction' that adopt similar approaches to those of Barad and Wilson. For example, Cary Wolfe suggests that 'second order systems theory' provides the pretext for a materialist 'reconstruction of deconstruction'. He takes Derrida's notion of writing as a model of the fundamental dynamics subtending meaning and mind, and links it to biological, social and historical conditions of emergence.[16] As Colebrook writes,

Cary Wolfe has argued that Derrida is not only compatible with systems theorists such as Luhmann and Maturana and Varela; he insists that the Derridean version of considering the world as system of relations rather than original presence is required if systems theory is not to fall into one more Cartesian dualism . . . What marks Wolfe's approach to Derrida is his alignment of deconstruction with a general trend to consider all life in terms of a single process of evolution. Linguistic systems would be no different in kind from other systems, all aspects of a co-evolving and necessarily de-centered life in which the organic and the inorganic interweave: 'psychic systems and social systems have coevolved, each serving as the environment for the other'.[17]

Here, we see Wolfe speaking approvingly of appropriating Derridean schemas to work out systems-theoretic accounts of life and material processes. Whether or not these sorts of 'reconstructions' would be sanctioned by Derrida, they ensure, according to Wolfe, that systems theory is not reinvested with traditional metaphysical dualisms as it seeks the common principles of all complex systems (whether biological, digital, linguistic or cultural).

Colebrook argues, however, that such materialist and naturalist 'appropriations' of deconstruction move too quickly. Her point is not to reject the possibility of formulating a deconstructive materialism, but to demand an approach to formulating it that takes the *materiality* of Derrida's texts seriously. If we wish to undertake a materialist 'reconstruction of deconstruction', such a reconstruction cannot proceed merely by supplementing deconstruction (or grammatology) with the theoretical framework of one's choice: systems theory, quantum theory or neuroscientific accounts of plasticity. If one or another theoretical framework must supplement grammatology, in order for the latter to become materialist, then its original limitations must first be made explicit. On the other hand, if grammatology always implied the textuality of matter, then the meaning of general textuality must first be clarified. Certainly, affirming the textuality of matter will not leave the meaning of 'matter' or 'nature' intact. Rather, to think matter and nature in terms of writing entails a 'radical destruction of figures and senses of nature'.[18] It follows that the theoretical supplements in question would be salient to deconstructive materialism inasmuch as they too participate in such a radical destruction.

In Colebrook's view, these materialist reconstructions correctly intuit that it is wrong to think that Derrida claims that 'we do not know matter as it is in itself because we are only given matter by way of some mediating system (of concepts, experiential stabilities or language)'.[19] Rather, we do not know matter because:

> matter 'itself' is not in itself. Matter *is* differential rather than sub-stantive, not only something that can only be presented differentially (though time and space) but 'is' differential. What we experience as

time and space has the form that it does because there are material forces that enable something like the subject and his syntheses.[20]

Where they fall short is specifying how we can get from a discourse about the materiality of the trace to claims about the textuality of matter. In the end, I think that new materialist approaches, including Bard's, Wilson's and Wolfe's, are compatible with Colebrook's idea of matter as differential. However, correctly in my view, she insists on the need to hesitate before equating the Derridean trace with the phenomena of diffraction in quantum physics, the material trace in connectionism or the *différance* of evolutionary systems theory.

If theorists such as Kirby, Barad and Wilson all point in various ways to Derrida's account of *différance* as a model of the sort of relations they believe must ground a new or reinvigorated materialism, and see his critique of metaphysics as offering philosophical insights into connectionist models (of neurons) and quantum entanglement, then this is enough to motivate us to revisit the question of general writing in Derrida's work. If the burgeoning speculative appropriation of the trace to domains beyond language and signification that we see among new materialists is warranted by grammatology, then there is no need to speak of appropriation at all. Grammatology will have been speculative all along.

If I have framed new materialist projects in terms of a radical critique of Representationalism and discursive enclosure, these issues are very close to the critique of correlationism which frames the speculative realist project. Correlationism, which speculative realism believes unifies all of post-Kantian philosophy, asserts that 'world' is always already the correlate of thought. If I have distinguished between new materialists and speculative realists, it is primarily on the basis of their distinctive relationship with post-structuralist and deconstructive philosophy. While new materialists seek to extend and radicalise the insights of the latter, speculative realists have argued that they are both instances of the correlationism that needs to be overcome.

I will turn now to speculative realists and the problem of correlationism in particular, before returning to the problem of formulating the project of deconstructive materialism. As I argue, we can better understand both Derrida's strategy in grammatology and its materialist implications if we also understand grammatology as a distinctive strategy for overcoming the problem of correlationism.

## Speculative Realism

In the introductory essay to *The Speculative Turn* (2011), philosophers Levi Bryant, Nick Srnicek and Graham Harman argue that, however much continental thought appears to gradually decentre the idea of a form-giving, world-constituting or world-disclosing transcendental subject, its critiques restore and rehabilitate this same subject in the guise of language, discourse or structure. The latter retain all the philosophical functions of the 'self-enclosed' Cartesian subject that they apparently disperse or 'extend'. Crucially, reality retains its meaning as 'a *correlate* of human thought' even as these critiques contest the meaning of 'human' and 'thought':

> It has long been commonplace within continental philosophy to focus on discourse, text, culture, consciousness, power, or ideas as what *constitutes* reality. Despite the vaunted anti-humanism of many of the thinkers identified with these trends, what they give us is less a critique of humanity's place in the world, than *a less sweeping critique* of the self-enclosed Cartesian subject. Humanity remains at the centre of these works, and *reality appears in philosophy only as the correlate of human thought.* In this respect phenomenology, structuralism, post-structuralism, deconstruction, and postmodernism have all been perfect exemplars of the anti-realist trend in continental philosophy. Without deriding the significant contributions of these philosophies, something is clearly amiss in these trends ... The danger is that the dominant anti-realist strain of continental philosophy has not only reached a point of decreasing returns, but that it now actively limits the capacities of philosophy in our time.[21]

According to Bryant et al., the displacement of first-personal, conscious activity (Descartes and Husserl) or transcendental structures (Kant) transfers the *activity* of the transcendental subject to textual or discursive structures. Because the latter designate the conditions enabling thought and its relation to an object, thought remains both the point of departure and the critical limit of philosophical inquiry.

By contrast, the 'speculative turn' promises to complete the critique of Cartesianism at which continental thinkers aimed, but which, out of deference to the Kantian critical tradition, they were unable to achieve. Speculative realism rejects the centrality of 'hermeneutic' questions in twentieth-century continental anti-realist philosophy. Philosophy will no longer be 'obsessed with the critiques of written texts' because it will no longer be inclined to treat the things of this world as though they were so many texts to be interpreted. Instead, philosophers will be concerned with developing a 'positive ontology' which, as Harman writes, will identify the 'basic structural features shared by all objects' and allow us to generate an account of the relations between objects, including the sorts of relations that make distinctive forms of *human* knowing possible.[22]

As Bryant, Srnicek and Harman suggest, prominent twentieth-century continental critiques of Cartesianism and transcendental subjectivity were improperly motivated. Concerned to debunk the idea of an ahistorical, 'self-present' subject directing and mastering its own world-constituting activities, thinkers such as Foucault and Derrida aimed to release the subject from its 'Cartesian closure' and demonstrate this subject's constitution and conditioning by worldly, impersonal/intersubjective processes that it neither masters nor controls. These critiques, however, failed to release us from the more general problem of world-constitution that requires thinking of the world as subjective correlate. This notion that *constitution* and its end product, the correlate, are the explanandum of philosophy is the implicit organising assumption of all modern and contemporary philosophy.

Quentin Meillassoux, in *After Finitude*, defines this organising assumption as the correlationist thesis. The correlationist thesis is the belief that 'we only ever have access to the correlation between thinking and being, and never to either term considered apart from the other'.[23] For Meillassoux, the mark of any correlationist philosophy is a critique of the naive realism of perceptual experience that posits the objects of perception as simply being there outside and independent of any perceptual activity. Critiques of what Husserl referred to as the 'natural attitude' claim that the latter takes as original and independent what is inextricably the effect of a certain kind of engagement or relation. The correlationist says: while it may be true that in perceiving we feel ourselves to be directly in touch with the world, critical reflection shows this belief to be naive and impossible to justify; it is formed by 'forgetting' or erasing the constitutive activity that makes the appearance of the object possible.[24]

Importantly, if Meillassoux argues that the mark of

correlationism is its critique of naive realism, not all correlationist philosophies will affirm anti-realism, that is, the view that references to an objective reality are nonsensical. Indeed, many contemporary critiques of naive realism – whether in the analytic or continental tradition – aim to vindicate the intuitions of the naive realist. However, Meillassoux argues that correlationism can never be compatible with an acceptable scientific realism, that is, the sort of realist framework that would preserve the meaning of scientific statements. We shall return to these issues below and in the chapter that follows. What I want to underscore, for the moment, is only that, generically, the mark of correlationism is not anti-realism per se, but rather the *unsurpassability* of the correlate.

Meillassoux's argument aims to debunk the apparent compatibility of correlationism with scientific claims. Because the correlationist cannot conceive a world that is independent of the disclosive relation – a world radically cut off from the structures that disclose it cannot be thought – they cannot make any sense of scientific statements referencing a world *logically* prior to the possibility of any correlation. 'Ancestral' events – to which we might also add radically posthumous events – make explicit the absurdity of correlationism and sharpen the philosophical choice to be made: either we choose correlationism or we choose science.

Importantly, Meillassoux's point is not that correlationism cannot account for and explain *unwitnessed* events. On the contrary, he insists that correlationism's manner of treating the unwittnessed *is* plausible and, indeed, it is this plausibility that gives it the realist legs that it has. Correlationism can treat statements about unwittnessed events counterfactually, as events that would have been given or evidenced in a certain way had there been a witness. However, according to Meillassoux, the correlationist cannot conceive a world that is in principle outside of the conditions of its evidentiary givenness. It is precisely such uncorrelated objects, events and phenomena that are unthinkable for the correlationist. If this were right, though, we could not say anything about the greater part of the earth's history.

Speculative realists, therefore, see no reason to choose between correlationisms that are compatible with realism and those that are explicitly anti-realist. Indeed, they argue that philosophers have attacked the notion of givenness as too tied to a subjective, first-person perspective only to become mired in another set of 'accessibility' problems, which have 'not only reached a point of decreasing returns, but ... actively limit the capacities of philosophy in our time'.[25] Correlationism sets out with the aim of vindicating scientific realism and reaches a dead end in the anti-realist, post-structuralist philosophies.

### Derrida's Critique of Correlationism

As we saw in the previous sections of this chapter, when philosophers have rejected forms of correlationism compatible with realism, it has often been in the interest of denying the (self-) evidentiary character of givenness: that is, its epistemic status. What is *given* is given not as the 'thing itself' but as 'sign', and is therefore subject to all the hermeneutic indeterminacy and instability of a text. In fact, there are two main versions of this critique of givenness. The first version claims that givenness cannot be self-evident because it is necessarily structured *like* a sign, and as Charles Peirce argued, no sign can be self-interpreting. The second version of the critique claims that the givenness cannot be self-evident because it is always already structured *by* (linguistic) signs.

Both versions of the critique question the epistemic status of givenness, but in different ways. The first argues that anything that could play the grounding epistemic role assigned to givenness could not be a given (simple, self-evident, non-inferential). Or, in Derridean terms, the conditions of possibility for givenness are the conditions of its impossibility. The second points out that linguistic, conceptual or cultural categories are constitutive of anything we might take to ground our beliefs. Givens are effects (of language) rather than linguistically expressible grounds for belief – effects that mask themselves as grounds. At their epistemic best, attempts to understand the relationship between our representations of the world and the world these representations *purport* to be about will teach us about the *discursive activity* producing these ideas and representations.

Both versions of the critique of givenness undermine the case that correlationism is compatible with naive realism. However, neither is a critique of correlationism. Indeed, critiques of givenness seem to replace the view that the correlate of mind and world is unsurpassable with the view that the world presents itself first naively as world, then as a (realist-preserving) correlate, and finally as the dissimulative effect of discursive or significative activity.

Derridean deconstruction is usually identified with either or both of these critiques of givenness. Most often, interpreters take it for granted that Derrida's critique of the transcendental signified demands rethinking givenness as 'internal' to language (or textuality). However, as I have already begun to argue, Derrida's critique of givenness – his critique of presence and the transcendental signified – is done not in the name of vindicating anti-realism, but of critiquing correlationism. In this sense, deconstructive critique is not the ineffectual dead end of correlationism as speculative realism has diagnosed it.

Derrida's critique of the metaphysics of presence is not a critique of the idea of self-evidence in the name of irreducible mediation. The claim of generalised textuality does not transform the world, correlatively disclosed, into a book. Rather, as I shall argue in the subsequent chapters, Derrida's critique of the metaphysics of presence should be read as a critique of the very idea of a mind-world correlate, a critique *avant la lettre* of what speculative realism calls correlationism. Rereading the early Derrida – particularly *Of Grammatology* – as a critique of correlationism will transform our understanding of its aims and motivations while resolving interpretive challenges that have long exercised Derrida's readers. The meaning of textuality and writing and the warrant for Derrida's claim that writing is absolutely general simply cannot be grasped outside the framework of his critique of the metaphysics of presence/correlationism.

Philosophical notions of object and form are, Derrida argues, indissociable from the form of presence (or correlationism). If, as Husserl insisted, lived experience puts us in touch with the things themselves (rather than putting us in touch with internal representations or 'effigies'), this can only be because of a parallelism, an identity-in-difference, of the *form of experience* and the form of the *object* experienced.[26] The object disclosed is the same (but different) from its appearance, identical but absolutely other. Restating Husserl's stipulated parallelism, Derrida writes:

> Form is presence itself. Formality is the presence of whatever aspect of the thing *presents itself*, lets itself be seen, gives itself to thought. That metaphysical thought – and consequently phenomenology – is a thought of Being as form.[27]

The philosophical concept of form, the *form* of givenness as the givenness *of* the object, assumes that the materialisation of matter as meaning or intelligibility perfectly translates or expresses the essence of the worldly object. Attempts to critique or deflate givenness (as self-evidence) have been limited inasmuch as they retain, so Derrida argues, the same notion of form as presence (as meaning, objectivity, relation to a subject). By contrast, for Derrida, the critique of presence (or the critique of correlationism) must proceed by a radical critique of philosophical conceptions of *form*.

If I am correct that Derridean deconstruction is best understood as a thoroughgoing rejection of correlationism, it is important to note that this critique proceeds not by way of a transformation of givenness (the original self-presentation of the object in the immediacy of subjective experience) into representation (the 'internal effigy' of the purportedly external thing). Again, it is not a matter of questioning the warrant for realism that givenness offers. Rather, by positioning himself as a critical phenomenologist – but a phenomenologist nonetheless – Derrida considers what the *structure* of givenness reveals about itself, what it evidences itself as.

It is perfectly true that objects appear perceptually, but phenomenologists should not be as impressed by this idea of appearance as they are. In her fascination with the how of givenness, the phenomenologist behaves like a would-be reader indefinitely captivated by the calligraphy of a text. The phenomenologist is supposed to be after accurate descriptions of the structures of consciousness that produce meaning in all its forms. If Derrida argues that the phenomenologist should better attend to the structure of texts and signs, this is not in spite of but because the structure in question does not correspond with any appearance. Texts reveal the structures that the phenomenologist seeks better than the phenomenologist. For example, an analysis of the experience of 'inner time consciousness' should lead us to reject any account of time in terms of a present-now. The experience of time has a manifest trace structure, of retention and protention, as Husserl himself demonstrated. It thus turns out that the 'now', the very form of 'the correlate', is both excessive and deficient with respect to presence, shot through with absences. The subsequent question should have been: what can this trace structure, or time as the originary reinscription of the past, tell us? What does it mean that experience is always *différance*?

Minimally, as Derrida argues, the structure of experience evidences itself as 'spaced'. The 'outside' of materiality, spatiality – everything that phenomenology has always sought to bracket and reduce to reach a pure interiority – shows itself on the 'inside' (of consciousness) as absence. If the outside is on the inside, there is no inside. The trace structure is the non-transcendental condition of experience. This is what the phenomenologist should have concluded. Instead, Husserl interpreted the trace structure as answering the question: how is experience of a present now possible? The 'conditions of possibility' (a structure of non-presence) are interpreted exclusively in terms of what they are said to make possible, namely, the *experience* of presence.

This structure – Derrida calls it 'spacing' – should have evidenced to the phenomenologist that time's necessary relation with an 'outside' was no longer thinkable in terms of correlationism or transcendental consciousness. Spacings, effects of *différance* (whether said of the structure of perception, sense experience or 'inner time'), are *how* the non-transcendental or non-correlational conditions of experience appear to consciousness. Or, as Derrida states the point in *Of Grammatology*, spacing evidences the (non-conscious, non-transcendental) structure or 'warp' through which the 'woof' of consciousness and experience is woven.

It is worth dilating, for a moment, on the analogy that Derrida uses in this context: that of the warp and woof structure of textile weaving. The 'warp' describes the threads held taut and lengthwise through which the 'woof' is interwoven. In *Of Grammatology*, Derrida writes that spacing reveals that the phenomenology of experience, and the language which describes it, are a 'woof' on a 'warp' that is 'not its own'. In fact, Derrida is, characteristically, more circumspect than I have just suggested. However, his analyses of Husserl's inner time consciousness not only warrant but explicitly assert the interpretation he presents in *Of Grammatology* as merely a suggestion.

> [I]s the phenomenological model itself constituted, as a woof of language, logic, evidence, fundamental security, upon a warp that is not its own? And which – such is the most difficult problem – is no longer at all mundane? It is not by chance that the transcendental phenomenology of the internal time-consciousness, so careful to place cosmic time within brackets, must, as consciousness and even as internal consciousness, live a time that is an accomplice of the time of the world. Between consciousness, perception (internal or external), and the 'world,' the rupture, even in the subtle form of the reduction, is perhaps not possible. (OG, 76)

It is only on account of spacing that Derrida can suggest that the warp through which the woof of phenomenological experience – and the descriptive language attuned to it – is woven is 'not at all mundane'. Mundane, in this context, refers to the world of the natural attitude, that is, a pre-critical, uncorrelated understanding of the world. If spacing evidences an exteriority entangled with the pure interiority of consciousness, this exteriority cannot be identified with the mundane 'world' that phenomenology put into brackets in order to investigate consciousness.

'The most difficult problem' that spacing presents us with is that the 'trace' or 'shadow' of exteriority – the warp through which consciousness is woven – is not mundane. Therefore, we may not interpret it as either empirical, real or material. Why not? The latter are each determined by the language and logic of the phenomenological woof. What we are authorised to say is that the exteriority in question is entangled with interiority and produces it. As I will argue, thinking this sort of entanglement will require us to abandon the weaving metaphor altogether. However, as a first pass, we can say that this exteriority is non-transcendental, its status is not that of a condition of possibility but of a non-correlational or uncorrelated structure. If 'no rupture', no reduction to a pure interiority of consciousness is possible, this is because consciousness is not the noetic correlate of the world. It is 'woven' into the world. To understand consciousness requires understanding spacing, which is more general than consciousness. Its absolute priority more than justifies, despite Derrida's precautions, speaking of the trace structure in realist (non-correlational) terms.

On the reading I have just proposed, Husserlian phenomenology's fault is not a failure to discover or make visible the 'constitutive' structures of perceptual experience – its failure has been to mis-describe its discovery at the very moment of its appearance, in order to insist on the identity of givenness with the subject. If Derridean deconstruction diagnoses the move to secure correlationism at the expense of the earned insights of phenomenological analyses, then bringing us back to these very insights – to the processes which can be said to *underwrite* lived experience – would open up the possibility of a genuinely speculative enterprise: namely, making sense of the 'speculative structures' using whatever non-phenomenological, empirical, or theoretical considerations are available.[28]

Derrida's deconstruction of givenness requires us to give an interpretation of *différance* or spacing where phenomenology has failed. This interpretation must not make the Husserlian mistake of defining the 'differantiality' of the trace structure in terms of a homogeneity or purity of time. Husserl continued to think 'time [as] a general form, the homogeneous element of this differential-ity'.[29] 'Rather [the trace] must be thought *in return*.'[30] We must explain time, on the basis of 'this differential heterogeneity'.[31]

This idea of 'thinking in return' is crucial to understanding the logic of Derrida's argument. Indeed, I take it to be one of the hall-marks of deconstructive thought. 'Givenness', 'presence', 'time' can only be explained or accounted for when thought 'in return', that is from the point of view of a successful deconstruction. Thinking in return requires re-traversing the path in thought that led to a deconstruction. For example, when the phenomenologist discovers that there is something in presence (givenness) which disturbs presence but can make no sense of it (except to say it is 'constitutive' of presence), then this disturbance and excess must be the impetus and guide for seeking a perspective that can resolve this disturbance or 'differential heterogeneity'. Such an enterprise or project, if successful, will allow us to think both the heterogene-ity and what it seems to make possible – the experience of pres-ence, givenness and self-evidence.

The structures in question are speculative not because they go *beyond* givenness (in the strict or literal sense of what is given to us, evidentiarily speaking), but rather because that which in given-ness 'overflows the (given) presence of the present' requires us to speak of a *speculative structure*.[32] Such structures will, indeed, be 'difficult to describe in the classical logos of philosophy ... the order of that which represents itself or presents itself clearly and easily in order to coordinate itself with the value of presence which governs everything that is self evident in experience'.[33]

In this context – a text that tracks Freud's attempt to evidence and evince something that is in principle resolutely 'negative' or 'beyond' the pleasure principle – Derrida calls 'speculative' not those claims that illicitly go beyond the '(self) evidenced' or given, but rather that which shows itself through what is given as 'over-flowing [the form of] presence' and leads us to go beyond the clas-sical logos whose language and concepts deny any reality or access to the speculative structure.

Transforming the notion of givenness in order to reveal *diffé-*

*rance* as a speculative structure, Derrida dismantles correlationism from within. Having shown that there is no 'inside' to textuality, he still has to make explicit the sense in which there is no pure outside (or exteriority). How does the trace – the sort of entangled form irreducible to presence – permit us to think exteriority in a non-mundane sense? To think of materiality and matter 'in return' – in terms of the trace? This is the alpha and omega for any deconstructive materialism.

## Conclusion

With regret, Derrida observed in an interview with Maurizio Ferraris in 1994 that his notion of text has most often been interpreted as a replacement for the crossed out or discredited notion of reality. On this (mis)reading, 'text' is shorthand for the claim that the constitutive role of language in producing our sense of reality makes language the 'authority of final jurisdiction'. Yet, as Derrida insists:

> Deconstruction . . . was always a protest against the 'linguistic turn' which under the name of structuralism was already well on its way. The irony – painful at times – of the story is that often, especially in the United States, because I wrote '*il n'y a pas de hors-texte*', because I deployed a thought of the 'trace', some people thought they could interpret this as a thought of language (*it is exactly the opposite*) . . . I take great interest in questions of language and rhetoric, and I think they deserve enormous consideration; but there is a point where the authority or final jurisdiction is neither rhetorical nor linguistic, nor even *discursive. The notion of trace or of text is introduced to mark the limits of the linguistic turn.* This is one more reason why I prefer to speak of 'mark' rather than of language. In the first place the mark is not anthropological; it is pre-linguistic; it is the possibility of language, *and it is everywhere there is a relation to another thing or relation to an other.* For such relations, the mark has no need of language.[34]

Here, perhaps more assertively than elsewhere, Derrida distinguishes his notion of textuality from that of an absolute discursivity with which it has been confounded. Insofar as it has to do with relations – and in particular with relations to others – it is more general than language and not to be confused with the human, either transcendentally or anthropologically speaking.

Nonetheless, deconstruction does not simply break with or turn away from the philosophies of access. Derrida, I argue, considers phenomenology's critique of naive realism ('the natural attitude') – to be a necessary point of departure.[35] If Derrida would agree with the correlationist critique that the philosophical tradition is mired in epistemological questions of access, the roots of this obsession need to be thoroughly understood and diagnosed.

In *Of Grammatology*, Derrida writes:

> It is to escape falling back into naive objectivism that I refer here to a transcendentality that I elsewhere put into question. It is because I believe that there is a short-of and a beyond of transcendental criticism. To see to it that the *beyond* does not return to the *within* is to recognize in the contortion the necessity of a pathway [*parcours*]. That pathway must leave a track in the transcendental text. Without that track, abandoned to the simple content of its conclusions, the ultra-transcendental text will so closely resemble the pre-critical text as to be indistinguishable from it. (OG, 61)

The deconstructive critique will not return us to a mundane, pre-critical world, nor will it permit us to retain the use of many of our concepts, since the latter are structured by the very metaphysical oppositions that produce the transcendental problematic. The deconstructive or ultra-transcendental text allows us to rewrite the terms of metaphysics in a way that will not reinscribe the old oppositions. Without 'traversing' critiques of naive objectivism (or realism), 'post-critical' or 'post-correlationist' philosophies risk falling short of, rather than going beyond, the correlationist position of which transcendental philosophy is one example.

In the chapters that follow, I characterise deconstruction in terms of its displacement of correlationism and explain in what this displacement consists. In particular, I argue that Derrida's displacement of the correlationist problematic leads us to a metaphysical realist interpretation of text and writing. If this anti-correlationist, realist reading is right, then speculative realism is wrong to oppose or reject deconstructive philosophy. Rather, deconstruction should be seen as a powerful philosophical ally.[36]

The reading I propose makes it possible to integrate the realist-sounding claims that Derrida makes, but that are often bracketed or under-emphasised, into a coherent interpretation of deconstruction. Derrida argues, negatively, that his notion of the text was never meant to underwrite an anti-realism that extended the 'reassuring' notion of the book to the 'outside world'.[37] The world is not to be seen as a text in this sense.[38]

> [A]n hour's reading, beginning on any page of any one of the texts I have published over the last twenty years, should suffice for you to realize that text, as I use the word, is not the book. No more than writing or trace, it is not limited to the *paper* which you cover with your graphism ... It is in the interest of one side and the other to represent deconstruction as turning inward towards an enclosure by the limits of language, whereas in fact deconstruction *begins* by deconstructing logocentrism, the linguistics of the word, and this very enclosure itself.

Interestingly, Derrida suggests here that both realist and anti-realist positions have an interest in reading deconstruction as 'turning inward towards an enclosure by ... language'. This characterisation has allowed the debate between different species of correlationism to continue unabated.

## Notes

1. Braver (2007: xix).
2. Barad (2003: 802).
3. Spivak (1989: 150).
4. DeLanda (2012: 43).
5. Malabou (2016: 36).
6. Butler (1993). See Kirby (2005b) for a powerful critique of Butler's account of 'materialisation'.
7. Bhaskar (2008).
8. Bhaskar (2008: 21).
9. In fact, the phenomenologist has more resources to offer the realist than this description suggests. Husserlian 'transcendental' phenomenology describes the object of perception in terms of a difference dividing the 'presence' of the object. This difference is internal to the 'materialisation'. There is the *object* that appears and the *appearance* of the object. The former is the intelligible object. Husserl argues that appearance and object are indissociable – two sides of the same coin. The object is disclosed through its appearance. Our investigations of the world presuppose this disclosive activity. It may seem that the world dissimulates itself in perception, insofar as it 'hides' or

'forgets' its own disclosive activity. But this is not essentially deceiving, since this difference 'internal' to perception reflects or evidences the reflective or expressive relation of mind and world. However, the phenomenologist can, again, only say that such a relation is evidenced rather than endorse its truth.

10. Dan Zahavi, one of Husserl's very best contemporary interpreters, offers just such an account of Husserl's notion of intentionality. According to Zahavi, Husserl's account of the correlation of mind and world in intentional consciousness makes him a perceptual realist while rejecting 'metaphysical' realism. A perceptual realist rejects representationalism – the idea that we are 'in touch' with internal effigies or signs, rather than 'the things themselves' – but also rejects the conceivability of an uncorrelated reality (Zahavi 2008).

11. As we have seen, feminists have argued that representations are not neutral and distinct from the reality they claim to represent. Feminist accounts of the body's discursive construction emphasise the power of representations to produce the reality they purport to reflect. In this case, representations may not only distort the reality they represent through various forms of cognitive and perceptual bias, they may, in an ontological reversal, produce reality. In this case, 'discursive construction' undermines 'Representationalism' insofar as it insists on the entanglement of representationalism and reality. For example, labelling a baby 'girl' has characteristically led, as Iris Marion Young (2005) famously argued, to an under-developed body and a depression of the body's physical potentials. This under-development is due to gendered cultural practices that have historically included constraining clothing, foot binding, and norms of comportment that dictate passivity as the mark of 'femininity'. More generally, Ian Hacking has argued that humans are essentially interactive or discursive kinds because they are uniquely aware and responsive to representation. Unable to remain neutral with respect to how they are represented, 'discursive kinds' end up being formed by these representations. By contrast, though (human) representations certainly bear on matter through various forms of intentional activity, this is not due to any awareness on the part of matter (1999: 34). Representations are not ontologically inert, then, but the entanglements of representation and reality are limited, apparently, to human kinds.

12. Barad (2010).

13. Wilson (1998: 202–3).

14. Wilson (1998: 161–2).

15. Wilson (1998: 189).
16. Wolfe (2010: 43).
17. Colebrook (2011: 20).
18. Colebrook (2011: 6).
19. Colebrook (2011: 7).
20. Colebrook (2011: 7).
21. Bryant et al. (2011: 3).
22. Harman (2007: 204).
23. Meillassoux (2008: 5).
24. Harman's (2009) notion of a 'philosophy of access' is perhaps a more intuitive label than 'correlationism', but both help us think a set of positions that are otherwise difficult to subsume. For example, Judith Butler's notion of discursive construction and Husserl's notion of constitution are antithetical philosophical positions in many respects. The latter is a dedicated realist – for Husserl, the objects that we experience are just 'the things themselves' (as they *appear*) – whereas Butler is staunchly anti-realist, arguing that it simply makes no sense to ask what is outside of the discursive constitution of subjects and bodies – since it is this very discursive constitution that makes that question possible. Harman's point is that a 'philosophy of access' is essentially concerned with the question of the status of the object – and with the objectivity of the object. Philosophies of access bracket questions related to ontology and focus instead on questions related to epistemology, and especially with the conditions of possibility for truth.
25. Bryant et al. (2011: 3).
26. I owe this term 'parallelism' to Paola Marrati (personal communication, 2011).
27. Derrida (1982: 172).
28. Or, to adopt Derrida's terms from his essay on Freud in *The Post Card*, 'givenness' shows itself to be a 'speculative structure' 'in the sense of that which overflows the (given) presence of the present' (1987: 284).
29. Derrida (1987: 280).
30. Derrida (1987: 280).
31. Derrida (1987: 280).
32. Derrida (1987: 284).
33. Derrida (1987: 289).
34. Derrida and Ferraris (2001: 76).
35. For an excellent account of the relation between deconstruction and critiques of naive naturalism, or what Husserl called the 'natural

attitude', see Joshua Kates's indispensable study of Derrida's relation to Husserlian phenomenology and transcendental critique (Kates 2005).

36. For a realist defence of 'the trace' and 'iterability' that interprets the latter in terms of possible kinds of objects, see Roden (2004). Roden defends the view that Derrida's notion of the trace implies that there are such things as iterable, or repeatable, particulars, whereas I argue that Derrida defends the more radical claim that there is nothing but such repeatable particulars.

37. 'It was never our wish to extend the reassuring notion of the text to a whole extra-textual realm and to transform the world into a library by doing away with all boundaries . . . but . . . we sought rather to work out the theoretical and practical system of these margins, these borders, once more, from the ground up' (Derrida and Venuti 2001: 84–5).

38. Derrida (1986: 77).

# 2

# From Ancestral Events to Posthumous Texts: Two Critiques of Correlationism

For my own part, I think that if one were looking for a single phrase to capture the stage to which philosophy has progressed, 'the study of evidence' would be a better choice than 'the study of language'.

A. J. Ayer, *Philosophy in the Twentieth Century*

## Derrida and Meillassoux: Two Critiques of Correlationism

Today the problem of correlationism and its pertinence to contemporary continental philosophy is well known. The term owes much of its current prominence, of course, to Quentin Meillassoux's *After Finitude* (2008). However, as Husserlian Dan Zahavi helpfully underlines, its philosophical use can be traced back to an earlier, less pejorative context.

As Zahavi recalls, Maximillian Beck in 1928 characterised phenomenology in terms of a solution to a series of philosophical antinomies:

'Correlationism' can here serve as the term for a position developed by Husserl and Dilthey, according to which the old alternative between idealism or realism, subjectivism or objectivism, philosophy of immanence and phenomenalism or philosophy of the real, must be overcome in favor of the following [negative] claim: Neither does a world in itself exist independently of consciousness, nor does only consciousness or a conscious subject exist and the world merely as a mode (experience, function, content) of consciousness or the subject. Neither do we know the world as it is in itself, i.e. independently of our consciousness, nor do we merely know an illusory world, behind which the real, true, world exists in itself. The positive counter-thesis of correlationism is the following: *Consciousness and world, subject*

*and object, I and world stand in a correlative, i.e. mutually depend-*
*ent context of being, such that the disjunctions mentioned above are*
*meaningless.*[1]

If, according to Beck, 'correlationism' names a positive solution to
a philosophical problem – a solution to the ontological indetermi-
nateness of what is meant by 'perceived object' – for Meillassoux
it names the overarching anti-realist framework for a modern
philosophy that stymies its development.

Meillassoux – no doubt unwittingly – rewrites Beck's 'positive
[correlationist] counter- thesis' as 'there are no objects, no events,
no laws, no beings which are not always-already correlated with
a point of view, with a subjective access'.[2] This correlationist
thesis is a problem because it consumes and exhausts philosophy
with the insoluble problem of access. 'Experience' and 'consciousness' are indices for access problems and testify to a form of
philosophical forgetting. What is urgent to think is the world in its
radical difference from and indifference to the human subject. For
Meillassoux, correlationism's inability to conceive of the radical
absence of the human from most of the Earth's past (and its prob-
able absence from its future) is sufficient grounds for rejecting the
correlationist thesis. This rejection implies the rejection of most
post-Kantian philosophy:

> The central notion of modern philosophy after Kant seems to be
> that of *correlation*. By 'correlation' we mean the idea according to
> which we only ever have access to the correlation between thinking
> and being, and never to either term considered apart from the other.
> We will henceforth call *correlationism* any current of thought which
> maintains the unsurpassable character of the correlation so defined.
> Consequently, it becomes possible to say that every philosophy which
> disavows naïve realism has become a variant of correlationism.[3]

Importantly, Meillassoux does not expect the sort of critique he
proposes to lead back to naive realism. That is, if the naive realist
takes the world disclosed through our perceptions to be the real
world, the world as it is independent of our perceptions, then
correlationism will properly point out that this effaces the role
and activity of the perceiver, which must be factored. The correlationist critique will not fall short of the transcendental critique.
As a critique of the critique it seeks a path beyond correlationism

that will allow us to again conceive of thought as adequate to the world. Such a critique, however, must first demonstrate its necessity. If, on Beck's telling, correlationism was necessary to overcome the problems of naive realism and to give an account of the relation between mind and world, what philosophical impasse motivates overcoming correlationism?

The title of this chapter mentions two critiques of correlationism. There are no doubt other candidates, but my aim in this chapter is to argue that, while it has gone strangely unremarked, Derridean deconstruction is a radical critique of correlationism and proceeds by a similar argumentative strategy to the one proposed by Meillassoux.

Both Meillassoux and Derrida motivate their critique of correlationism by identifying what I will call an 'extra-correlational instance'. As Meillassoux argues, a living body is a necessary condition for the instantiation of a transcendental subject, which accounts for its finite point of view on the world. An extra-correlational instance, then, is one that 'takes place' under conditions that logically preclude the taking place of the transcendental subject. Any instance is extra-correlational which is in principle unwitnessable or unrecognisable. Of course, the correlationist will deny that there could be any such instances in principle, or will at least claim that any such instances are transcendental illusions. The argumentative strategy I attribute to Meillassoux and Derrida lies in demonstrating the necessity of such instances.

Meillassoux argues that correlationist epistemology founders on 'the ancestral'. The ancestral is an unwitnessable event; by definition, it takes place prior to the appearance of life. For example, the accretion of the planet Earth five billion years ago would be such an ancestral event. The correlationist, Meillassoux argues, cannot *literally* believe in unwitnessable events and processes that occur prior to the appearance of life. Belief in ancestral events requires an epistemology that does not entail that objects or events outside of a possible experience are unthinkable.

Derrida, on the other hand, argues that the structure of texts is extra-correlational. Texts, he argues, remain 'structurally readable' in the absolute absence of any possible reader. Correlationism, wrongly, identifies the conditions of 'readability' with the transcendental subject. Only an extra-correlational account of these conditions will reveal this structure, which Derrida refers to as *sur-vival* (*sur-vivance*).

Meillassoux's critique of correlationism has been especially influential in contemporary continental philosophy. In particular, it has energised debates about the limits of phenomenology for thinking life, embodiment and the material world. As Catherine Malabou writes of Meillassoux: 'in search of noncorrelationist modes of thinking, [he] elaborates a notion of the absolute which would not be "ours," which would remain indifferent to us'.[4] She suggests that the idea of material processes radically disjunct from the transcendental subject – *self*-informing, ungoverned and ungovernable – is at the centre of contemporary new materialisms. In particular, these modes of thinking reject correlationism's attention to 'givenness', the centrality of the category of first-person experience, and the problem of the relation of thought to world.

Derrida's critique of correlationism, as already mentioned, is less well known. Indeed, it is usually not read as a critique of correlationism at all, but rather as endorsing an anti-realist variant of correlationism. As a result, *its* impetus to materialist thought goes unrecognised. As I argued in the previous chapter, Derrida's account of textuality is often misread as a post-structuralist variant of the correlationism that Meillassoux diagnoses. However, as a reading of Derridean *textuality* this interpretation is hard to credit as soon as we factor in that Derrida defines textuality in terms of its extra-correlational status. Indeed, he could not have been more explicit that written texts – properly understood – can be correlated neither with a subject, nor with lived experience, nor with transcendental activity.

Just as 'everyone' *knows*, for example, that for Foucault the 'author is dead', so too does 'everyone' *know* that for Derrida the text remains 'readable' after its author's death. However, in both cases there is a rather large gap between recognising the dictum and understanding its meaning. The text, Derrida famously writes in 'Signature, Event, Context' (1972), survives in the radical absence of any possible recipient, 'of any possible reader determined in general'.[5] The text (and its survival) transcends its recognition; it is not relative to a reader or any enabling acts.

The parallels between Derrida's claims about a written message being still 'structurally readable' in the 'absolute absence' of any recipients and Meillassoux's claims about ancestral events being still evidenced in the 'absolute' absence of any witnesses are unmistakable. Yet many of Derrida's readers deflate his claim about texts because it seems *prima facie* implausible. Yes, it is true that the text survives the death of this or that author or reader. After all, we regularly read the words, thoughts and intentions of those long dead. Their *words* survive thanks to writing. However, the same intuitions which will readily grant the latter will lead us to say that *texts* cannot be readable in the radical, let us even say terminal, absence of readers and writers in general.

The aim of this chapter is twofold. First, it demonstrates that Derrida's account of textuality is part of a radical critique of correlationism, or what he calls the 'metaphysics of presence'. Second, it explores the significance of the structural parallels and disjunctures between the critiques of Derrida and Meillassoux. The parallels are easily evidenced. Meillassoux's ancestral event and Derrida's posthumous texts both press the correlationist to admit a radical outside to transcendental activity. Both argue that the absolute exteriority of ancestrality and textuality, respectively, cannot be understood in terms of a *possible* relation to a knowing subject. Each of them wagers that demonstrating the necessary transcendence of these instances will present the correlationist – committed to the unsurpassability of the epistemic relation – with a crisis of their most basic philosophical commitments.

At this level of generality, the structural similarities between these two thinkers may tempt us to say that the main difference between their approaches is the placement of the temporal ruptures with the human that they introduce. Meillassoux's ancestral events point to a time radically anterior to the human (indeed to any life on Earth), whereas Derrida's posthumous texts point to a time radically posterior to human life. However, closer attention to the differences between the extra-correlational instances breaks the homology I have just set up. For Derrida, the extra-correlation instance refers to a structure, for Meillassoux it refers to an event.

## Extra-Correlational Instances

Written texts and natural events are very different sorts of things. One cannot easily generalise from one to the other. If the goal is to push the correlationist interlocutor to admit to a necessarily transcendental instance, written texts seem a uniquely challenging choice of object. Unlike natural events, which our spontaneous, naive realism already conceives non-correlationally – as unfolding in blind indifference to human concerns – we are not at all accustomed to thinking of written texts as radically independent of humans. On the contrary, texts seem like exemplary technical objects uniquely reliant on human makers.

It is, Meillassoux underscores, the dubious virtue of correlationism to make belief in extra-correlational events and objects seem incredible. It seems incredible, on the contrary, to think of texts in extra-correlational terms. Yet, as we shall see below, Derrida defines texts – exemplary linguistic artefacts – as 'absolute' in Meillassoux's sense, that is, as indifferent to human survival. Thus, Meillassoux's critique of correlationism on the basis of the ancestral premise vindicates (rather than challenges) everyday ideas about natural events. On the other hand, Derrida's notion of absolute textuality will entail a radical revision of our standard view of texts.

All things being equal – assuming both instances do the same kind of critical work – we might be tempted to adopt Meillassoux's approach. Ancestral events promise to generalise to any and all (material) events, processes and objects. It is not at all clear how truths about texts would generalise to non-textual items. But of course, all things are not equal, and the 'object' choice is anything but philosophically arbitrary; it defines their respective approaches to the problem of correlationism. Meillassoux's anti-correlationist project leads to Alain Badiou and his ontology of the event, while Derrida's project leads through grammatology, the project of a general writing.

Must we choose between Meillassoux's critique of correlationism and Derrida's? Does it matter if our escape from correlationism involves reflecting on the non-relative or absolute status of events or texts? In this chapter, I shall argue that it does matter. Reflecting on the difference between Meillassoux's and Derrida's choice of object will allow us to diagnose a problem with Meillassoux's argument, or what he understands to be the entailments of his argument. The distance between the two approaches narrows considerably once we correct for this problem.

Meillassoux believes that correlationists face a characteristic dilemma: patterns of reasoning that normally warrant belief in scientific statements do not warrant such belief in the case of ancestral events. Therefore, according to him, they must decide between their epistemic commitments to scientific evidence and their correlationist commitments to the inconceivability of uncorrelated events. However, on my reading, Meillassoux misunderstands the entailments of his own argument. As he formulates it, the problem of ancestrality actually challenges correlationists' beliefs about the nature of *evidence* and not the nature of events. If there is evidence of ancestral events, this evidence must itself be ancestral. If there is evidence *of* the non-correlational then there is also non-correlational evidence. But this violates the correlational account of evidence, that is, that all evidence is a form of givenness, which Meillassoux's argument assumes rather than challenges.

If my reading is right, Meillassoux's thought-experiment motivates not a non-epistemic conception of objects and events but a non-epistemic – or recognition-transcendent – conception of evidence. This difference has non-trivial consequences for Meillassoux's critique. By contrast, Derridean textuality just is, under a different description, recognition-transcendent, non-correlational evidence.

Non-correlational or recognition-transcendent evidence will sound as odd as recognition-transcendent texts. Indeed, as I will suggest in the conclusion of this chapter, the structure of textuality and what I shall call the structure of indicative evidence are the same. On the standard view of texts and indicative signs, which Derrida challenges, both are defined as correlates of transcendental activity. Texts and signs are only such when seen as indicating the meaning of something to a subject who recognises them as playing this functional role. If, on the other hand, this standard (correlational) view is wrong, then evidentiary traces, including those traces of ancestral events, and written texts both require a non-correlational account. Once we reinterpret Meillassoux's argument in a way that correctly identifies its pertinence to evidence rather than events, I argue that it entails revisions to our everyday notion of events of the same order and scope as those prompted by Derrida's notion of textuality.

In the remainder of this chapter, I reconstruct Meillassoux's account of correlationism, emphasising the realist variant, which is the target of his critique in *After Finitude*. As he argues, the correlationist believes herself to be a realist, roughly someone who can affirm the meaning of scientific statements, despite affirming the unsurpassability of the correlation.[6] Meillassoux's argument depends upon defeating the belief that correlationism is compatible with realism. I argue that Meillassoux does defeat the correlationist on the grounds he lays out, just not in the way that he thinks he does. A more granular account of correlationism's philosophy of evidence allows us to identify a critical equivocation in his argument.

I then reconstruct Derrida's critique of correlationism from textuality. Derrida argues that texts are necessarily extra-correlational – they retain their function autonomously from transcendental subjects or readers. This relates essentially to their structure. Non-correlational texts are what I call 'in-formed' or parasitic forms.

In the chapter's final section, I turn to the significance of Derridean textuality for Meillassoux's critique from ancestrality. Despite the fact that Meillassoux's account would deny any meaningful distinction between ancestral evidence and ancestral events, his argument from ancestrality implicitly preserves the opposition between indirect or indicative evidence and directly given events that is essential to the correlationist position. Deconstructing the opposition makes clear that a sufficiently powerful critique of correlationism will require, as a matter of priority, a non-correlational account of evidence. Derridean textuality provides a schema for just such an account.

## Meillassoux and the Critique of Correlationism from 'Ancestrality'

In *After Finitude*, Meillassoux argues provocatively that the truth of the correlationist can be found in the bad-faith science sceptic.[7] Consider the biblical creationist who believes in the literal truth of Genesis. When presented with radiometric evidence (radioactive dating) for the antiquity of the Earth, the biblical literalist can either argue that she is not interested in scientific evidence, or, if she wishes to avoid charges of irrationality, she can argue that such evidence does not *compel* belief.

Belief in an ancient Earth seems to be well supported by radioactive dating. But according to the sceptic, this belief does not warrant the credence that scientists assign to it. We must believe that the presence of the stable argon 'daughters' that we test for today, and that we use to calculate the age of rocks, were *not* present at the rock's accretion, but are exclusively effects of the very long process of radioactive decay (the half-life of potassium-40 is around 1,250 billion years). The sophistical sceptic will disarmingly agree that this *is* a reasonable assumption on the basis of the conditions we find *today*. But how can we be sure that these same conditions were present *then*, at the origin?

It is true: we cannot be certain of initial conditions at the Earth's genesis, a time before any possible witnesses. Scientific inquiry attempts to gain knowledge of these conditions by examining traces of these events as they persist in the present, for example in the geological record. The sceptic reminds us, however, that evidence is a relational game between inquirer and world; the game does not extend to a world that does not correlate to the inquirer. Scientists must assume (nature's) continuity and uniformity, that the conditions we find and observe today can be retrojected to the ancient past. But, the sceptic argues, this belief is unwarranted by scientific standards of evidence. We cannot validate that the same conditions that we observe today prevailed then, at the time of the Great Unwitnessable. Therefore, science too rests on faith.

The bad-faith sceptic emphasises the central role of the witness for establishing not only the 'initial conditions' but also the persisting uniformity of natural laws. The presence of corroborated evidence of these conditions validates the chain of inferences from initial conditions to the present inquirer. However, where there is a manifest break in this chain, the epistemic warrant for scientific inferences fails. The sceptic's argument assumes that the (ideal) standard of evidence is that which is seen with one's own eyes – or otherwise *given* to the senses – and that such givenness is also the ground for all inference. For evidence of any process or event to be sufficient, it must in some sense be contemporaneous with an observer, or at least a possible observer.

Meillassoux argues that bad-faith science sceptics avail themselves of all the best resources that correlationist philosophy has to offer. It follows that resisting the present wave of irrationalism will not require doing battle with biblical literalists in the name of scientific rationality. It will require doing battle with the seemingly responsible and institutionally respectable correlationist philosopher who unwittingly provides the science sceptic with so much sustenance. The sophisticated biblical literalist allows us to make explicit the correlationist belief that evidence divorced from witnesses, from a possible mode of givenness, is no evidence at all.

If the science sceptic depicted above is in bad faith, this is because their primary interest is not to consider the evidence of science from an indifferent point of view, but to defend their own dogmatic views as equally rational and warranted. Meillassoux does not think the correlationist in general is a bad-faith sceptic; indeed, he thinks that correlationists are usually not even aware that they *are* science sceptics. Thus, pointing out that the correlationist shares her epistemic bed with the biblical literalist is meant to serve as a wake-up call.

At this point it is worth emphasising that Meillassoux's argument does not aim at so-called post-structural correlationists who would doubt that even our best (witness-corroborated) evidence could ever (literally) be about the world. The correlationist who believes that what we call 'evidence' is really experience as it conforms to contingent conceptual or linguistic schemes is not likely to be moved by charges that she undermines scientific claims to objectivity. Often, her arguments call for radical revisions to accounts of scientific objectivity. Meillassoux aims rather at those correlationists who believe that their epistemic commitments do *nothing* to impugn the validity of scientific claims. In other words, he aims at realist-compatible varieties of correlationism and wagers that making explicit the link between correlationism and forms of contemporary irrationality will galvanise these correlationists to revise their views in the direction of a realism that will radically decentre the role of the finite observer.

Meillassoux's strategy assumes, then, that at least some correlationists – the realist ones – are in error about their own beliefs. But how can correlationists be so mistaken about their views – in particular the epistemic consequences of their views? For Meillassoux, the correlationist is mistaken about her ability to endorse the literal meaning of scientific statements. This misapprehension is clarified when we consider scientific statements about the distant – pre-human, pre-carbon-based life – past. Exemplary of such statements is 'the Earth accreted 4.5 billion years ago'. He calls these sorts of statements ancestral statements. In turn, they are grounded in statements about 'arche-fossils' and 'fossil-matter'. As Levi Bryant glosses:

> Meillassoux refers to 'arche-fossils' and 'fossil-matter' as not simply materials *indicating the traces of past life* in the sense of our familiar understanding of 'fossil', but also as materials *indicating the existence of ancestral realities or events anterior to all life*. An arche-fossil is thus not an ancestral being like the big bang 'in the flesh', but is rather something like the radioactive decay of isotopes that allows us to *infer* the ancestral or that which precedes all life. Meillassoux's question is thus two-fold: On the one hand, he asks, under what conditions are these statements meaningful? That is, what must be the case for ances-

tral statements to have any sense? On the other hand, and more fundamentally, how must the correlationist interpret these statements?[8]

The first question Bryant attributes to Meillassoux – 'what must be the case for ancestral statements to have any sense?' – seems easy to answer. According to a certain view, one knows the meaning of 'the Earth accreted 4.5 billion years ago' when one knows its truth conditions. 'The Earth accreted 4.5 billion years ago' is true if and only if the Earth accreted 4.5 billion years ago.

The second question, about how the correlationist must interpret the statement, is less clear. As Bryant glosses, the correlationist can unproblematically agree that fossils, in general, indicate the existence of past life. They can affirm this because the past life these fossils *indicate* is (presumably) correlatable, something that could in principle be given 'in the flesh' to a witness. However, arche-fossils are material indications (in the present) that allow us to refer to that which cannot, in principle, be given.

Herein lies the rub for the correlationist. For her there can be no evidence, indicative or otherwise, of what cannot in principle be given. The correlationist must insist that arche-fossils, unlike fossils contemporaneous with life on Earth, do not evidence anything. They cannot be indications, they cannot function as evidence. The correlationist reasons that we take the indicating evidence to be evidence of an event which, *were* there witnesses, would have appeared 'in the flesh' in such and such a way.

The conditions for givenness are retrojected backwards. Indeed, as Meillassoux emphasises, this is just how the correlationist makes sense of any and all appeals to unwitnessed events. However, the difference between the unwitnessed and the ancestral – the reason why the latter poses a problem to the correlationist that the former does not – is that, in the case of the ancestral, this retrojection violates the core correlationist view that an object that cannot *in principle* be given 'in the flesh' cannot be thought. Thus, Meillassoux argues that any statement equivalent to 'we have indicative evidence of ancestral events' cannot be meaningful to the correlationist. Or else, the correlationist must admit that there is evidence of the uncorrelated.

## Correlationism as a Theory of Evidence

Correlationism is, I argue, best construed as a theory of evidence. A brief detour through this theory will clarify the issues surrounding 'evidence of the uncorrelated'. For the realist correlationist – for example, the Husserlian phenomenologist – the (ideal) standard of evidence is that of self-evidence or givenness. As Husserl writes in the fourth *Logical Investigation*, 'the appearing object announces itself as self-given' in an 'originary giving intuition' – this object appears, in his formulation, 'in the flesh'.[9]

The object as it gives itself in perception testifies to its presence and, we might add, even to its ontological independence from its own appearance. For Husserl, part of the meaning of a worldly object's appearance is that it *transcends* its appearance. However, as with any other knowable feature of the world, this ontological independence is evidenced through the ways it is given. A phenomenological analysis makes the mode and manner of its givenness explicit.

Givenness, or self-evidencing, is not limited to perception, which remains nonetheless exemplary for the phenomenologist. Many things self-evidence beyond perceptual objects, including mathematical idealities, the meaning of proofs and theoretical entities. What all forms of givenness have in common is that they involve ideal content or meaning. In the case of a present perception, meaning (formulable as a logical statement) is intrinsic to its appearing. Meanings can, however, float free of the perceptions that make them meaningful. To understand the meaning of a statement such as 'the cat is on the mat' requires, for Husserl, knowing what sort of perceptual state of affairs would make that sentence self-evident.

Husserl calls this movement from language to meaning 'reactivation'. To get at the meanings of our statements, we must be able, at least in principle, to go back to the primary self-evidences upon which these statements are built. For example, we reactivate the meaning of Euclidean geometry when we go through the proofs and reawaken the sort of cognitive self-evidences that animated Euclid when he wrote his proofs. Reactivation is important for scientific activity, in particular, because of the long chains of inferential reasoning and judgements involved in scientific work and communication.[10]

Just as givenness is not limited to a present perception, evidence is not, strictly speaking, limited to forms of direct givenness. The correlationist admits a secondary form of evidence: indeed, one that is closer to the everyday use of that term. Evidence is either self-giving or it is what Husserl calls 'indicative'. However, indicative evidence is evidence only insofar as it leads back to a form of possible givenness. That is, indication points the observer to an absent or past form of presence. It is, as it were, a placeholder for meaning. The meaning of any indicative sign is never in its primary givenness – how it directly appears – and to take it as it is given is to miss that it is evidence *of* something, in short that it is a sign *of* something.[11]

Indication supposes an inferential leap from absence to presence. Non-presence is part of the way that indicative evidence 'gives' itself. Husserl's example: when we *see* smoke *indicatively*, we see it as indicating the 'presence' of (a perceptually absent) fire. The difference between seeing smoke directly (as it gives itself) and seeing smoke indicatively is not 'intrinsic' to the appearing object (that is, smoke); the difference is in how the perceiver 'takes' or 'intends' the perceptual object (*as* a given, or *as* a sign). Thus, for example, when the dendochronologist (who analyses and dates the growth rings of trees) discovers a spike in carbon-14 in a tree's rings, she recognises this presence as a marker or trace of a past event, say a solar flare. She can then date the event of the solar flare, knowing that each tree ring marks a terrestrial year. The meaning of any indicative sign is whatever more original, primary form of presence it points to. This meaning is established not by the sign, but by the knower's tutored inferences. Indeed, as Husserl writes in *Ideas I*, 'Nature *is* only in being constituted in regular concatenations of consciousness.'[12]

Indicative evidence, then, is no more recognition-transcendent than other primary forms of givenness. It requires seeing something as evidence, or as a sign of something else, which in turn requires making the sort of associations that will lead back to (a form of) possible givenness. The difference between indicative evidence and givenness is the sort of evidentiary warrant each gives. Givenness, Husserl specifies, is apodictic or self-evident.[13] Indication, by contrast, is never self-evident. We need a web of associations and empirical correlations to grasp something as indicative.

The detour through the correlationist theory of evidence is complete. We needed the distinction between indicative evidence and evidence 'in the flesh' or givenness in order to get a precise sense for why a correlationist cannot affirm indicative evidence of the ancestral.

### Evidence of the Absolute as 'Absolute Evidence'

As we saw above, Meillassoux seeks to weaken correlationists' intuitions that they can vindicate the *realist* meaning of scientific statements. He argues that the weakness of correlationism as a satisfactory interpretation of scientific evidence is manifest in correlationists' inability to affirm ancestral events. Ancestral events are prior to the possibility of self-evidence, thus they cannot be equated with any form of (direct) givenness. But neither can ancestral events be indicated, properly speaking, since as we just saw, indication must refer to a possible presence or form of givenness. Hence, the correlationist cannot affirm, after all, what the scientist affirms when affirming evidence for an ancient Earth – not because the events referenced are uncorrelated, but because there cannot be *evidence* of the uncorrelated.

Meillassoux focuses on the difference between the meaning of the scientist's statement for the scientist and its meaning for the correlationist. Unfortunately, he does not discuss whether the scientist would endorse the non recognition-transcendent status of their evidence. It is true that for the scientist the arche-fossil will count as evidence (a valid ground of inference for the ancestral event) whereas it cannot count as such for the correlationist. But why does arche-evidence remain a valid ground of inference for the scientist? It must be because the scientist, at least implicitly, has a different view of indicative evidence than the correlationist. The scientist does not (or need not) believe that indicative evidence is essentially tied to givenness. There can be evidence of the non-correlatable because evidence is uncorrelated.

Curiously, Meillassoux seems to retain the very correlational account of evidence that he otherwise puts into question. To paraphrase Meillassoux, what the correlationist cannot accept is that an 'arche-fossil can manifest [evidence] an entity's anteriority vis-à-vis manifestation [givenness]'.[14] But can the arche-fossil also manifest this anteriority without manifesting to someone? Apparently not, since Meillassoux writes just before the line quoted that 'fossil-matter is the *givenness in the present* of a being that is anterior to givenness'. Strictly speaking, he ought to have written, 'fossil-matter is evidence (in the present) of a being anterior to givenness'. This is what the correlationist cannot believe but what the scientist must believe, since, for both, the fossil matter will always have been traces of anterior being and not givenness qua self-evidence.

The question for Meillassoux is why he accepts the correlationist's description of evidentiary traces in the first place?

Given that the arche-fossil dates back billions of years – we are speaking here, again, of things such as radioactive decay, of the 1.2-billion-year half-life of potassium-40 – what does its *givenness in the present* matter to the evidentiary worth of the arche-fossil? Unless we are inclined to agree with our biblical literalist, we would like to say that the decay 'clock' of potassium-40 continues to tick whether it is manifesting (to someone) in the present or not, which is what makes it such good evidence of the remote past. We would want to say, simply – in order to take the scientist literally – that we have evidence of the ancestral because the evidence is itself ancestral. The evidence *evidences* the ancestral, it *indicates* this event, even in the absence of any possible correlation.

Put another way, if evidence can be of the ancestral, if this evidence can itself be ancestral, then indicative evidence ought no longer to be defined by the inferential activity of the scientist any more than the ancestral event ought to be defined by the enabling activity of a knower. Evidence itself must be thought in non-correlational terms.

What I have suggested is that Meillassoux's argument from ancestrality motivates, in the first instance, a non-correlational or recognition-transcendent account of evidence (or, as he puts it, 'traces') rather than a non-correlational account of the event. This sets a rather different path and agenda for the anti-correlationist than the one he anticipates – since he is interested in disentangling both the thought of the event from the thought of evidence, and thought of the ontological from that of the epistemological. However, if evidence were 'absolute' in this sense, then these distinctions no longer mean what they mean for the correlationist. Absolute evidence deconstructs these distinctions because it entails thinking of evidence as independent of transcendental activity. For such a view we find surprising resources in Derrida's notion of textuality, to which we now turn.

## The Critique of Correlationism from 'Posthumous Texts'

The philosopher John Searle, addressing a meeting of literary scholars at the height of deconstruction's influence in the United States, attempted to correct what he saw as literary theory's increasingly unhinged views about texts and meanings.[15] There are, he insisted, exactly two options to review when considering theories of textual (and by extension, linguistic) meaning. The first is to cash out textual meaning in terms of authorial intention. The second is to think of meaning as assigned by the recipients of the text. Meaning, then, is a matter of what is present at the text's inception or reception, through the activity of either the author or the reader. In either case, meaning implies the reduction of the material signifier, an exit from the text towards meaning.

For Searle, it seems obvious that Derrida's dictum 'there is no outside-the-text' would imply not only that texts have no assignable or determinant meaning, but simply no meaning at all:

> For Jacques Derrida meaning is a matter of, well, what? Meanings are 'undecidable' and have 'relative indeterminacy', according to Derrida. Instead of fully determinate meaning, there is rather the free play of signifiers and the grafting of texts onto texts is within the textuality and intertextuality of the text.[16]

Searle's critique of the 'generalised' intertextuality that he attributes to Derrida is an auspicious starting point for elucidating Derrida's concept of textuality. This is not because it offers us the right account of Derridean textuality (it does not), but because it presents, with admirable economy, how Derridean textuality appears from the correlationist's point of view. Since for the correlationist a text only has meaning when and if it is being read by a reader or written by an author, to affirm 'no outside-the-text' means that there is no reader/writer whose transcendental activity can bring the text 'home', returning meaning to the written words. It reduces the text to a heap of insignificance.[17]

As Searle argues, philosophers have typically understood written texts in terms of the sort of subjective activities they make possible: reading and writing, communication at a distance. Just like speech, written texts communicate meanings. However, following Searle's descriptions literally, texts (and speech) do not have meaning; *speakers* and *readers* have meanings. Texts *signify* or *indicate* 'transcendental' or correlational Meanings through a certain economy of the (artefactual) linguistic mark. This picture of texts as vehicles for meanings assumes, Derrida argues, a radical distinction between textual signifiers and their (transcendental) meanings or signifieds. From this it follows that texts can neither be construed in non-relational terms nor considered exclusively from the side of their objective materiality. The idea of an extra-correlational text or sign is a transcendental illusion. To be a text is to be readable, an unreadable text is no text at all, and texts without any possible readers are unreadable. The possibility of reading refers to the possible presence of a reader who can restore their meaning. Meaning, on the other hand, is essentially non-textual.

Contrary to this tradition, Derrida argues that the read*ability* of a text – the essential possibility defining it – is not dependent upon the existence of any reader. Asking us to consider the status of a radically orphaned text, outside the horizon of any transcendental subject, Derrida makes the case for the non-correlational status of texts. 'A writing that is not structurally read*able* – iterable – beyond the death of the addressee – would not be writing.'[18] Here, as will become clear, Derrida is not referring to the death of this or that potential addressee – as is often supposed in the secondary literature – but to the radical absence of all possible addressees. Hence, the readability to which Derrida refers – and which connects with the more unfamiliar term 'iterability' – would redefine the nature of texts, and by extension the nature of meaning.

Let us consider in some detail the moment in Derrida's 1972 essay 'Signature, Event, Context' when he defines texts and writing in terms of this posthumous readability. After arguing, unobjectionably, that writing distinctively functions in the absence of its author or intended reader – a text may always be intercepted, its recipient lost or confused for another – Derrida argues that the same possibility that ensures that texts survive their authors and intended audiences also entails that texts function in the radical absence of all readers:

> In order for my 'written communication' to retain its function as writing, i.e., its readability, it must remain readable despite the *absolute* disappearance of any receiver, determined in general. My communication must be repeatable – iterable – in the *absolute* absence of the receiver or of any empirically determinable collectivity of receivers. Such iterability – (iter, again, probably comes from *itara*, other in Sanskrit, and everything that follows can be read as the working out of the logic that ties repetition to alterity) *structures* the mark of writing itself, no matter what particular type of writing is involved . . . a writing that is not structurally readable – iterable – beyond the death of the addressee would not be writing.[19]

While the classic definition of texts that Searle's analysis calls upon assumes that a transcendental, meaning-giving activity defines texts, Derrida insists that the absence of such activity defines writing of 'no matter what particular type' from the start. If written messages are readable ('retain [their] function as writing') at the two standard termini of the communicative circuit (writer and intended audience), then it follows that the message remains readable (and also interceptable) at any point in its itinerary. If a text is readable at any point in the itinerary, even when it is not being read, is it not strange to think that it would lose its readability in the case of the sudden, apocalyptic and, let us further stipulate, terminal disappearance of any and all possible readers?

The structure of texts accounts for the possibility of reading. Yet this is precisely what the classic definition of a text – the one to which Searle subscribes – denies: the possibility that readability names is located on the side of the transcendental subject that is capable of restoring a text's meaning through the mnemonic associations of exteriorised textual marks with 'internal meanings'.[20] On the other hand, if a text is readable in the absence of all possible readers, then what, now, is reading?

One may object that Derrida's argument, here, depends upon conflating 'legibility' and 'readability'. It seems possible to deflate Derrida's radical-sounding claim about readability to a seemingly less radical claim relating to the formal features of any text. Readability above translates the French *lisabilité*, which signifies equivocally between two distinctive English terms, 'legibility' and 'readability'. Is Derrida, then, making the less interesting claim that the text retains its legible *form* after the radical disappearance of all reading life: that a text's structural *features* are recognition-transcendent? Or is he making the incredible-sounding claim that the text remains readable (and hence meaningful) outside of reading life? In fact, as I will now argue, Derrida means both; indeed, a proper understanding of textual form will forbid any clear distinction between structure and signification.

At the conclusion of the text cited above, Derrida writes that the text remains '*structurally* readable [*lisible*]' beyond the death of the addressee. This death is qualified first as the 'absolute disappearance', then as the 'absolute absence' of any receiver 'determined in general'. The notion of 'structural readability' that Derrida is after must be interpreted in terms of the text's radical 'sur-vival' – or *sur-vivance*, literally (in French) its 'living on' and/or 'living beyond'. What is the meaning of the 'structure' that qualifies readability? The subsequent line appears to offer a response. This readability should be understood in terms of the structure of iterability. But iterability is a neologism – it designates a kind of 'future concept' (should we discover the need for one) – for a relation logically linking repetition and alterity. Why should the structure of readability require recourse to such an unheard of relation?

Iterability, it is seldom enough emphasised, is not identical with the concept of a repeatable structure in general. It is not a synonym for repetition. Iterability is not a novel way to designate the old idea or 'paleonym' of a linguistic mark (e.g. the letter 'e') or a pattern of elements (e.g. a word or sentence). Indeed, it is *because* the available concept of repetition does not specify the nature of the textual (readable) structure that Derrida justifies the introduction of iterability, which will now designate the distinctive sort of repeatable structure that a text is. If Derrida selects the term iterability to designate this structure, it is because, on the basis of his speculative etymology, the particle 'itera-' captures economically the idea of a repetition 'always already' entailing alterity. The alterity in question is not the 'once again' of an ideal repetition (of the same). It is the idea of a heterogeneity implicit in each such repetition, a heterogeneity that remains obscure, unremarked in the classic concept. 'Such iterability . . . structures the mark of writing itself, no matter what particular type of writing is involved.'[21]

What does it mean to say that iterability structures the mark of writing '*itself*'? Iterability both produces the mark itself and makes the mark something other than itself. The 'othering' in question is not the one implicit in the difference between tokens of an ideal type. Attempting to distinguish the structure of iterability from the latter, Derrida introduces the image of parasitism: 'iterability alters, contaminating parasitically what it identifies and enables to repeat "itself"'.[22] The mark is never simply identical with itself because it always already 'hosts' another mark that structures it. The infrastructure of a mark is a heterogeneous mark. The mark is 'in-formed' by another, in-formed form.

Texts are parasitic structures; the relation between textual signifier and its presumed 'transcendental signified' is something like the relation between a parasite and its host, where the parasite exists in and through the body of its host.[23] If we follow this metaphor, the signifying stratum, composed of its pattern of differential marks, would be the host or medium in and through which the parasitic signified elements are expressed. A nested structure, the parasitic pattern in-forms the host pattern. The form of the host is always already due to the form of a heterogeneous other. While this description of a text may sound unfamiliar and even fantastical, Derrida suggests that such structures are, in fact, perfectly ordinary and common. They describe, for example, the written texts all around us. The extra-correlational 'life' of texts is a parasitic life.

I have just argued that Derrida's neologism, 'iterability', specifies the sort of in-formed structure that permits writing to function both within and beyond the horizon of any subject. This structure, 'foreign to the order of presence', binds repetition to alterity. It repeats a heterogeneous difference (signified) in repeating itself. Textually speaking, differences live on or *sur-vive* only in the 'flesh' of the heterogeneous differences that they alter or transform. Whatever is structured *like* a writing – and this includes, minimally, language – will involve differences or systems of differences characterised by the modifiability or in-formability of their elements. The repetition characteristic of language is not limited to, nor can it be exemplified by, the story of a conventionally adopted, arbitrary mark, which would be indefinitely repeatable. Such an account of linguistic repetition suffers from a one-sidedness that the account of iterability corrects by drawing our attention to the potentially incalculable manifold of encoded differences repeated along with any repetition of the surface or host text.

On the basis of Derrida's non-correlational account of the structure of texts, we can say that one experiences something *as* a signifier, or understands the meaning *of* a signifier, when one performs – however spontaneously or unconsciously – something like a reverse translation, retrieving the parasitic or nested pattern from the manifest, host pattern. However, this possibility – the possibility of reading or translation – is not a function of the reader. Translatability is a function of the structure of the text. Therefore, as Derrida points out, a text remains structurally readable without anyone actually performing such an act of translation – or even recognising it as a text. An empirical example will help illustrate the point.

James Gleick, in his book *The Information* (2011), retells the famous story of the drum language of the Kele people in Central West Africa.[24] Gleick describes the 'talking drums' as patterned after spoken Kele, a tonal language with two sharply distinct tones: each syllable is either low or high. The Kele language is 'spoken' – or more properly, 'written' – by a pair of drums that, isomorphically, produce two distinct tones. Kele words are 'pronounced' on the drums in a sequence of high and low tones that repeat the tonal pattern in the spoken language.

Kele, like any spoken language, is rich in contrastive oppositions. Tonal differences are just some of these 'marked' contrastive magnitudes. But tonal differences are important enough contrasts to allow other marked differences to be dropped without too much loss of information – jst lk w cn drp vwls frm phntc nglsh – while still allowing the drum-writing to convey differences marked in speech. Gleick notes that European travellers and missionaries did not know how to 'read' the drum language and were always surprised that news of their impending arrival preceded them. They simply could not hear the 'readable' messages that were everywhere around them.[25]

It is true that the textual iterability exemplified by the drum-writing – the same iterability that we find in English phonetic writing – may seem a very poor model for understanding the difference between signifier and signified, generally speaking, precisely because phonetic writing does not seem to implicate the signified or conceptual element in language. Indeed, drum-writing as described makes it a form of phonetic writing, where the signified (structuring) element is, perhaps non-standardly, another signifier, differences in speech. We will concern ourselves further with the question of meaning in the next two chapters. For now, I want only to note that, *if* iterability generalises to all linguistic structures, it must apply to the link between signifier and signified – or, as Derrida emphasises, 'to writing of whatever sort'. If this claim is warranted, then the signified or semantic content can also be preserved within and/or as the differential patterns that define speech or the signifying strata of language.

## From Posthumous Texts to Ancestral Evidence

As with Meillassoux's anti-correlationist strategy, Derrida's account of writing asks us to think the status of the written text under conditions that exclude the possibility of any correlation taking place. He defines the text in terms of a recognition-transcendent structure – iterability – that also suggests a new way to think about reading. Reading will no longer be understood in terms of the movement from indicative signs (signifiers) to conscious meanings (transcendental signifieds). Instead, reading involves a reverse translation, the reconstruction or reconstitution of the parasitic text. The iterable text has no vital need of a transcendental subject to be a text or retain its function as written communication. Derrida's non-correlational account of textuality thus entails challenging the standard, correlationist view of texts as indicative signs that point to transcendental signifieds.

What I want to argue now, however, is that Derrida's rejection of the view that texts are structurally explicable in terms of cor-relational, indicative signs is not limited to *linguistic* texts. Indeed, the claim is not simply that written texts do not function *indicatively*, that is, that they cannot be understood as the correlate of a transcendental activity connecting them to a signified. The claim is also that there are no purely indicative signs. The mark in general, in whatever domain it is found, will not be indicative in the correlationist sense. This has repercussions for Meillassoux's anti-correlationism and his notion of the absolute, that is, non-subject-relative structure or being.

As we saw above from Levi Bryant's gloss, 'Meillassoux refers to "arche-fossils" and "fossil-matter" as not simply materials *indicating the traces of past life* in the sense of our familiar understanding of "fossil", but also as materials *indicating the existence of ancestral realities or events anterior to all life*.'[26] Arche-fossils, though they refer to ancestral events, are still interpreted correlationally; they are signs grounding inferences.

How does Derrida's notion of textuality permit an understanding of arche-matter in non-indicative, non-correlational terms? The arche-matter is not an indication of ancestral realities, if this means that it ceases to be readable outside of inferential activity. Arche-matter, its evidence and traces, must remain legible outside any and all transcendental activity. If we were to understand arche-matter textually, in Derrida's sense, how should we now describe it? If we use the schema of textuality, we would be looking at the present indicative marks of ancestral events as structured by a heterogeneous pattern or mark.

Let us return to the example of the dendochronologist, who finds in one of the central (that is, oldest) rings of a tree a 'spike' of carbon-14. How shall we describe the pattern of discovery? Shall we say she sees the spike as an indicative sign, by linking the presence of carbon-14 to the known efflux of solar flares and then inferring that a solar flare happened, say, 250 years ago? Such a description seems perfectly plausible. Is another description possible? Can we also say that she 'reads' the solar flare in the carbon-14 markers? What is the difference in these two descriptions? Is one more apt than the other? What is *seeing* and what is *reading*?

The carbon-14 can function as a marker or indication *of* something because it is differentially present in the tree rings. Each distinct tree ring, we have learned, marks a terrestrial year of tree-life. This clear demarcation makes the tree a sort of almanac. The differential pattern of carbon absorption in each ring records the differential quantities of carbon in the atmosphere each year. The differential marks of carbon are already spatially and temporally structured, without which they could not be read. These differences, or carbon marks, we might suggest, form a text within the text of the tree rings. The 'burst' in carbon, which we find spaced let us say in ring 12 – that is, the *difference* between it and the surrounding carbon marks – is the trace of the solar flare event. Indeed, the distinction between the trace (of the event) and the event now seems problematic. Surely the absorption and retention of the carbon-14 is part of the event. Minimally, this textual description motivates more theoretical attention to the *structure* of evidentiary traces, while the competing description assumes that the structuring activity happens in the associational activity of the scientist.

There is, of course, much more in this living record or archive of the tree. For example, differences in the width of the tree rings 'signify' differences in the length of the growing season. What makes something a significant mark or indication is first of all the presence of other marks, a differential pattern. What makes these marks textual, in Derrida's sense, is that the form or pattern is in-formed by a heterogeneous pattern. Scientific discovery does not amount to adding to these marks their transcendent meaning, but learning to read what in-forms these marks. The different widths of the tree rings indicate the fluctuating length of growing seasons; the density of the rings indicates different levels of rainfall. We can continue to say that the dendochronologist's activity consists in inferring past events from these present traces, but this inferential activity is possible because of the textual structure of the evidence, which is neither defined by nor dependent on it. The point would be that not just ancestral events but *all* events are best understood not as correlated with a transcendental subject but as correlated to textual evidence or 'written' traces.

Texts, then, are not inherently linguistic; they describe, as we demonstrated above, an iterable structure. Differential marks are the material 'substrate' of the signified. The signified is, as it were, inscribed in the signifier, or vice versa. This structure of entanglement characterises textuality, writing 'of whatever kind'. Derrida's notion of ultra-transcendental or post-human texts transforms our understanding of the structure and materiality of language and writing. In doing so, it also provides a general or speculative schema for any kind of textual or grammatological structure.

## Conclusion

Why has Derrida's critique of correlationism been so difficult to recognise as such? Unlike Meillassoux, Derrida's aim is not to dispel the spectre of correlationism by pointing to the sort of object – a readable text – that cannot be described or, indeed, can only be essentially mis-described by correlationism. His aim, or so I shall argue in the following chapters, is to dismantle correlationism from within. Not only language but phenomena 'internal' to the correlation will turn out to be textual.

Derrida does not move from an anti-correlationist argument with respect to texts to a general argument about the viability of a materialist programme where nothing would be outside 'the formation of form'. Nor does he explicitly investigate how thoughts about the absolute (non-relative) are possible, as does Meillassoux. Rather, Derrida moves from an anti-correlationist argument about the status of *texts* to an anti-correlationist argument about the textual status of *consciousness* or lived experience.

Written texts and their purported meanings (signifieds) are not only independent of subjects and subjective life. They are the broad possibility of what Husserl called 'reactivation'. Consciousness and perception, understood as the very essence of 'the correlation', are thus equally mis-described by correlationism. Indeed, correlationism (or the metaphysics of presence) would be plausible in the first place only because of correlationist descriptions of texts and belief in transcendental signifieds.

## Notes

1. Beck, quoted in Zahavi (2016: 306, emphasis mine).
2. Meillassoux (2008: 9).
3. Meillassoux (2008: 5, emphasis in original).
4. Malabou (2016: 41).
5. Derrida (1988: 7).
6. The phenomenologist believes, in other words, that even though she rejects the naive metaphysical realism implicit in scientific statements, her perceptual realism retains the meaning of these statements. The 'translation' from metaphysical to perceptual realism preserves the sense and validity of the statement.
7. Bad-faith sceptic because the sceptic in question is not interested in the truth or falsity of scientific statement; they do not have a genuine concern for the truth of scientific statements. Seeking to justify their *a priori* disbelief, they attempt to show that scientists have no better grounds for their beliefs than biblical literalists do for theirs. Correlationism – and hence unwittingly contemporary philosophy, which is overwhelmingly correlationist – gives resources to the sceptic, precisely by linking credence, on the one hand, to proximity to testimonial evidence and, on the other, to the possibility of, as Husserl described it, reactivating each link of an unbroken chain of inference to the primary self-evidences that ground belief.
8. Bryant (2009: n.p.).
9. Husserl (2000: 252).
10. Husserl (2000: 376).
11. Husserl (2000: 103).
12. Husserl (1983: 116).
13. Seebohm (1995).
14. Meillassoux (2008: 14).
15. Searle (1994: 634).
16. Searle (1994: 637).
17. In *Introduction to the Origin of Geometry*, Derrida writes:

> Writing, as the place of absolutely permanent ideal objectivities and therefore of absolute Objectivity, certainly constitutes such a [subjectless] transcendental field. And likewise, to be sure, transcendental subjectivity can be fully announced and appear on the basis of this field or its possibility. Thus a subjectless transcendental field is one of the 'conditions' of transcendental subjectivity. But all this can be said only on the basis of an intentional analysis which retains from writing nothing but writing's pure

relation to a consciousness which grounds it as such, and not its factuality which, left to itself, is totally without signification [*insignifiante*]. (1989: 89)

Transcendental writing, in other words, can dispense with the possibility of actual (existent) readers, and think of writing as among the transcendental conditions of objectivity. However, precisely because it is conceived correlationally in terms of a pure (possible) relation to a consciousness, such an analysis must determine factual writing (equally deprived of actual readers) as essentially insignificant (without Meaning). Thus, when we look at empirical phenomena such as hieroglyphics, we get a sense of what Derrida calls a 'transcendental sense of death', the appearance to consciousness of its own (impossible) radical absence.

> But if the text does not announce its own pure dependence on a writer or reader in general (i.e., if it is not haunted by a virtual intentionality), and if there is no purely juridical possibility of it being intelligible for a transcendental subject in general, then there is no more in the vacuity of its soul than a chaotic literalness or the sensible opacity of a defunct designation, a designation deprived of its transcendental function. (Derrida 1989: 90)

In short, the text must appear as both unreadable and *a priori* readable. In *The Introduction to the Origin of Geometry*, Derrida does not resolve the 'paradox' of transcendental death, he announces it. On my reading, in this announcement we can find a central key to his project.

18. Derrida (1988: 7).
19. Derrida (1988: 7).
20. Indeed, as Peter Bornedal argues, Derrida ought to have come to exactly the opposite conclusion from the one he did: rather than testifying to the possibility of their function under conditions of radical absence, texts testify to the need for a reader's radical presence (1997: 201–5). Texts need some – any – possible readers (together with whatever empirical conditions are required to decode them) – at least when we assume that written texts are supplementary to some original (form of) living presence. If a text's inner meaning or content is radically exterior to the text, it follows directly that the survival of a text is radically dependent upon the life of its possible readers. Bornedal's interpretation is interesting, because unlike some

of Derrida's interpreters who see him as arguing that the definition of a text is to transcend any particular reader or writer, Bornedal reads him correctly as claiming that the radical absence of all readers defines all texts. This pattern of interpretation is unfortunately widespread. Derrida's detractors tend, on the whole, to be more likely to take his claims literally and seriously. On the other hand, Derrida's defenders tend to deflate his claims, even where these deflations lead either to distorting the text or to implausible positions, or both.

21. Derrida (1988: 62).
22. Derrida (1988: 62).
23. 'Transcendental signified' economically captures the twin assumptions of a correlational interpretation of texts: 1) a text is a pattern of signifiers whose signified is presumed to be transcendent to the text and 2) the signified element is the effect of a transcendental activity.
24. Gleick (2011: 19).
25. The story of the talking drums and the way that they 'speak' Kele is even more interesting if we consider that the distinctive sounds of the talking drums account, according to some musicologists, for some of the distinctive structure of American popular music and dance forms, including jazz, rock 'n' roll and tap. One might speculate that the musical structures descended from Kele drumming are still replete with readable messages, though such messages would be produced without any sort of intention on the part of the drummer or tap dancer. The readability of such messages is entirely unaffected by the presence or absence of Kele speakers. In the drum-writing, Kele spoken language is found in and as the pattern of differences that the drums repeat – in much the same way, we might add, that spoken language is found in phonetic writing.
26. Bryant (2009: n.p., my emphasis).

# 3

# Texts without Meanings: Deconstructing the Transcendental Signified

Without writing, you cannot think; at any rate you cannot think with any intellectual train of thought.

Niklas Luhmann, *Zettels*

Anyway you cut up the pie, Meaning just ain't in the head.

Hilary Putnam, 'The Meaning of "Meaning"'

## Textuality and the Transcendental Signified

In the previous chapter, I argued that Derrida's account of textuality motivated a radical revision of our understanding of the structure of written texts. In defining written texts non-correlationally – that is, as independent of the activity of a transcendental subject – Derrida challenges those views – he calls them logocentric – according to which meaning is radically transcendent to the text. Indeed, when Derrida writes, in *Of Grammatology* and elsewhere, of the need to deconstruct the doctrine of the *transcendental signified*, he intends by the latter the idea of meaning as 1) *transcendent* to signifying strata and 2) correlated to the activity of a *transcendental* subject. To paraphrase Hilary Putnam, for logocentrism the meaning of meaning is Meaning or 'the transcendental signified'. (In this chapter, where I capitalise 'Meaning', I refer to the idea of the transcendental signified; where it is not capitalised, I refer either to a naive or revisionary account.)

The mark of logocentric theories of meaning is the *opposition* between a subjective interiority, where Meaning is present, and a textual exteriority, where Meaning is absent. For such accounts, Meaning is essentially non-textual, first-personal, in short, the correlate of subjective acts aiming at it. Derrida's critique of logocentrism involves demonstrating 'the myth of the transcendental signified', as Wilfrid Sellars might put it. Derrida argues that the history of Western philosophy is the development of this myth.[1]

As with Sellarsian 'givenness', transcendental signifieds are pure theoretical posits introduced to explain how language or thought functions. They answer to the intuition that language and thought 'bottom out' in Meanings, and that reading (and thinking) entail reducing any textual or signifying elements *to* the Meanings signified. I call this thesis about linguistic function the reducibility thesis. The non-linguistic transcendental signified founds the linguistic signifier. Derrida's argument consists in demonstrating – and here the parallels with Sellars's argument are, again, instructive – that nothing *could* successfully play the theoretical role of Meaning. Or, as Derrida puts it in the 1968 essay 'Ends of Man', no 'reduction *to* Meaning is possible'.[2]

If Derrida is right, the failure of the reducibility thesis has grave consequences for logocentric theories of language. Derrida will have shown that the condition of possibility for linguistic function, Meaning, is impossible. This leaves us with no workable account of how our language functions, or what happens when we communicate, read, write and translate. If Derrida's account were purely negative, we could interpret it as a kind of philosophical nihilism. Indeed, many of his readers (and half-readers) have accused him of just such a project. However, as I shall argue, the nihilistic interpretation is ill founded.

Derrida's account is not unremittingly negative; it does not demonstrate that no account of meaning is possible, because Meaning is impossible. But Derrida does not tell us that Meaning is impossible in order to give us an alternative, revisionary account of Meaning. This would obviously be incoherent. Yet, as we shall see, this is precisely the impossible demand that 'readers' such as John Searle have made. I have put 'readers' in quotes because, as I outline in detail below, by Searle's own lights, reading is a success term involving the (successful) communication of a Meaning-intention. Demanding an account of Meaning from Derrida makes crystal clear that no such communication has occurred.

If Derrida does not offer a revisionary account of Meaning, his critique of the transcendental signified does provide ample resources for a reconstruction of the meaning of meaning, or at least a viable account of linguistic function. Derrida, however, for the most part eschews reinvesting 'meaning' with a different, non-logocentric sense, because he believes the term has been over-invested by logocentrism. As a Meaning eliminativist, Derrida outlines an alternative account of linguistic function in terms of 'translatability', a notion he borrows and develops in a reading of Walter Benjamin.[3]

Translatability is the condition for meaning-effects. In a logocentric discourse, translatability would designate the possibility of the exchange of transcendental signifieds from an original to a target language. In Derrida's non-logocentric, eliminativist account, translatability refers to the *modifiability* of one text by another. The regulated modification between texts implies an *exchange* of form. Translation in-forms, by 'regulated transformation', one text with another. As I argue in the conclusion of this chapter, contemporary 'sensory substitution devices' function according to the (non-logocentric) principle of translatability; consequently, they offer an image of how texts without Meanings can function and produce meaning-effects.

The plan for the rest of this chapter is as follows. I first consider Derrida's critique of logocentrism and the reducibility thesis through the lens of translation. I reconstruct Derrida's argument for why a reduction to Meaning is impossible. Simply put, for anything to function as Meaning, Derrida argues, it must be formally indiscernible from what is said to have no Meaning, namely the textual signifier. But in order to function as a Meaning, Meanings must also be formally discernible. By the identity of indiscernibles, Meanings and texts, because they are indiscernible, are identical. The reduction to Meaning is impossible; each reduction would yield another text. Of course, we might imagine that the transcendental signified is a very special sort of text: a self-intimating, self-reading, self-reducing sign.[4] But since such a text would be 'magical' – that is, utterly inexplicable – a philosophical account must exclude it. I then consider Derrida's revisionary account of (the meaning of) meaning as translatability and conclude with a brief examination of Derrida's speculative account of the origin of the myth of the transcendental signified in the 'phenomenological voice'.

## 'The thesis of philosophy is translatability'

In *Of Grammatology*, Derrida recalls that Aristotle's theory of signs is *eo ipso* a theory of translation, a theory of a mind and a theory of truth (as correspondence).

Just as all men (*sic.*) have not the same writing, so all men (*sic.*) have
not the same speech sounds, but mental experiences, of which these
are the *primary symbols* (*semeia protos*), are the same for all, as also
are those things of which our experiences are the images (*De interpre-
tatione*, 1, 1 6a). (OG, 11, emphasis added)

That 'all men (*sic.*)' share the same ideas is the condition of possibility both for truthful communication and translation. Common
ideas are not sufficient conditions, of course, for (successful) translation or communication. It must also be the case that these ideas
have a *communicable* or *expressible* form. Otherwise, we would
never know that we shared common ideas. Derrida emphasises
that for Aristotle, ideas take the form of primary symbols. These
psychic symbols can then be expressed by conventional symbols,
which are exchangeable or translatable between themselves.

Aristotle's theory of signs, however, relies upon a prior, more
original translatability:

[B]etween being and mind, things and feelings, there would be a relationship of translation or *natural* signification; between mind and
logos, a relationship of *conventional* symbolization. And the first
convention, which would relate immediately to the order of natural
and universal signification, would be produced as spoken language.
Written language would establish the conventions, interlinking other
conventions with them. (OG, 11)

To share the same ideas (about the world), the mind must be
capable of translating or signifying being, which it then communicates according to conventional signs. What circulates between
being, 'protean' signs and logos is Meaning. Derrida is clear that
logocentrism refers to *this* (Aristotelian) account of language,
which defines logos as the correlation of being and sign at its
centre.

This definition of logocentrism is, perhaps, not terribly controversial. What is controversial, however, is Derrida's claim that
logocentrism structures and limits Western philosophy to this day.
One way to put the claim is that, from Aristotle to today, philosophy has been characterised by the agreement that language
functions as the exchange and essential fungibility of Meanings. In
turn, this common, shared thesis about linguistic function determines both what language does – it transports semantic content

into another signifying form, it expresses and communicates Meaning – and what makes it possible, Meanings.

When Derrida argues that the 'thesis of philosophy is translatability', he means that its core belief is that the exchange of Meanings is possible. Underlying the surface diversity of languages and cultures, there is a possibility of shared agreement, a common way of articulating the world, and a correspondence of these articulations to the (original) articulations of nature.

Philosophers and 'lay' speakers assume that words refer to and are underwritten by cognitive entities or items distinct from the languages we use. To access these underlying Meanings, it follows that we must, as it were, cash in the 'materiality of the signifier' – the material element of language exemplified by a written mark or spoken word – for the value it represents. Successful uses of language – reading, writing and translating – would each involve restoring to mind ('re-presenting') the underlying Meanings that have been transferred through language. Philosophical accounts propose various theoretical entities that serve the required functional role of Meaning.

Through a reduction to Meaning, we escape the opaqueness of the linguistic signifier in any particular language and the Babelian diversity of languages more generally.[5] Assuming the possibility of reduction, Derrida argues, has permitted philosophers to bracket empirical language altogether when considering Meaning.[6] Even linguistic theories that emphasise the free play of the signifier – the functional flexibility or plasticity that militates against assigning signifiers fixed Meanings – *must* be 'constituted upon a fundamental immobility and a reassuring certitude, which is itself beyond the reach of the free-play'.[7]

These sorts of categorical claims rile many of Derrida's readers, and perhaps not without reason. Such statements eliminate or erase philosophical diversity – such as it is – both historically and within any given philosophical milieu. For example, it paints twentieth-century analytic philosophers with the same brush as those of the continental tradition, and it identifies both with debates in Scholastic philosophy; it seems to deny any real distinction between ancient, modern and contemporary philosophy. In each case, everyone is rewriting Aristotle, or at least operating within the set of possibilities opened up by the core views of logocentrism.

It is undoubtedly true that Derrida intends logocentrism to comprehend the entire history of Western philosophy, and any category so sweeping will necessarily minimise internal differences and invite controversy. Nonetheless, it might help to underscore that Derrida is not arguing that no philosopher before him has ever opposed Aristotle, opposed logocentrism or opposed its doctrine of Meanings. What he is arguing is that any and all attempts to oppose logocentrism have ended up reinscribing themselves within logocentrism. They oppose one version of the transcendental signified, let us say a language of thought, only to replace a language of thought with a perceptual state. The diversity of philosophy would amount to the rhythm of partial critique and reinscription, exit strategies aimed at 'false exits'. By contrast, an adequate critique of logocentrism would entail nothing short of the reduction (or elimination) of Meaning.

The sort of massive agreement that Derrida refers to – which if warranted would have to include even those theorists who have argued that Meaning is essentially linguistic and that thought cannot be conceived as distinct from language – is not, of course, simply the result of a kind of a lamentable group-think or an unavowed but nonetheless potent theological commitment to the pure living Word (though Derrida often suggests that these motivations are at work). It has, principally, to do with the difficulty of thinking otherwise. This difficulty is what leads to what Derrida calls 'false exits'.

One of the principal problems for thinking otherwise – against logocentrism – even when philosophers recognise that belief in transcendental signifieds is exorbitant with respect to the evidence in its favour, is that *negation* of the reducibility thesis seems to lead to a *reductio ad absurdum*. And, as is well known, a *reductio* is indirect proof of the thesis in question, the reducibility thesis, and hence of the transcendental signified. Thus, when we demonstrate that the reduction to Meaning is impossible (logically inconsistent), the logocentrist can always counter that the impossibility of Meaning leads to absurdity. Therefore, to deconstruct logocentrism requires not simply rejecting or negating the reducibility thesis, which preserves Meaning, even in its negation, as the now-impossible ideal. It requires demonstrating that the reducibility thesis relies on a *petitio principii*: that signifiers and signifieds are radically distinct, and that meaning is Meaning. Negating the reducibility thesis only leads to absurdity if we also accept that signified elements are either Meanings or do not exist at all.

## The Textuality of Meaning and the Im/possibility of Meaning

What reasons do we have for opposing the reducibility thesis? What sort of problems does it systematically pose, and what makes Meanings 'impossible'? Derrida argues that there can be no reduction to Meaning, because Meaning or the transcendental signified is necessarily textual, or it has the same structure or form as the signifier.

Derrida demonstrates, over a number of texts, that logocentric accounts of Meaning assign 'writing' a constitutive function.[8] That is, Meaning could not appear to the subject as an object of thought, could not become communicable or expressible, without taking the articulated *form* of written language – where the latter refers broadly speaking to the ideally repeatable structure of a signifier. Notably, when Derrida says that writing is constitutive of Meaning, he is not claiming that thinking literally requires a subject who writes, or that thought consists in the empirical production of written marks. He is arguing that the transcendental signified is conceived, paradoxically, as something absolutely distinct from linguistic signifiers (especially writing) and as *formally* indistinguishable from empirical writing. Meaning has to be *a priori* 'written', in the form of writing, for the same reason that there cannot be private languages.

To be communicable or expressible in language, even to be available to thought, Meaning must be ideally repeatable. The difference between this writing that is constitutive of Meaning and mundane, empirical writing has, first of all, to do with the *materiality* of the mark. Meaning cannot be *like* empirical writing, because this would mean that in order to know or 'read' what we are thinking, we would first have to reduce the signifier to get to Meaning. But since writing is constitutive of Meaning, we cannot, finally, reduce it. If Meanings were *a priori* written, then the condition of their possibility (writing) also names the condition of its impossibility. Meanings are textual or written, but this means that they cannot function as they are supposed to. Textuality excludes reducibility.[9]

We can attribute this argument to Derrida, but in fact we can find versions of it elsewhere: for example, in objections to a language of thought, or in critiques of what Samuel Wheeler (2000) has called 'magical languages'. Indeed, Derrida offers several versions of this argument, one of them in his reconstruction of Charles Sanders Peirce's semiology in *On Grammatology*. On Derrida's reading, Peirce's semiology affirms the textuality of the transcendental signified.[10] However, the latter's account falls short of a deconstruction of the transcendental signified, which means that the deconstruction of logocentrism is not the same as the 'discovery' of Meaning's textuality. While Peirce's account recognises that the irreducible referral and deferral of the sign is the condition (of possibility) for Meaning, according to Derrida he does not adequately factor that it is also a condition of its impossibility.

> Peirce goes very far in the direction that I have called the deconstruction of the transcendental signified, which . . . would place a reassuring end to the reference from sign to sign. I have identified logocentrism and the metaphysics of presence as the exigent, powerful, systematic, and irrepressible desire for such a signified. According . . . to the 'phenomenology' of Peirce, manifestation itself does not reveal a presence, it makes a sign . . . 'the idea of manifestation is the idea of a sign.' There is thus no phenomenality reducing the sign or the representamen so that the thing signified may be allowed to glow finally in the luminosity of its presence. The so-called 'thing itself' is always already a representamen shielded from the simplicity of intuitive evidence. The representamen functions only by giving rise to an interpretent that itself becomes a sign and so on to infinity. The self-identity of the signified conceals itself unceasingly and is always on the move. (OG, 49)[11]

Here, Derrida describes Peirce's position but also distinguishes the final or adequate deconstructive position from it. The *absence* of the transcendental signified still structures and determines Peirce's definition of the sign. 'From the moment that there is meaning, there are nothing but signs. *We think only in signs. Which amounts to ruining the notion of the sign* at the very moment, as in Nietzsche, its exigency is recognised in the absoluteness of its right' (OG, 50). Signs produce signs as their interpretents, which then, in turn, require interpretents *ad infinitum*. When it comes to those items at which signifiers point – where we would expect to find the Meaning of signs – we find only more signs.

Derrida does not say much more about the significance of Peirce's ruination of the concept of the sign in this context; he instead moves forward with his discussion of Saussure. It seems clear, though, that the ruination of the notion of the sign results from

Peirce's rejection of a pure signified element. Any interpretent will involve the same structure of delay and deferral. Paradoxically, the notion of the sign is ruined once it is generalised in this way, because the very notion of the sign depends upon its contrast with a non-signifying element. Because Peirce's account continues to rely on the very notion of the sign that his own account undermines, he offers an account not of linguistic or semiotic function but of its dysfunction. His is only an incomplete rejection of the opposition between signifier and signified.

To see what Derrida is getting at with this notion of conceptual ruin, let us try to describe the structure of the signified in the terms Peirce proposes. If it is true that we think only in signs – as opposed to imagining that the contents of our thoughts are, at some level, self-present and self-transparent – then, in order to *access* the meaning of our thoughts, we would have to *interpret* these thought-signs. If thought involves such a sign language, this would have the unhappy consequence that we (thinkers) could never, in principle, know what we were thinking. That is to say, we would never have access to the contents of our own thoughts; such access would be infinitely deferred.[12]

As Derrida underscores, the (logocentric) logic of the sign assumes a signified that puts an end to referential play – an end, that is, to the difference and deferral of Meaning that characterises its operation. On Derrida's gloss, Peirce has discovered and affirmed the sign as *différance*, and the impossibility of its reduction. However, because he leaves intact the radical distinction between signifier and signified, which determines the meaning of sign, instead of affirming that the signified is also a 'sign', Peirce's account ends up affirming that there are only signifiers (and no signifieds). On the one hand, Peirce demonstrates that there cannot be Meanings, but only signifiers (signs, representaments, interpretents); on the other, if there are only signifiers, there can be no meaning (signified elements).

Peirce has gone far, but not far enough in the direction of the deconstruction of the transcendental signified. He has failed to factor in the extent to which he has ruined the concept of the sign. He has demonstrated the impossibility of the reducibility thesis, but has left himself open to a counter-argument: namely, that the negation of the reducibility thesis leads to absurdity, which is just what Searle argues in what he takes to be a decisive refutation of Derrida's claims.

## Negating the Reducibility Thesis and the Reduction of Meaning

In 'Literary Theory and its Discontents', Searle recognises that Derrida challenges the reducibility thesis, but still faults him for failing to offer any alternative account of Meaning. At no point does Searle consider that the account he demands entails accepting the very thesis that Derrida has just rejected. Just after noting that Derrida refutes the 'possibility' of 'fully determinate' Meanings, Searle quips that 'instead . . . there is rather the free play of signifiers and the grafting of texts onto texts within the textuality and the intertextuality of the text'.[13] Searle is not citing Derrida here; he is just summarising Derrida's arguments from somewhere, as he has understood them. What Searle has understood is that textuality offers a revisionary account of Meaning – an account of Meaning without Meanings – and he is, understandably, vexed to find no account of Meaning there at all. This *is* no doubt absurd, but the fault does not lie with Derrida or textuality.

For Searle, Derrida's rejection of the reducibility thesis is self-refuting. Therefore, he does not need to do the work of refutation himself. He correctly surmises that if Meaning were textual, this would make Meaning impossible: there would just be 'texts, grafted onto texts in a general intertextuality'. But Meaning cannot be impossible. Saying so makes texts meaningless and texts are clearly not meaningless (unless they are Derrida's). They function. Therefore, there must be Meaning. Q.E.D.

So taken is Searle with his *petitio principii*, if there is meaning, it must be Meaning, that he never stops to consider that Derrida's argument might be eliminativist rather than revisionist with respect to Meaning, or that his aim might be to demonstrate that texts function without Meanings. Searle is not always so dismissive or condescending as he is when he is reading Derrida. Elsewhere, in a famous thought-experiment, Searle considers with a bit more seriousness and rigour a view of language (and mind) that challenges the reducibility thesis. However, his method of refuting the view is approximately the same. He seeks to demonstrate that any account of linguistic function that does not assume the reducibility thesis is absurd. However, his argument assumes what it claims to demonstrate.

In 'Minds, Brains, Programs' (1980) Searle proposes a thought-experiment that has become known as the 'Chinese Room'. He asks us to imagine an English monolinguist, alone in a room, charged with the task of replying to a text written in Chinese characters. While the monolinguist does not speak or read Chinese, the thought-experiment stipulates that they have all the resources necessary to produce a legible and apt response. Searle imagines, for example, that the monolinguist has full access to all the rules for constructing a text ('the program'), such as the rules governing permissible syntactical transformations, along, perhaps, with the statistical knowledge that specifies the likelihood that a certain syntactical string will follow another string.

Searle's argument functions as a *reductio ad absurdum*. Assuming the monolinguist has sufficient time, it is perfectly plausible to think that they could produce relevant responses to incoming messages. However, Searle argues that the possibility of this performance does not warrant saying that the monolinguist *understands* Chinese, or that this is all there is to linguistic or cognitive function. Something important, something critical, is missing from the account.

Understanding is something more than the successful syntactical transformation of a phrase – if only because any account of the operation's success or failure would seemingly need to reference a language-user capable of *judging* the aptness of the text produced. To perform this task, the judge would have to possess precisely what the occupant of the Chinese Room lacks: Meanings. Therefore, Searle concludes, there *must* be something extra-textual about language and thought. If there were not, with respect to our own language and our own thoughts, we would all be like the monolinguist in the Chinese Room, with no insight into whether our words had meaning or what meaning our words had.

In the case of the Chinese Room, Searle's target was a certain view of language and of artificial intelligence in particular (the 'Strong Program for AI') that would reduce language to what Searle calls 'syntax'. Searle insists that 'syntax is not by itself sufficient for, nor constitutive of, semantics'. This indicates that syntax may be partially constitutive for semantics, but that syntax cannot tell the whole story. Unfortunately, Searle does not specify how we might understand a *partially* constitutive relation, which is too bad, since if syntax were even partially constitutive of semantics, this too might pose a hard problem for Meaning. Despite this fascinating aside, Searle's account otherwise enforces and reinforces a rigorous opposition between semantics and syntax, texts and

Meanings, programs and minds. To explain linguistic – and by extension cognitive – function, rather than its simulation, we need something that is *beyond* the text: Meanings. Though Searle's argument is aimed at the idea of reducing language to texts, it pertains to any theory that rejects the reducibility thesis.

As we saw in the previous section, Derrida's critique of Peirce's general semiology in *Of Grammatology* covers some of the same ground as Searle's 'Chinese Room'. That is, Peirce seems to argue that language can function without transcendental signifieds: that is, without the reducibility thesis. However, Derrida writes that Pierce's way of challenging the reducibility thesis 'ruins the notion of the sign' at the moment when he extends it to the transcendental signified. If thought were *only* sign-involving, moving from interpretent to interpretent without rest or end, thought could not function. Rather than an account of cognitive function, Peirce's is an account of cognitive dysfunction.

There is, however, an important difference between Searle's argument from the Chinese Room and Derrida's qualified disagreement with Peircean *différance*. While Searle argues that the negation of the reducibility thesis – the proposition that language can function without a reduction of the signifier – leads to absurdity, Derrida argues that it leads to absurdity only if negating the reducibility thesis involves collapsing the *difference* between the signifier and signified.[14] On Derrida's reading, Peirce's way of rejecting the transcendental signified collapsed the difference, turned all signifieds into signifiers, *because* it left the opposition structuring the concept of the sign untouched. As we will see below, Derrida argues that while we can deny the reducibility thesis, we cannot explain linguistic function without affirming the difference between signifier and signified.[15]

It may seem that Derrida is trying to have it both ways: rejecting the reducibility thesis and affirming the difference of the signified from the signifier. But these would only be incompatible if the only way to think the relation or difference between signifier and signified was as opposition. But there are, perhaps, other possibilities.

Derrida does not just argue that reduction to Meaning is impossible, but argues that we need a reduction *of* Meaning: or, what comes to the same thing, a new conception of the sign that does not require thinking it in terms of the radical opposition between signifier and signified. *Pace* Searle, rejecting reducibility only leads to absurdity when we accept the logocentric assumption that signifiers and signifieds are opposed. However, if they are not opposed – if their difference can be explained in other terms – then no absurdity results. Derrida easily refutes Searle's argument from absurdity.

## From Meaning to Translatability

The sort of radical critique of logocentrism at which deconstruction aims does not seek to collapse the difference between signifier and signified, but rather to radically rethink the nature of this difference. Deconstruction aims to think the *différance* of language in a way that gives us a revised account of linguistic function. However, as Derrida explains, the deconstruction of the transcendental signified must be undertaken 'with prudence' to avoid losing the theoretical means to account for their difference. That is, we must be able to account for the difference between signifier and signified without making such a difference absolute.

Without preserving the difference, we could not explain linguistic function – in particular, the possibility of translation which relies on this difference.

> [It is not a question] of confusing at every level, and in all simplicity, the signifier and the signified. That this opposition or difference cannot be radical or absolute does not prevent it from functioning, and even from being indispensable within certain – very wide limits. For example, no translation would be possible without it . . . In the limits in which it is possible, or at least appears possible, translation practices the difference between signified and signifier. But if this difference is never pure, no more so is translation.[16]

If the possibility of translation – and language use more generally – depends upon a difference between signifier and signified that 'is never pure' or absolute, then conceptions of linguistic function that assume this purity must be revised. Thus, '[f]or [the logocentric] notion of translation' which assumes the transfer of extra-textual signified elements, 'we would have to substitute a notion of transformation: a regulated transformation of one language by another, of one text by another'.[17]

How shall we understand translation as transformation? And how, in particular, can we understand such a projected account as offering some insight into linguistic function in the absence of

Meaning? We can turn to Derrida's reading of Benjamin's 'The Translator's Task' for some guidance to answering these questions. Benjamin argued that 'translation is a form. In order to grasp it as such, we have to go back to the original. For in it lies the principle of translation, determined by the original's translatability.'[18]

In what sense is translation a form? In 'The Translator's Task' Benjamin writes that 'word-for-word translation completely thwarts the reproduction of sense and threatens to lead directly to incomprehensibility'.[19] Translation, then, does not reproduce the *outward* form of a source text. Instead, Benjamin writes, translation consists in 'liberating the language imprisoned in the work by rewriting it'.[20] This notion of a language 'in' language that would be liberated by translation risks a logocentric interpretation. We might think that what Benjamin has in mind by liberation is a process that would first reactivate the Meaning intended by a text in order, then, to translate it into the target language. However, this does not seem to be what Benjamin envisions by translatability. This is evidenced by what he writes a few lines after the text quoted above: '*Accordingly*, the translatability of linguistic structures would have to be considered *even if they were untranslatable for human beings*.'[21]

Whatever Benjamin means by a possibility of translation beyond the human, he is clear that what translation implies is best grasped by putting the human out of play. 'Relational concepts gain their proper, indeed their best sense, when from the outset they are not connected exclusively with human beings',[22] and translation, for Benjamin, is a relational concept. By the latter, Benjamin seems to mean that the source and translated text are relata constituted by translation, and assume their prior translatability. Translatability describes an essentially relational form. The translated text is the source text different and differed. This form is made possible not by the transcendence of the signified (to the text) but by the *translatability* of the original, which is to say that the original is already a translation, already the effect of *différance*.

Benjamin is careful to emphasise that translation is not indexed to human capacities, and hence translatability cannot depend on Meaning or transcendental signifieds. It has to do, as he writes, with the form of the original, its original translatability. Translation does not begin after the original text has been produced or written. Nor is Meaning the *a priori* of all translation. On the contrary, translatability must be thought *first* and then meaning (and a new meaning of meaning) can be thought 'in return'.[23] The possibility of translation can only be original if the original was already the effect of a translation; or what comes to the same thing, if there was no untranslated original. Benjamin's thinking here seems so enigmatic because it counters, as Derrida emphasises, everything that is central to logocentric accounts of meaning.

The notion of a 'pure language spellbound' in a text suggests that textual forms are entangled texts. The spellbound text in the original, which demands translation, is the signified element or *difference*. This is why, for Benjamin, the 'original' text *requires* translation and this is even so when and if there is no translator 'fit to respond to this injunction, which is at the same time demand and desire in the very structure of the origin'.[24]

Derrida relates the form of translatability to what Benjamin calls 'survival'. According to Derrida, the original translatability characteristic of texts requires us to understand a text 'independently of its living conditions – the conditions, obviously, of its author's life – and to understand it instead in its *surviving structure*'.[25] Benjamin, Derrida notes, is not entirely clear about the nature of this surviving structure.

> At times [Benjamin] says 'Uberleben' and at other times 'Fortleben'. These two words do not mean the same thing: 'Uberleben' means above life and therefore survival as something rising above life; 'Fortleben' means survival in the sense of something prolonging life, even though they are translated in French by the one word 'survivre'.[26]

Before glossing the meaning of this difference, I want to remark on the performative dimension of this citation. Derrida is discussing the nature of translation, but he is also discussing the question of *how* to translate Benjamin's text. Here we see him engaged in 'the critical task of the translator', as he corrects or modifies what he sees as a problematic translation of both as *survivre* in French. Benjamin's conceptual equivocation – which he marks linguistically – will be collapsed in the French translation. Its philosophical relevance will no longer be legible or structurally readable. The difference between *fort-* and *uber-* is important enough, philosophically, that it will be difficult to understand how translatability might do the work of Meaning in accounts of linguistic function without remarking this difference. Where a difference does not already exist (in the target text), it must be wrought.

Derrida finds a way to remark this difference in his translation of Benjamin's text. He adds the graphic operator '-' to remark the difference in the original. This transforms, in a regulated fashion, the French word *survivre* into *sur-vivance*, or, in English, survival. Benjamin's difference between *fort-* and *uber-* is preserved in the differential spacing of the neologism. Derrida modifies the target language so that it can take on, in *differantial* form, the form or differences in-forming the source text. Such an act of translation makes *sur-vive* in the term 'sur-vival' the difference in the original. This exercise of translation that Derrida makes visible to the reader is, characteristically, performative; it demonstrates the principle of translatability.

Having made explicit this performative dimension, which is present in almost every one of Derrida's texts, I want to return now to the question of the philosophical significance of sur-vival. Benjamin is speaking of texts and their essential translatability. Texts sur-vive human life (*Uber-leben*) but they also make this life sur-vive (*Fort-leben*): they transcend life to extend or supplement its finitude. On the one hand, we can think of textuality as *Fortleben*, as allowing something of the author's life to survive. Texts prolong this life by preserving a life's work, that is, its thought and intentions. On the other hand, the structure proper to the text – or the sort of survival that defines texts and that texts make possible – cannot be understood in terms of the life it preserves, and in particular the *finitude* that is the mark of human life. Textual survival is *Uberleben*.

With respect to the finitude of the author's life, textual structures indefinitely postpone death and forgetting, even if this form of memory is always threatened by a loss of legibility.

> This structure is the relation of life to sur-vival. This requirement of the other as translator, Benjamin compares it to some unforgettable instant of life . . . it is unforgettable even if in fact forgetting finally wins out. It will have been unforgettable . . . The requirement of the unforgettable – which is here constitutive – is not in the least impaired by the finitude of memory. Likewise the requirement of translation in no way suffers from not being satisfied, at least it does not suffer in so far as it is the very structure of the work.[27]

That which is 'remembered' or remains 'unforgettable' in the text is not conditioned by the finitude of human memory or human life. The necessity and the possibility of translation is part of the 'very structure of the work', a requirement, furthermore, that does not suffer from not being satisfied. The task of translation can wait, indefinitely, as the in-forming text sur-vives, dormant or spellbound.

As we saw in the last chapter, in the same way that the death of all readers functions to define the form of textual sur-vival in 'Signature, Event, Context', Derrida argues here that neither the death of all possible translators, nor the finitude of human memory, nor the empirical impossibility (in the case of humans) of *not* forgetting impugns a text's translatability. The structure of the work – that is to say, the structure of sur-vival – is constitutively linked to that which in it is 'unforgettable'. Hence, so long as there is a text, there is the requirement or demand for translation/ remembering. This is the same as saying that the text is, primarily and before it is anything else, structurally an (in-human) form of memory. An archiving/archival form, a form of preservation that involves the modification or rewriting of that which cannot be defined in terms of what it makes possible – the familiar uses to which humans may put this form – the text provides all the necessary conditions for its own translation.

What sur-vives in language – according to Derrida's gloss of Benjamin – is revitalised in and through translation. Successful translation liberates the pure language imprisoned within the source language – that which we habitually refer to as the text's meaning. In contrast to the ideal of a translation governed by the reproduction of a source text's meaning, for Benjamin this liberation is not reproductive but productive.[28]

The liberation of pure language/meaning produces (more) meaning.

> The original gives itself in modifying itself; this gift is not an object given; it lives and lives on in mutation: For in its survival, which would not merit the name if it were not mutation and renewal of something living, the original is modified. Even for words that are solidified there is a postmaturation.[29]

The original language or text survives only in its translation – in its modification-transcription in another text. The life of language and texts is a parasitic life. Structurally speaking, texts imply inscribed or compressed patterns, patterns of difference that store or encode other, heterogeneous patterns. Translation *restores* through the regulated transformation of the patterns in the target language something like the resonance patterns (Benjamin uses the image of an echo) achieved in the 'source' language.

Derrida figures the task of translation both in terms of preservation and transformation, of reproduction and creation. There is, of course, nothing particularly innovative about this description. What makes Derrida's view of translation distinctive, however, is that it is not linguistic Meaning that a translator reproduces or represents in a target language. As we have seen, Derrida understands language not as a vehicle for Meanings, but from the point of view of its structure. The task of the translator involves waking up language – or unfolding or decompressing the patterns stored in language – and putting language to work in order to make one language resonate in another.

### Meaning in Translation

To get a more intuitive sense for how such an account of translation could explain linguistic function, and in particular how translation produces the characteristic meaning-effect, I propose a simplified case study of translation without Meaning. The case is not linguistic, in the narrow sense, but pertains to intermodal (or intersensory) translation. The structural translatability of the senses is demonstrated by what are commonly referred to as sensory substitution devices (SSDs). SSDs are most often used as sensory prostheses, when subjects have lost the use of certain sense modalities, such as hearing.

'EyeMusic' is an example of such a prosthetic device. As the name suggests, researchers developed it to translate patterns or differences in the visual field (colour, for example) into sound. According to the lab's description, EyeMusic is a system for the congenitally blind that transforms visual images into sequences of sound.[30] The language of 'image' somewhat obscures what we might call the principle of translatability. Sequences of sound can convey visual information because of what Benjamin called 'original translatability'. And if visual images are originally translatable, this also entails that they are not originally visual. In turn, users of the device can be taught to read or translate the sound sequences as visual differences even though they are congenitally blind, because, in principle, the structured differences in sound can be heard as a heterogeneous text (of structured differences). In a double sense the user of the device can learn to 'see' through the sound.

The differences that structure visual images are transformed into and made to appear in and through differences in sound. For example, the differences characteristic of visual images (e.g. light/dark) are transformed into differences in sound (e.g. high/low frequency). In Derrida's words, the program for the device 'practices the difference between signifier and signified' in and through the regulated transformation of one text by another. The very possibility of intermodal translation indicates that sensation too is iterable or textual.

One of the insights that we can glean from this example and those of Kele drum-writing and English phonetic writing from the previous chapter is that the object or signified of any signifying modality cannot, in principle, be identified with respect to its origin or its essence. To borrow from the language of perceptual and cognitive studies, texts are, originally speaking, intermodal. The original translatability (or iterability) of essentially intermodal phenomena forecloses the possibility of identifying any signified with an original field of appearance. With these examples, I hope to have made clearer how, having reduced Meaning, Derrida's account of original translatability allows him to redescribe meaning-effects in terms of translation. Derrida's account transforms Meaning into the effect of generalised translatability. This translatability involves the dimensions of both protention and retention. As attention to SSD devices shows, translation entails the modifiability and retentiveness of textual elements and their relations – or, as we will see more clearly in the chapters to come, the plasticity of the text.

Sight is retained 'in' sound, and if we can 'see' through hearing, this is because the structures in-forming vision can be retrieved through a movement of 'reverse' translation. The signified structures now appearing through and structuring sight may be retranslated in yet another sense modality, or displaced and reorganised by another iteration of the same movement that makes the original substitution or translation possible. The dimension of survival that structures the horizon of translatability implies both the indefinite possibility of reinscription and also erasure in the form of the text's essential modifiability – which up until now I have referred to in terms of parasitism.

All of the 'success words' related to linguistic function and understanding, including 'hearing', 'reading', 'understanding', 'meaning' and 'translating', would involve either a reverse translation or a new translation. We can thus speculate that the phenomenon of a 'voice of consciousness', hearing-oneself-speak, is not a puzzling, empty repetition or even merely *auto*-affective, but that this inner 'hearing' or subvocalisation initiates a movement of translation: that in a curious sense, 'thought' designates the movement through which we affect ourselves with words, with language and with texts.

## Conclusion: Speculating on Subvocalisation

By way of conclusion, I would like to develop a speculative thought occasioned by the SSD EyeMusic and Searle's account of the Chinese Room. EyeMusic offers an illustration, I argue, of the principles of translatability. It is also a prosthetic device that might give us some insight into how sensory systems are structured. But what if language were originally *like* an SSD, like EyeMusic? What if the patterns of sound or the pattern of written marks involved the same principle of intermodal translation?

We might think that what language 'translates' and 'substitutes' itself for is thought. On some level, this must be right if the analogy is to work. Here, 'thought' does not designate the stream of transcendental signifieds, but rather heterogeneous intermodal structures. There is, however, a sense – and this is what interests me here – in which such a prosthetic device would also produce thought, and this in at least two senses. If we follow the EyeMusic analogy, language would not just translate pre-linguistic texts into speech. EyeMusic translates vision to be sure, but its characteristic feature is to produce vision in the user, where there was no vision. If we follow this analogy, language would also produce thought or thoughts where there were none before. I can 'see' what I could not otherwise 'see' through EyeMusic. What I have in mind is not that without language, and in particular without speech or writing, there would be no thinking, but rather that language does not simply translate thought; it is a form of auto-affection. I will return to this notion of language as auto-affection below. But first, I want to point out another quite distinctive or original sense in which language and speech in particular produce 'thought'. The thought that is in question is not thinking per se, but a certain experience or image of thought. The type of experience in question may indeed be quite marginal or ineffective. Its effectiveness is an empirical question. The speculative point, however, is that it has had an inordinate effect on what philosophers have thought about thinking and goes some way to explaining why the 'myth of the transcendental signified' is so tenacious.

The experience I have in mind is subvocalisation, or what Derrida calls in *Speech and Phenomena*, 'the voice that keeps silent'.[31] Subvocalisation, as the voice in your head, is a mode of speaking. It is not imaginary, in the sense that, as researchers show, your jaw and vocal apparatus are engaged and move when you subvocalise (this allows for mind-reading devices). Subvocalisation seems reliably to accompany reading but also thinking, though it does not seem necessary to reading, at least. Husserl argued that subvocalisation or silent monologue did not count as *effective* speech. In silent monologue (with ourselves) we are communicating nothing, least of all to ourselves. He was keen to avoid the very idea that communicating with ourselves was possible. If we communicated to ourselves, all the misfires that occur in communication could occur in thought. We might fail, for example, to hear ourselves speak, or know what we were saying. More to the point, 'speaking' to ourselves silently cannot be the way that thought works because this would imply that the problem of reduction (to Meaning) is internal to thought. In order to have Meaningful thoughts, Husserl believed, the materiality of the signifier cannot interfere on pain of infinite regress.

Husserl, Derrida is clear, was an exemplary logocentrist who attempted to give a particularly vigorous defence of the transcendental signified. At the same time, having refused the effectiveness of 'silent speech' when he attempted to give an image or model of thought, he offered the image of silent monologue. He is, of course, not the only philosopher to have done so. Hannah Arendt famously described thinking in similar but more dialogical terms as a 'two-in-one', as the possibility of being in dialogue with oneself. Indeed, this model of thought is true not only for philosophers. When we are asked what we are thinking, this is often thought of as a request to 'speak up', to vocalise or express our thoughts, as if these thoughts were already speech.

Derrida objects to Husserl's view that subvocalisation is not effective speech. It is silent to be sure, it keeps to itself, but what is remarkable about the phenomenology of subvocalisation is that it involves (or seems to involve) *hearing*. Without making any sound, in subvocalising I can hear myself speak as if, or almost as if, I were really speaking. It is a ghostly, uncanny phenomenon. How can I hear something (a voice in my head) when there was no sound made? What sort of auto-affection is this?

Thought appears to sensibilise itself – to appear 'in the flesh' – as silent monologue. Moreover, it appears not as real (emitted) sound, but as the phenomena of hearing-oneself-speak. What am I thinking – right now? I may ask myself this, quite literally: I can silently subvocalise and hear a voice in my head. This hearing myself speak, Derrida argues, *feels* like immediacy, it feels like *self*-presence. Moreover, it is the phenomenological locus for consciousness. Consciousness gives or evidences itself as this voice that hears itself in an absolute interiority, that affects itself with itself. Of course, this appearance or evidence is dissimulative. It is made possible by the peculiar operation of the subvocalising voice. Here, 'I' am directly present to myself in a way that is even more direct than in 'silent' proprioception, in particular because I can affect myself voluntaristically, seemingly immediately without any mediation. The meaning of the words that I 'utter' seems readily present, even though this meaning nowhere appears or evidences itself beyond the *sense* that I have understood myself.

One might object that thought also sensibilises itself through writing – as Luhmann's epigraph at the opening of this chapter suggests. Why give subvocalisation a certain pride of place in provisioning us with an image of 'thought'? It is certainly true that writing sensibilises thought in the same way as speech. But there is no such phenomenon as 'sub-writing', and even if there were, it would not give rise to the peculiar simulation of presence that subvocalisation does. However intimate a form of self-relation or auto-affection writing is, the effect of immediacy or being in touch with oneself that subvocalisation produces has had a more profound effect on how we think about thought.

Writing provides us with the right sort of dissimulative self-experience (that of self-presence) only inasmuch as it involves subvocalisation. The silent reading voice accompanying writing produces a reassuring sense of proximity and immediacy or presence. Of course, while the voice that keeps silent can sustain the illusion of immediacy and pure interiority, its very structure as 'hearing oneself speak' testifies to the same difference and delay, *différance* which, Derrida argues, philosophy refuses to think or countenance.

This auto-affecting inner voice – the voice that rouses our attention, that alerts us to ourselves, that allows us, as Arendt writes, to be in dialogue with ourselves – implies necessarily and essentially a gap or absence that paradoxically produces this sense of self-presence or proximity. The self-reading or self-translating sign is an illusion in a double sense. It requires us to think that thought produces or expresses itself to itself first as endogenous signs, as a particular meaning or object exactly as it is meant – in a form that is both linguistically communicable or expressible – but *without* the possibility of miscommunication or misfire. Yet if we can only understand thought or meaning in terms of an expressible though not yet linguistically expressed $x$, in terms of that which has all the features of language, do we not thereby admit that it is already indiscernible from the form of expression? Wherever we point to thought, we point to what is always already, irreducibly, formally linguistic.

I want to return, as promised, to the question of auto-affection. Researchers have shown that when subvocalisation happens there are tiny but perceptible movements of the jaw and vocal apparatus. From a motor perspective, I *am* speaking. If thinking were really indistinguishable from subvocalisation, then what we call thinking would be nothing more than affecting oneself by speaking, listening to oneself, hearing what one was saying. In speaking, as with the EyeMusic device, I am conveying to myself or affecting myself with 'meanings' or heterogeneous, intermodal patterns. (One might also say *infecting*, recalling William Burroughs's quip about language being 'a virus from outer space').[32]

This speculation, which is indeed Derrida's speculation in *Speech and Phenomena* – which, as I am not the first to note, would be more relevantly translated as *Voice and Phenomenon* – is not meant to imply that thought *is* originally speech, nor that speech or subvocalisation is all there is to thought, but that a certain sensory substitution device or intermodal prosthesis – call it language – and its dissimulation as subvocalisation – the voice that keeps silent – has determined to a large extent how philosophers have thought about thought.

It may well be that subvocalisation is no more than idle chatter or background noise, something like tuning into a radio station, and that it has very little to do with cognition and real or 'effective' thinking. It may be as well, as Luhmann's epigraph suggests, that the prosthesis of writing has had far more effect on what philosophers have called 'thinking' than speech. Nonetheless, as Derrida argues, the phenomenology of the voice, and its apparent self-proximity and auto-affective quality, may account for our attachment to the transcendental signified.

The first and primary task of this chapter was to get a sense of why Derrida thinks that the transcendental signified is impossible, why logocentrism has no workable account of linguistic function. Derrida, if he has been successful, will have argued that the transcendental signified is finally the *petitio principii* of logocentrism that would have no more reality than the structure of hearing-myself-speak – the self-affection that is thought – and the feeling that in hearing myself I have reduced the voice and am in the full presence of a meaning or understanding. Hearing, like reading or understanding, functions as a 'success' term without offering an account of what success consists of, beyond the fantastical posit of a self-interpreting, self-reading sign.

The secondary task of this chapter was to demonstrate that if we *ought* to think otherwise, then we can think otherwise. The deconstruction of the transcendental signified does not commit us to a philosophical nihilism, or a rational argument for the *a priori* incomprehensibility of thought and language. Or at least, there are enough indications throughout Derrida's *oeuvre* that he himself is not committed to any such philosophical nihilism. Instead, Derrida argues that we need to attend to the 'formal' structures that make our experience of meaning possible.

### Notes

1.  By 'myth' I mean to evoke the resonances with Sellars's 'Myth of the Given' (Sellars 1956). There are important and fruitful comparisons to be made here between Derrida's critiques of phenomenological givenness and the Sellarsian notion of 'givenness', in particular his attention to its epistemic function. However, it is easy to show that Sellars's thought remains within the correlational frame. He is interested precisely in the idea of a logical 'space': a 'space of reason' or meaning, as opposed to an exterior space defined against the possibility of Meaning. Derrida interestingly also equates the myth of the transcendental signified with the dream of unequivocal translatability, which rests precisely on the idea of transcendental signifieds.

2. Derrida (1982: 134).
3. Derrida (1985).
4. For deconstruction as a critique of magical or self-interpreting language or signs, see Wheeler (2000).
5. According to Derrida, the logocentric or Meaning-centric accounts of linguistic function have determined how philosophers and theorists have thought about translation. However, a certain understanding of translation may also have given rise to logocentrism. Derrida writes that the theological ideal of unequivocal translatability may be behind our logocentric beliefs. 'In effect, the theme of a transcendental signified took shape within the horizon of an absolutely pure, transparent, and unequivocal translatability' (Derrida 1981: 20).
6. The reducibility thesis does not initially have a phenomenological specification, but Derrida is clear that phenomenology makes this thesis explicit in its (more) rigorous account of Reduction. See in particular *Speech and Phenomena* (1973).
7. Derrida (1978: 279). In the context I cite, this claim is asserted but not argued for. In the chapter on 'Linguistics and Grammatology', however, particularly in Derrida's treatment of Saussure, it is directly argued for. I defer the question, then, of the extent to which theories that insist on the constitutive value of language (for thought and ideas) effectively challenge the logocentric ideal of Meaning to the next chapter.
8. Derrida argues for this claim most directly in his readings of Husserl. See particularly the essay 'Form and Meaning' in *Speech and Phenomena* (1973). In *Introduction to the Origin of Geometry* (1989), Derrida offers an extensive critical reading of the transcendental role that Husserl assigns to writing. However, this reading is a critique in the more traditional philosophical sense rather than a deconstructive reading of Husserl. For an extensive analysis of Derrida's arguments on the constitutive value of writing, see Kates (2005: esp. ch. 2).
9. Derrida's interpreters have often argued, wrongly in my view, that Derrida's aim is to show that the ideal of univocal meanings is impossible. Writing will demonstrate the impossibility of *this* account of Meaning, while offering a novel theory of meaning that factors the impossibility of univocity. Derrida will have shown that some absolute or ideal case is impossible. Writing is the condition of possibility of meaning (in general), but it is the condition of impossibility for Meaning (understood in a particularly narrow way). Reading will never be *perfectly* successful or meaning*ful*. This ostensibly leaves

room for another theory of reading/meaning/language that is sensitive to the fact that any reading will always be ambiguous, contextualised, relative to a context, etc. That is, Derrida's theory of reading is understood as encouraging us to deflate what we mean or understand reading/meaning to be. It will not be univocity, but always equivocity, it will not be absolute, but relative, it will not be literal, but always already metaphorical.

For example, Simon Glendinning concludes that, 'for Derrida, language is made possible by, and must ultimately be understood in terms of, structures of writing (in his new sense)' (2004: 6). This is literally right, but what it omits is that these structures of writing seem to make language impossible because they make Meaning impossible. Hence, we need an account of language that does not define it in terms of the general possibility of the *successful* transmission or expression of Meaning. If, as Glendinning writes, language cannot be distinguished from writing in Derrida's 'new sense', language must be understood ('in return') in terms of writing *in this new sense* rather than in terms of Meaning. What writing in this new sense is is not just a structure of repetition that implies a break with any context, though this is also literally true, but iterability, as a 'parasitic' structure, a structure in-formed by alterity.

These deflationary readings, it seems to me, miss Derrida's point in precisely the same way that Searle misses Derrida's point regarding the logical possibility of Meaning. Searle argues that he cannot understand why it is that Derrida insists that he, or any other philosopher, believes or trades in 'perfection' or rigid ideal cases – for instance, that either there is something like pure intentions, absolute reading, univocity, or there is nothing. Indeed, Searle thinks that Derrida fails to factor in, or simply ignores, all of the progress and innovation made by contemporary philosophy – contemporary Anglo-American philosophy of language in particular.

10. Derrida's reading and critique of Peirce is very truncated. He credits Peirce with being more attentive to the genetic structures of signs than Saussure. In particular, Peirce shows how the particular domain of language (arbitrariness) is rooted in the non-arbitrary (the becoming-arbitrary, the becoming-unmotivated of the sign). This specification of language (or linguistic strata) in terms of a more general semiotics parallels Derrida's own generalisation strategy. Peirce also seeks to deconstruct the transcendental signified (particularly as the form of an intuitive presence), substituting for this phenomenological ideal the notion of manifestation as a sign. However, I have argued that,

according to Derrida, the way he does this leads to too much 'play' – and not enough signification. To evaluate Derrida's critique of Peirce on this point, or the one I have attributed to him above, would require a more specialised grasp of Peirce's semiotics than I possess. However, I am not aware of any particularly satisfying treatments of Derrida's critique of Peirce. No doubt this is because critiques of Derrida's account of Peirce usually attribute to the former a notion of *différance* as Saussurean opposition or contrast, which, as I argue in the fourth chapter, is easily refuted. What Derrida retains from Saussure is the insistence on the indissociability of the signifier and signified. For Saussure, this indissociability is precisely maintained to make sense of how manifestation or phenomenologisation 'makes a sign'. The sign produces 'intuitive' presence. For Derrida, the *entangled* structure of signifier and signified are non-transcendental conditions for 'presence'. To evaluate Derrida's critique of Peirce, I believe, requires examining the latter's triadic structure of signification as a competing account of the possibility of meaning or signification.

11. See also the text Derrida quotes from: Buchler (1940: 9).

12. An image might help to show the logic of Derrida's argument. Picture the spinning pinwheel that appears on a computer screen as the processor attempts to carry out a command. The pinwheel, we assume, represents the time it takes for the command to be executed. We hope, when such a pinwheel appears, that it will eventually disappear. The operation will come to a happy ending and we will be able to continue with the task. Now imagine the process of thought in Peircean terms as a series of steps. In order to interpret a sign, we are directed by the sign to open another file (the interpretent); this interpretent redirects us to open another file, which, in turn, sends us to a third. If this process were literally without end, as Peirce suggests, it seems that rather than an account of the possibility of thought, we have an account of its radical impossibility. The right conclusion to draw would not be that our thoughts are indeterminate in the sense that we do not know *all* that is in our thoughts, because we do not have time to open all of the files. The point is that the picture of thinking/language that Peirce leads us to is, from a theoretical perspective, a picture of dysfunction.

13. Searle (1994: 637).

14. In *Positions*, Derrida writes that 'translation *practices* the difference between signifier and signified' and that without this difference no language could function (Derrida 1981: 20). Here, he clearly flags the problem of collapsing the difference between signifier and

signified. Derrida does, however, deny that the difference between signifier and signified is *pure*. The difference between signifier and signified must be understood in non-oppositional terms. Perhaps Derrida never emphasised this enough.

15. Derrida (1981: 19).
16. Derrida (1981: 20).
17. Derrida (1981: 20).
18. Benjamin (2012: 76).
19. Benjamin (2012: 81).
20. Benjamin (2012: 83).
21. Benjamin (2012: 76).
22. Benjamin (2012: 76).
23. See the previous chapter for a discussion of the idea of thinking a deconstructed concept 'in return'.
24. Benjamin (2012: 76).
25. Derrida (1985: 202).
26. Derrida (1985: 202).
27. Derrida (1985: 205).
28. Derrida (1985: 182–3).
29. Derrida (1985: 183).
30. Maidenbaum et al. (2014).
31. Derrida (1973: 70). To preserve the centrality and function of 'the voice' in Derrida's deconstructive reading of Husserl, a text entitled *La Voix et le phénomène* might have been more aptly translated as *Voice and Phenomenon*. More recent translations have corrected for this. However, since *Speech and Phenomena* is still the most common citation, in this book I refer to the 1973 Allison translation.
32. Burroughs (1986: 48).

# 4

# Rewriting the
# *Course in General Linguistics*:
# From Sign to Spacing

The name 'my ink pot' seems to overlay the perceived object, to belong sensibly to it. This belonging is of a peculiar kind . . . not word *and* inkpot.

Edmund Husserl, *Logical Investigations*

To think the 'holding together' of the *disparate* itself. Not to maintain together the disparate, but to put ourselves there where the disparate itself holds together, without wounding the dis-jointure, the dispersion, or the difference, without effacing the heterogeneity of the other.

Jacques Derrida, *Spectres of Marx*

Multiple heterogeneous iterations all: past, present, and future, not in a relation of linear unfolding, but threaded through one another in a nonlinear enfolding of spacetimemattering, a topology that defies any suggestion of a smooth continuous manifold.

Karen Barad, 'Quantum Entanglements'

## The Most General Concept of the Gramme

The grammatologist, founder of an autonomous science of writing, must first clarify its central concept, writing. In order to do so, they must clarify grammatology's position vis-à-vis linguistics. If Saussure indicated that, 'by rights', the field of linguistics belonged to the (more general) field of semiotics, so would semiotics be covered by the field of grammatology.[1] To free grammatology from linguistics requires grammatology also to declare its independence from the concept of writing generated by linguistics.

Who, then, is the grammatologist for whom, in particular, arche-writing would be so pertinent? *Of Grammatology* appeared in 1967, and the expansion of writing, Derrida argues in the first chapter of the book, was in the cybernetic *air du temps*. In popular and scientific thought, 'writing' no longer meant what it once did. It was no longer a technical appendage to human language. It was already, to all appearances, becoming general, extending from the code of life (genetics) to computer programs (informatics).

The expansion of writing in scientific, technical and aesthetic discourses was essentially speculative, both in the sense of inflationary, demonstrating a certain willingness to capitalise on a metaphor, and in the sense of using the model of writing to think or explain that which underwrites and supersedes experience. This change in the concept of writing, Derrida insists, calls for philosophical explanation and explication, a critical justification of this speculative discourse. *Of Grammatology* answers these calls.[2]

The grammatologist aims to think writing in the broadest possible terms – that is, in terms that both subtend and extend beyond the human. The grammatologist requires the most general concept of the gramme. How then to get at this general concept? Does the generalisation of writing imply that graphic writing serves as the model for what has not traditionally been thought of as writing? There is no doubt that the model or metaphor of writing had been productive – especially for linguistics. But the generality of writing will not refer to the fecundity and productivity – the general appeal – of this metaphor.

Certainly no science of general writing can be founded on a metaphor. Minimally, grammatology will require principles for determining what makes something an instance of writing. In the context of grammatology, phonetic and graphic writing would constitute instances of writing that have been mistaken for the whole. But how to get from the example or model of writing, in the narrow sense of phonetic or graphic writing, to the general concept of writing? Is it a matter of taking into account the structural features of phonetic writing or of linguistic signs generally? If so, how would grammatology differ from structural linguistics, particularly the formalist analyses of a linguist such as Louis Hjelmslev, who resolved to think of systems of signification exclusively in terms of form and irrespective of the 'substance' of expression (OG, 61)? More generally, in what sense has the project of general linguistics failed at precisely this project? Do quantitative models of message, information and communication – such as those provided by Claude Shannon – recommend themselves as substitutes for more traditional linguistic models?

To specify the domain of writing, the grammatologist must generate a general concept of writing – to make explicit what we talk about when we talk about 'writing'. Curiously, as just mentioned, Saussure's successors in the field of structural linguistics appear to offer a more grammatologically apt model of writing than Saussure did himself, ones, moreover, that are more apt for quantification. Curiously because, in the second chapter of *Of Grammatology*, entitled quite simply, 'Linguistics and Grammatology', Derrida directs the grammatologist *not* to follow in the path of Saussure's formalist successors, who appear to transcend the master's teachings by taking rather more seriously than did Saussure his own dictum that 'language is a form and not a substance'.[3]

Indeed, Derrida insists that the grammatologist must follow Saussure precisely where the grammatologist might be expected to part ways with him. We ought, he counsels, to resist the temptation to break with Saussure too soon, for then we will fall short of the most general concept of writing. This strategy seems paradoxical because, in the *Course in General Linguistics*, Saussure begins his investigation of the linguistic sign by excluding writing. It is as if writing needed first to be excluded or bracketed in order to attain to an account of its generality.

To generalise writing, then, we must first exclude its 'popular' and even its technical conception. Saussure was right to claim that writing misleads the linguists by providing a *false* image of language and the linguistic sign. To let empirical writing guide our intuition, then, will lead us, every time, to the wrong account of the sign. Unfortunately, Derrida notes, Saussure does not consider excluding only a *certain* image of writing – in particular phonetic writing – while leaving open the possibility that excluding *this* model will permit a better account of writing and the linguistic sign to emerge. This is certainly a problem. Nonetheless, excluding a certain model of writing permits Saussure to generate an account of the linguistic sign that is much closer, Derrida argues, to the account of general writing that the grammatologist requires. Furthermore, unlike many of those who followed him on the question of the structure of language, Saussure's inquiry into general linguistics was also a radical investigation into the origin and genesis of the linguistic sign. Indeed, he arguably subordinated the question of structure to that of genesis. It will be the problem of genesis, rather than structure, that permits the general concept of writing, or arche-writing, to appear.

It seems, then, that to generate the most general concept of the gramme, to get to arche-writing, we have only to follow in Saussure's footsteps and see where Saussure errs in his determination of writing. The grammatologist must demonstrate not only that everything Saussure says about language is also true of the writing he excludes, but also that the most general concept of writing accounts for both language (speech) and writing. Language and writing cannot be thought in terms of their radical heterogeneity but rather as sharing the same conditions: namely, arche-writing. Indeed, as we will see, this is just what Derrida does in *Of Grammatology*, and more specifically in the second chapter entitled 'Linguistics and Grammatology'. There, we can find the passage between narrow writing and arche-writing via Derrida's reading of Saussure. Not, however, without difficulty.

Indeed, this passage has eluded (as we will see in a moment) many of Derrida's best readers. And for good reason. It is a tortuous path, and one easily loses the trail. This is because, perhaps somewhat contrary to readers' expectations, Derrida connects arche-writing to the apparently transcendental problem of *experience*, which seems orthogonal both to the goals of the linguist, who seeks a scientific account of language, and those of the grammatologist, who wishes to show writing's generality and autonomy rather than its dependence upon consciousness and transcendental subjectivity.

It seemed that the generalisation of writing would require excising it from the phenomenological and experiential horizon rather than insisting on its pertinence. Yet Derrida unmistakably connects writing to transcendental experience, and he does so on the basis of Saussure's analysis of the linguistic sign:

> Origin of the experience of space and time, this *writing* of difference, this fabric of the trace, permits the difference between space and time to be articulated, to appear as such, in the unity of an experience. (OG, 66)

Even if, as Derrida writes, writing has always marked off a position of technical exteriority ('supplementarity') vis-à-vis the human life it purportedly served, arche-writing appears to lead writing back to the interiority of (transcendental) life. This move seems, as well, to erase the sort of conceptual advances that structuralism achieves – namely of thinking about language and its structure objectively, in particular in terms of linguistic value.

If arche-writing will not be limited to experience, but will be absolutely general, as Derrida claims, the passage from narrow writing to arche-writing requires a passage through the problem of lived experience. To get to generalised writing, even one that will eventually lose touch with the category of experience, we must pass through the transcendental 'text'.

What has been difficult to explain is, on the one hand, what necessitates, justifies or prompts the intervention of the transcendental problematic in Saussure's account of language. Why exactly does Derrida think that we must situate the transcendental question as a moment in the grammatological inquiry? If it turns out that Saussure's analysis of the sign leads to these transcendental questions, would this not count as a reason for the grammatologist to reject Saussure's analysis?

Certainly, the necessity of this 'transcendental' passage will not always be obvious to the grammatologist, or it will only be justified in retrospect. Without this passage through the transcendental, Derrida writes, we will likely confuse the ultra-transcendental notion of 'writing' or 'text' (arche-writing) with a pre-critical ('objectivist') sense of these terms (OG, 61). In any case, we cannot, without traversing the transcendental text, understand what Derrida means by 'spacing' and why this term is a cognate for arche-writing. Spacing is, indeed, so far apparently from the narrow notion of writing as to lose touch with it entirely.

Let us grant, then, that the path to the most general notion of the gramme – arche-writing – requires a passage through Saussure's text and through the problem of the relation of the linguistic sign to conscious experience more generally. 'Requires' may be too strong a term. This suggests a grounding relation, such that arche-writing depends upon the truth of Saussurean linguistics (its being right or wrong). This cannot be right in any simple sense, since we know in advance that Saussure is wrong – especially about the nature and status of writing. It may be, however, that he is crucially right about something else – and that this will permit us to forge not only a notion of general writing but also to demonstrate its absolute generality. Minimally, Saussure is right that the popular conception of writing is wrong, and that this conception of writing, insofar as it determines the meaning of language, leads us to misunderstand language. He is also right, according to Derrida – and herein lies his relative uniqueness in the linguistic tradition – that the linguistic bond is constitutive and, hence, that the two faces of the sign, the signifier and signified, are indissociable.

If Saussure is useful to the grammatologist, it is, then, to extent that his work is already deconstructive, seeking to oust traditional concepts that have made it impossible to think about the nature of linguistic signs as anything but secondary and derivative with respect to an original (non-linguistic) consciousness. In insisting on the originality of the linguistic sign vis-à-vis consciousness, Saussure's approach is proto-grammatological, soliciting the inherited concepts of a tradition in order to conceive what they, in their present formation, exclude. In this respect, finally, Saussure's treatment of writing will be an index of the extent to which this solicitation (of the tradition) has failed – of the extent to which the tradition still solicits him and therefore limits his analysis.

## Rereading 'Linguistics and Grammatology'

In the second chapter of *Of Grammatology*, Derrida invites the grammatologist to turn to Ferdinand de Saussure's *Course in General Linguistics* (*Cours de linguistique générale*) to develop a general concept of writing. The choice seems obvious at first, but becomes increasingly puzzling. It is true that the founders of grammatology are apparently in the same position with respect to writing as Saussure was with respect to language. Founding a general science of writing will entail an inquiry into the nature and limits of writing – and hence, the grammatologist may find Saussure's foundational text instructive. Yet, *prima facie*, the grammatologist is sure to find Saussure's treatment of writing not just unsatisfactory, but deplorable.

Derrida is clear about the fact that the founding gesture of the father of modern linguistics was to exclude writing. Saussure, Derrida emphasises, begins by uncritically defining writing as 'exterior' to language proper, but bases this exclusion on the most cursory, uncritical consideration of writing. Indeed, he limits his attention exclusively to phonetic writing. For Saussure, 'writing' always designates the 'sign of the [linguistic] sign', the 'representation' or 'image' of speech. Had he but considered examples of non-phonetic writing, from so-called ideographic writing to mathematical systems of notation, Saussure could not have so easily characterised writing as a derivative, inert supplement to speech. If we look just to those places where Saussure attempts to sharply

distinguish language (proper) from writing, we find so much con-
tradiction that one can easily doubt his value as a linguist.

Saussure's exclusion of writing is not only a problem for grammatology but for *general* linguistics. He risks the latter's claims to
generality. Even if phonetic writing were the only and universal
instance of writing (which it is not), why, Derrida asks,

> [d]oes a project of general linguistics, concerning the internal system in
> general of language in general, outline the limits of its field by exclud-
> ing, as exteriority in general, a particular system of writing, however
> important it might be, even if it were to be in fact universal? (OG, 39)

If one were trying to find the limits of language – that is, to mark
off the regional boundaries of a science – why not take better
care to ensure that systems of 'graphic writing' were not in fact
a subset of linguistic systems? Even if Saussure's intuitions were
that language had a *distinctive* form and function, which it did
not share with *phonetic* writing, why not wait to confirm these
intuitions by first establishing this form and function and then
clarifying the status and nature of writing? Why not consider
that if a certain model of writing has given us the wrong image
of language, this model also gives us the wrong model of writing?
No doubt this uncritical and unsupported exclusion of writing
evidences what Derrida calls Saussure's 'phonocentrism'. But the
latter is not simply another word for blind prejudice. Saussure,
who was otherwise so alert to the problem of inherited preju-
dices, is not motivated to resist a philosophical tradition that has
systematically elevated speech over writing. The linguistic sign is
phonocentric not because it excludes writing, but because, as we
shall see, it positively affirms the view that sound and thought are
essentially, constitutively entangled.

Based on the rationale that Saussure offers, one might well
conclude that the *Cours de linguistique générale* will not be productive for grammatology, and for similar reasons that it will
be of limited use to the linguist. Would it not, then, be more
productive to begin again? And with a more promising text?
For example, we might start with Hjelmslev's *Prolegomena to a
Theory of Language* (1953). The latter's theory of glossematics,
as a general semiotics, aimed to abstract the form common to all
linguistic systems. Hence, it included rather than excluded writing,
and introduced the generic term *glosseme* to designate any linguis-

tic signifier. Indeed, glossematics seems, in every respect, closer to grammatology than Saussurean linguistics. If Saussure gave us the tools to think of all systems of signification in formal terms (as an open system of values or differences) – and if, in terms of structure and function, systems of writing are formally indistinguishable from systems of signification – then why does Derrida tarry so long with the archaic *Cours de linguistique générale*? Why does he stage partings and breaks, only to return again to Saussure's account of the sign?

Derrida is hardly unaware of Hjelmslev or other formalist approaches. Indeed, he indicates that, with respect to Saussure, these approaches, in 'trying to go beyond the master', fall short. Indeed, Saussure tells us why. They work with and implicitly rely upon the model of popular writing. Therefore, they miss the constitutive relation between the signifier and signified. Instead of thinking the genesis of linguistic form, they abstract from the constituted form.

Saussure insists upon the entangled, mutually constitutive relation of the signifier and the signified, while the formalists treat language like a system of writing (where this constitutive relation is, according to Saussure, absent). If Saussure is wrong about the nature of writing – if it too is constitutively entangled with the signified – then Saussure's analysis of the structure and genesis of the linguistic sign will help the grammatologist understand the nature of writing. But to see how, we must think with and against Saussure; we must stay with him longer than seems reasonable or promising.

Saussure's analysis of the sign is radical in the sense that – unlike the glossematics approach – it does not subordinate the question of genesis to that of structure; his analysis of the sign's form is always articulated with the question of the genesis of this form. Saussure grants speech primacy over writing not because of the purported order of linguistic acquisition – this would ground writing's derivativeness in a contingent fact – but on the basis of his analysis of the *origin* of the dual-sided sign. For Saussure, as we shall see, the constitutive role of sound is decisive. If Saussure is wrong to centre sound – that is, if the grammatologist should break with his phonocentrism – they should continue, with Saussure, to think the genesis and structure of writing together.

In the remainder of this chapter, I will track Derrida's writing of arche-writing into the founding text of linguistics. In my reconstructive reading, I will focus on the grammatological significance of Saussure's phonocentrism. Why did Saussure think that sound was originally constitutive of the sign and what happens to our account of 'language' when sound is decentred? How does rejecting Saussure's exclusion of writing modify or transform the project of a *general* linguistics? What is the extent or scope of general writing? What do terms such as arche-writing, trace and spacing do with or make of the narrow, standard understanding of writing and of Saussure's account of the linguistic sign?

## The Enigma of Arche-writing

I have read and re-read these passages many times. I still find them enigmatic.

J. Hillis Miller

I want to begin this proposed rereading by remarking the enigmatic appearance of the unfamiliar term arche-writing in the text. 'Arche-writing' describes the 'gramme' of grammatology and, like its cognates, trace and spacing, 'communicates' with the 'vulgar concept of writing'.[4] This communication enables the regulated extension and generalisation of writing, while assuring that, however much arche-writing displaces everyday intuitions about what writing is, and however general it becomes, it will account for writing in the 'narrow' sense. Yet arche-writing often appears to lose touch with narrow writing entirely. This is nowhere more palpable then in the connection of arche-writing to what Derrida calls spacing.

In addition to being the possibility of 'the *graphie*, a possible unit of graphic expression' (OG, 65), arche-writing, we read, is also the articulation of time and space, which Derrida calls spacing. Spacing, in turn, is also the 'articulation of the living on the non-living' – which seems to be a different, but related sort of articulation (OG, 65). Why should we use 'writing' to speak generically about time and space and the relation of life to its others? What justifies these dramatic leaps away from the narrow linguistic context?

Of course, it is true, as Derrida writes in *Of Grammatology*'s opening pages, that the inflation of writing has been, for some time now, well underway. But the work of the grammatologist is not to 'give in to this movement' but to justify it. The point is not to assume that writing is pertinent beyond its narrow linguistic domain, but to demonstrate its pertinence, to keep the lines of communication between narrow and general writing open and clear.

The puzzle for *Of Grammatology*'s readers, however, is not just the question of what terms such as arche-writing *mean* but how Derrida gets the words to mean what they mean. As J. Hillis Miller notes in a close reading of several key pages in the chapter of *Of Grammatology* under consideration, 'trace', like 'writing', is a perfectly ordinary English word, with a more or less determinable meaning. But it comes to mean something else, something seemingly extraordinary in Derrida's hands. 'Just what does Derrida make the word "trace" mean?', Miller asks:

> Why does he twist just this word? Here my difficulties begin. I do not think what Derrida means by the word is at all self-evident or clear, in spite of the fact that everyone knows it is a key Derridean word. The word 'trace' can be traced all through Chapter 2, like a red thread in a tapestry. Read Chapter 2 again for yourself, dear reader. I'll bet you will still find what Derrida means by 'trace' obscure, occulted. Derrida says as much . . . I have read and re-read these passages many times. I still find them enigmatic.[5]

Now Miller, I should underscore, is not just one reader of Derrida among others; he is one of Derrida's best readers. Perhaps because he does not doubt his reading abilities, and nobody else does either, Miller can afford to say what often goes unsaid among Derrida's readers. We, the readers of *Of Grammatology*, are often unsure what these words mean.[6]

What Miller says of 'trace' can be said of 'writing'. Again, the terms are cognates, in the way that sign and speech are cognates in Saussure's texts. Writing, of course, is a term familiar enough – and certainly indispensable to grammatology, a science of writing. But arche-writing is no longer familiar; Derrida admits that the term cannot be found in the mundane text of any science, or even in the text of metaphysics. Indeed, 'no metaphysics can describe it' (OG, 244). None of this should be taken to mean that these terms have no meaning. The point it to remark that these terms remain enigmatic, despite over fifty years of critical readership.

Miller formulates a critical interpretive question: 'what does Derrida *make* [these words] mean?' To which I would like to add: *how* does Derrida make these words mean what they mean? How are they wrought – weaned from their 'narrow', 'familiar' designations and 'generalised'? I will begin by considering a complex passage in which arche-writing appears, in order to take the measure of the interpretive task I have set. The one with which I begin offers, apparently, a definition of arche-writing:

> Arche-writing, at first the possibility of the spoken word, then of the *'graphie'* in the narrow sense . . . this trace is the opening of the first exteriority in general, the enigmatic relationship of the living to its other and of an inside to an outside: spacing. The outside, 'spatial' and 'objective' exteriority which we believe we know as the most familiar thing in the world . . . would not appear without the gramme, without différance as temporalization, without the nonpresence of the other inscribed within the sense of the present. (OG, 71)

We note at the outset that to understand arche-writing we will have to understand it in terms of a network of other, more or less unfamiliar terms, including gramme, *graphie*, spacing and temporalisation. What, then, according to this definition, is arche-writing? Arche-writing names a common 'possibility'; first of speech, then of writing in the narrow sense of the *graphie* – a possible unit of graphic expression – and also perhaps of language in general. But, moving on, arche-writing is equally the possibility of appearance and of general relationality ('of an inside to an inside'). Arche-writing is 'spacing', which Derrida defines a bit further on in the text as 'the becoming-space of time and the becoming-time of space'. But what is the logic that binds all these disparate relations?

Arguably, what is most surprising in this passage (which is merely exemplary) is the claim that time and space, language and writing refer to a common possibility, namely arche-writing. The latter seems to function as the name of a hitherto undiscovered principle, gathering together seemingly disparate phenomena not previously held together by a single logic.[7] Because we are missing a sense for what logic 'hold[s] together . . . the disparate', this definition of arche-writing delivers something like the shock to thought that Michel Foucault described experiencing while reading the taxonomic entry for 'animal' in Borges's fictional 'Chinese encyclopedia', the *Celestial Emporium of Benevolent Knowledge*.[8] Echoing Foucault, we might ask of *Of Grammatology*'s entry for arche-writing: How is it possible to think these things together?

Derrida presents these disparate attributes of arche-writing as if summing up what has been previously established. Yet, as with the logical connections between all that arche-writing is said to make possible, the connection between arche-writing's debut in *Of Grammatology* and the discussion preceding it is unclear and the reader may be unprepared for it.

The proximate context to the quote above is a discussion of French linguist Roman Jakobson and his description of the structure of speech. According to Jakobson, speech cannot be understood – as it usually is – in terms of a *continuous* (temporal) stream; speech is made up of 'bundled', 'distinctive features' – it has a 'manifestly granular structure and is subject to quantile analysis' (OG, 69–70). These distinctive phonological elements or bundles are no more spatial and simultaneous than temporal and successive. If this is right, Derrida argues, then phonologists should renounce any sharp distinction between the spoken and written word; succession and simultaneity, temporality and spatiality characterise both speech and writing.

Jakobson claims to be describing speech, but he may just as well have been describing writing. Having apparently established just this much, namely, that speech and writing are structurally indistinguishable but that phonologists are reluctant nonetheless to relinquish a distinction that their own analysis undermines, Derrida concludes – somehow – that 'signification is *a priori written* . . . in a "spatial" element that is called "exterior"' (OG, 70). He then reserves the term 'arche-writing' for the 'opening of the first exteriority in general'. If speech and writing share a common structure, why call both of them 'writing' and why designate exteriority and its opening as 'writing' (rather than 'speech')? What or where is the 'first exteriority' and why should the 'first exteriority' be bound up with questions or problems of signification?

It is true that if we think of writing as a concrete possibility for a subject, the possibility of writing down and hence exteriorising and materialising particular intentions or thoughts, it might make a kind of *analogical* sense to denote the relation in which any inside is expressed in any outside with the name 'writing'. On this interpretation, arche-writing would name the generic possibility of this particular kind of exteriorisation or expression. But one should also note that speech apparently performs the same sort of expressive function, exteriorising thought. What, then, do we gain from the 'grammatological' substitution that Derrida proposes?

Perhaps the substitution of 'writing' for 'speech' is strategic or rhetorical. It decentres the latter and thereby loosens the *doxa* that leads us, wrongly, to think of writing as always exterior and derivative to speech. Indifferent between speech and writing, archewriting would name the 'opening of the first exteriority in general'. Countering uncritical habits is certainly all to the good. But 'first exteriority in general' seems a poor translation for 'expression'. Matters are further complicated by the fact that both Saussure and Derrida explicitly reject the view that language can be thought in expressive terms. Language does not *express* ideas, thoughts or meanings – it is *constitutive* of these.

Indeed, Derrida emphasises that even as Saussure insists – against the tradition he inherits – that expression is the wrong model for linguistic function, he accepts, without expending any critical energy, that it is the right model to understand writing (OG, 11). For Saussure, signifier and signified, word and thought, are indissociable. The linguistic bond is constitutive of what it relates. From this perspective, two things seem to be at stake in Derrida's substitution of writing for Saussure's speech: 1) correcting Saussure's uncritical exclusion of writing from language, and 2) thinking the relationship of linguistic 'inside' and 'outside' differently, otherwise than as expression.

Saussure's critique of expressivism (as a theory of linguistic function) is primarily motivated by his unorthodox view of the linguistic sign's structure. He believed that the two aspects of the sign, the signifying and signified elements, are not mutually exterior and independent. If form follows function, then the function (of the linguistic sign) cannot be the expression of a signified element that is already constituted elsewhere. The function of the sign must rather be, Saussure speculated, the individuation and articulation of the signified element. That the two faces of the sign are indissociable means that thought's exteriority to language is an illusion. 'In language, one can isolate neither sound from thought, nor thought from sound; one arrives at neither except by abstraction.'[9]

Yet as Derrida points out, despite Saussure's best efforts to explain the structural entanglement of signifier and signified, or what Saussure calls thought-sound (*pensée-son*), via a novel account of the sign-form, Saussure's account ends up reasserting the priority and independence of the signified element. In other words, his theoretical efforts fall short of their aim: theorising the constitutive entanglement of signifier and signified. This failure, Derrida suggests, is related to Saussure's failure to adequately interrogate the relation between speech and writing. The entanglement of signifier and signified, essential to the linguistic sign, may also characterise the relations of speech and writing. In any case, Derrida introduces arche-writing as the name for this other relation: the entangled, indissociable relation of thought to language, and of speech to writing.

If arche-writing registers the need for a novel schema of entanglement capable of specifying the relations between speech and writing, between signifier and signified, and between language and thought, Derrida's definition of arche-writing still reads as too inflationary, over-generalising and hyperbolic. Rather than speak specifically about the relation of thought to language – the problem of the 'articulation' of thought-sound in Saussure – Derrida describes arche-writing as 'the enigmatic relation of the living to its outside', and then generalises this relation to describe the relation 'of an[y] inside to an[y] outside: spacing'.

What justifies this apparent leap from the linguistic context, and the limited problem of whether or not writing is expressive or constitutive with respect to what it signifies, to the general problem of the relation of life to its 'outside'? The latter sounds like a problem facing a systems theorist attempting to think the relation of the organism to its environment, which seems different from Saussure's problem. It may be fascinating to speculate about the extent to which the problems are the same. More interesting still is to consider how these disparate problems may be subsumed under the heading of grammatology, but again the logic guiding Derrida's analysis is far from explicit. Does arche-writing say that *all* things are entangled (with their outside) in the way that thought is entangled with language and speech is entangled with writing? But why should we think that?

These questions are not meant to impugn Derrida's reading of Saussure, nor to imply that these are so many unanswerable questions. Rather, these questions underscore that the fame of Derrida's reading of Saussure has not resulted in the sort of insight into the key concept of Derrida's early work, arche-writing, that we might have expected. If the meaning of arche-writing were well known or well attested, the sort of reconstructive reading I propose here would be by now redundant. It would be possible to answer the question of what the project of grammatology consists of, and to understand its pertinence or obsolescence for today. However, I am aware of no reading that satisfactorily makes explicit the logic that leads from the seemingly limited problem of writing's linguistic inclusion or exclusion to an enlarged notion of 'writing' that encompasses seemingly fundamental ontological relations.

The central interpretive problem, I think, can be stated in the following way: what connects arche-writing both to language *and* to what Derrida calls spacing? The meaning of the grammatological project, and in particular its claims about the absolute generality of writing, hinge upon the answer to this question.

I am, of course, not the first person to pose some version of this question. Indeed, it has taken on some urgency recently with the materialist and realist turns in continental philosophy. In *Telling Flesh* (1997) Vicki Kirby offers a reading of Saussure's account of the sign as evincing the indissociably entangled relations between language and world. But here, Kirby's reading departs from Derrida's reading in *Of Grammatology* by attempting *another* reading of Saussure and his successors, one that will make clear, in the way that Derrida apparently does not, how we can move from an account of the Saussurean sign to an account of language's entanglement with its 'others', and, finally, to the generality of entanglement. The supplement to grammatology that Kirby's innovative reading offers, however, seems to attest to the incompleteness of the original, as if Derrida's claim about the generality of writing was a speculative promissory note rather than the conclusion of a philosophical argument.

Kirby's reading has influenced Karen Barad, among others, who generates, via a reading of Niels Bohr and contemporary experiments in quantum physics, an account of generalised entanglement or 'space-time mattering' – without, for that matter, connecting this 'space-time mattering' with the 'vulgar' concept of writing. Both Barad's and Kirby's accounts of generalised entanglement are arguably in the spirit of grammatology, while giving up on the letter of the text. It seems that arche-writing falls short, as Saussure's account of the linguistic sign did before, of thinking both entanglement and its generality, which would support Catherine Malabou's influential argument about the limits of grammatology.

Malabou has argued that supplementary readings such as Kirby's cannot vindicate Derrida's claims about general writing.

The latter was 'programmed to fail'.[10] The warrant for Derrida's generality claims is missing because this generalisation is impossible – on account of the limitations of the graphic model of writing with which Derrida begins. His starting point in empirical writing blocks the route to writing's generalisation projected in *Of Grammatology*.[11] Kirby, in a recent response, argues that Malabou's account of Derrida's failure to generalise writing is based on the (false) assumption that Derrida's 'graphematic structure' was intended to answer the demands of representational accuracy.[12] That is, on Kirby's reading, we should not expect arche-writing to look like (empirical) writing. It is rather that the 'riddles of writing' (not least of all the relation between repeatable form and material substrate) – as with the 'riddles' of the two 'faces' of Saussure's linguistic sign – are *generalised*, and hence gesture towards the thought of generalised entanglement. While I agree with Kirby's contention that arche-writing does not 'represent' graphic writing, this does not release us from the obligation to account for the difference between narrow and general writing. Without such an account, Derrida's claims about the generality of writing appear as ungrounded speculative gestures in the guise of rigorous philosophical claims. Despite his philosophical claims about the impossibility of strict literality, Derrida everywhere expends remarkable efforts to take a text at its word. It is therefore the letter – rather than the spirit – of *Of Grammatology* to which we must attend, and this is a text that insists on demonstrating the *necessary* generality of writing.

Martin Hägglund, in *Radical Atheism* (2008), has perhaps gone the furthest in defending Derrida's generality claim. He argues that the generality claim gets its necessity from the *form* of arche-writing. Hägglund's reconstruction of Derrida's argument moves from a stipulated generalised 'finitude' to the form that generalised finitude logically imposes: the material trace. For anything to be, it must persist, and persistence entails material supports. The trace is necessarily materially inscribed; it is what Malabou would call graphic. The trace does not persist forever, however: this is because the 'arche-materiality' of the trace entails its future erasure.

Whether or not Hägglund's argument succeeds in justifying the generality of the trace, it is anything but a generalisation of writing. His argument moves from the stipulated generality of finitude to the arche-materiality of the trace – exemplified by the image of inscription. That is, it reverses the trajectory of Derrida's own argument, which moves from narrow writing to arche-writing.[13] However, even if Hägglund accurately reconstructs Derrida's argument for the generality of writing, this argument seems to entail precisely the limits on writing's generality that Malabou diagnoses.

As soon as we think the trace in terms of graphic inscription, it cannot be generalised or enlarged, and it cannot support a speculative argument about the ultra-transcendental necessity of finitude. This is because matter will always be the condition of the trace, and as condition, it will be logically exterior to it – as the appeal to a material substrate suggests. We will return to Malabou's diagnosis of arche-writing's 'graphism' in the following chapter. For the moment, I take it that this sort of debate, between some of the most interesting and innovative materialist readers of Derrida, would not be possible if the meaning of arche-writing and its relation to narrow writing were clear and explicit.

In the next sections, I will challenge Malabou's claim that no account of writing's generalisation exists because no passage from narrow to general writing (or arche-writing) is possible. Or rather, I will to take her claim as a challenge to hazard this passage. Malabou's argument assumes that arche-writing, the most general concept of the gramme, does not transform our common-sense understanding of writing as *graphie*, a 'possible unit of graphic inscription', in a way that would make it generalisable. Her argument, I believe, is persuasive in the absence of an alternative, non-graphic account of arche-writing. The aim of this chapter, then, is to offer just such an alternative account, one that distinguishes between arche-writing (as generalised writing) and the *graphie* (OG, 46).

How does arche-writing compel us to revise what Derrida calls a 'popular' – or, as Malabou suggests, 'graphic' – conception of writing? The fact that Derrida sides with Saussure in insisting that the popular conception of writing does not offer the right model for the linguistic sign gives us at least one reason in favour of thinking that arche-writing may entail a substantial revision to this popular, graphic conception of writing (OG, 60).

## Language and Appearance: Saussure's 'Transcendental Semiotics'

For the grammatologist, Saussure's exclusion of writing from language is problematic. The reasons he gives are puzzling. On the one hand, Saussure seems to open up the possibility of grammatology by insisting, famously, that 'language is a form and not a substance'.[14] On the other, he (fore)closes this possibility by insisting that this form is indissociable from the phonetic substance of the signifier. The essentially phonic nature of the sign, in turn, is related to its entanglement with the signified element, which has a psychic provenance.

Saussure's structural analysis would seem to obviate any reference to experience, or its conditions of possibility. The Saussurean sign, according to Thomas Pavel, is that of an open system of differential marks.

> Saussurean signs ... constitute an open network where each position is defined and valued only by its non-identity with the surrounding positions ... The linguists have identified differential (contrastive) networks precisely there where language, disposing of limited means, must arrive at a maximal rendering.[15]

This description of the Saussurean sign is, however, almost certainly wrong – at least as a reading of Saussure.[16] Pavel conflates Saussure's definition of writing (or a system of writing) with his definition of a linguistic sign, unwittingly erasing the difference between linguistics and grammatology, between speech and writing, which Saussure insisted upon.

Wherein lies the difference? For Saussure, a system of writing is *solely* defined in terms of its contrastive value. The terms of such a system are purely arbitrary and purely quantitative. This is not the case with linguistic signs, which are dual-sided, composed of both signifier and signified. Saussure likens the dual-sided linguistic sign to two sides of a sheet of paper. This means that linguistic signs cannot be defined in terms of linguistic value, grounded only in relations of difference; signs are rather the *condition* for linguistic value. The contrastive relations between signs produce linguistic value. Insofar as the function of language has to do with contrastive elements, it behaves like a system of writing. But such contrastive relations presuppose the existence of signs.

Saussure offers an image that he hopes will help us understand the distinction he is drawing between the relations that constitute linguistic value and those that *originally* constitute the linguistic sign. If language were like a sheet of paper (with its two sides), dividing this paper into strips would produce linguistic value through the contrastive relations between the strips. However, this possibility is dependent on the more originary relationship that constitutes the indissociable linguistic sign.

> Language is a system of interdependent terms in which the *value* of each term results *solely* from the simultaneous presence of the others ... Putting it another way – and again taking up the example of the sheet of paper that is cut in four, *it is clear that the observable relation between the different pieces A, B, C, D, is distinct from the relation between the front and back of the same piece as in A/A'*.[17]

What can this account of language tell us about writing and the relation between language and writing? For Saussure, systems of writing are like language (or perhaps language is like writing) insofar as the 'value of each term results solely from the simultaneous presence of the others'. But writing differs from language insofar as its terms (unlike language) may be analysed solely in terms of linguistic value. This is what makes systems of writing relatively simple and characteristically substitutable, one for the other. Language is different; we cannot understand linguistic form solely by considering linguistic value. This would be to mistake, as Pavel does, language for writing, and it misses the fact that the linguistic sign is constitutively dual-sided. It will turn out, according to Saussure, that we cannot account for the form of the linguistic sign without including the perspective or point of view of the speaker.

In his classic text, 'Saussure and the Apparition of Language' (1976), Samuel Weber connects Saussure's account of linguistic form to temporalisation and spatialisation. On Weber's reading, the latter rejects inherited views that define language as 'a representation or expression of thought by sound', thinking of language instead as an *intermedium*. Language moves between the two spheres of sound and thought, delimiting each sphere through decomposition – before reorganising these intervals, primarily through relations of opposition.[18]

Linguistic intermediation articulates thought by also articulating sound and then binding the two. Weber specifies, in a valuable footnote, that:

> Among the meanings of *intermedium*, the O.E.D. lists: '1. Something intermediate in position: an interval of *space*. 2. Something intermediate in *time;* an interlude; an interval of time' . . . The first two meanings are considered to be obsolete. *The confusion of the spatial and the temporal interval*, combined with the fact that these meanings are historically obsolescent renders the word an appropriate sign for the ambiguous position [in Saussure] of 'la langue'.[19]

Here, Weber makes explicit how the 'confusion' of the spatial and the temporal interval, or what Derrida calls 'spacing', emerges as central to Saussure's account of language. That is, it is Saussure (and not Derrida) who demands that we think *la langue* in terms of intermediation, temporalisation and spatialisation or spacing.

For Saussure, the *effects* of linguistic intermediation are spatial intervals (in thought) and temporal intervals (in sound).

> [A]gainst the floating realm of thought, would sounds by themselves yield pre-delimited entities? No more so than ideas [thoughts]. Phonic substance is neither more fixed nor more rigid than thought; *it is not a mold into which thought must of necessity fit, but a plastic substance divided in turn into distinct parts to furnish the signifiers needed by thought.* The linguistic fact can therefore be pictured in its totality – i.e. language – as a series of contiguous subdivisions marked off on both the indefinite plane of jumbled ideas and the equally vague plane of sound.[20]

The intermediation of language does not just produce intervals of sound (time) and intervals of thought (space). It produces these intervals, Weber emphasises, as entangled – or, as 'the confusion of the spatial and the temporal interval'.

The dual-sided linguistic sign is the reciprocal articulation of sound and thought. These entangled intervals are then rearticulated through relations of opposition. Though it is often said that Saussurean signs are constituted through relations of opposition, Patrice Maniglier argues that this interpretation mistakes what Saussure calls the 'post-elaboration' of the sign for the genesis of the sign. Saussure's account makes clear that 'the game of opposition is played between terms *already given* . . . rather than supposing that [this game] *constitutes* signs ... it *redetermines* them'.[21]

The game of 'redetermination', which produces contrastive terms or values, is not limited to speech. Indeed, Saussure defines writing as a system of *purely* contrastive terms. This means, according to Maniglier, that most of the features that we associate with Saussure's account of linguistic signs – differential elements, terms constituted through oppositional relations – are actually attributes of what he calls 'writing'. What makes Maniglier's and Weber's readings of Saussure different from more familiar accounts, such as Pavel's, is that both recognise Saussure's rigorous distinction between the constitution of the sign and its redetermination in the game of linguistic value.

Language, for Saussure, cannot be defined by its expressive or communicative function with respect to thought because it is constitutive of that which is expressed or communicated. Indeed, Saussure argues that what individuates a thought is constitutive of the thought as such.

> Psychologically our thought – apart from its 'expression' in words – is only an amorphous and indistinct mass. Philosophers and linguists have always agreed in recognizing that without the help of signs we would be unable to distinguish ideas in a clear and consistent fashion.[22]

Interestingly, Weber remarks, Saussure appeals to tradition at the precise moment he breaks with it:

> If it is doubtless true, as [Saussure] asserts, that 'philosophers and linguists' have almost always concurred in attributing to language an indispensable function 'in distinguishing two ideas in a clear and constant fashion,' [philosophers] have still distinguished between the *process by which ideas are distinguished* from one another, involving language, and the *process by which they are constituted* in themselves, which has been construed as transcending language, de jure if not de facto.[23]

In other words, 'the tradition' may grant that, without the right sort of identity conditions – one of which is language – we could not distinguish thoughts clearly and distinctly. However, Weber points out, 'the tradition' is not likely to agree that the conditions for distinguishing thoughts are the same as those constituting thoughts. If there are thoughts to be distinguished, the assumption is that there are differences according to which they may be distinguished. Despite what Saussure claims, the idea that articulation, differentiation and constitution are the same seems to be uniquely Saussure's.

For Saussure, intermediation 'decomposes' or articulates thought and sound into intervals. '[W]ithout language, thought is a vague uncharted nebula. There are no pre-existing ideas, and nothing is distinct before the appearance of language.'[24] Indeed, for Saussure, language – coeval with its 'apparition' – is the condition of possibility for thought's appearance. Language describes the reciprocal demarcation of units. Thought, for Saussure, is not yet the elaborated, signified element that will emerge through what Maniglier describes as 'the game of opposition'. Prior to its individuation, thought can only refer to something like inchoate sense variations, albeit variations not yet spaced or intermediated by language. We must imagine, it seems, something like a language without syntax. If we grant Saussure this much, however, it is still unclear why sound – as opposed to another sense modality or signifying 'substance' – should do the work of individuation? Is sound exemplary, for Saussure, of the signifying substance in general, or does it have a *necessary* constitutive role? By all indications, it is the latter. 'The original, indissociable bond is between thought and sound [*pensée-son*].'[25]

Weber notes that a philosophical tradition, which extends back to Aristotle, takes natural languages to be grounded in shared (non-linguistic) ideas. This tradition does not give language a radically constitutive role vis-à-vis thought. Indeed, it assumes, as Weber writes, that the processes constituting thought are *de jure* language-transcendent. However, as we will now see, even if this view is dominant in the Western philosophical and linguistic tradition, there are other, 'minority' traditions that make Saussure's position appear far less radical. That is, Saussure's position may not be as novel as Weber's reading suggests – something that Derrida also seemed to recognise. Recalling this other philosophical tradition will help explain why Saussure assigns sound the role that he does.

\* \* \*

Thinking of language in radically constitutive terms was not foreign to Saussure's philosophical milieu. Indeed, a lively post-Kantian lineage assigned to the form of the linguistic sign the same transcendental role that Saussure assigns it. This milieu was apparently familiar to Derrida as well, who reminds us of it in the course of his reading of Saussure, via a quote from Main de Biran: 'the word is intention "sensibilized"' (OG, 73).[26] For this tradition, sensibilisation, and not expression, is the original function of language.

For Herder, von Humboldt and other figures within post-Kantian German philosophy, language had a distinctive transcendental function. As Michael Forster writes, this tradition shared the view that '[1] one cannot think unless one has a language and [2] one can only *think* what one can express linguistically'.[27] The second, 'expressibility' thesis is grounded on the first, 'constituting' thesis. Language, or linguistic form more precisely, makes thought possible in making it sensible. Language renders thought sensible by provisioning or shaping it with the right kind of form.

'Transcendental semiotics' is how Markus Messling and Kurt Mueller-Volmer (2003) refer to the view that language provisions thought with the form of sensibility. Humboldt's account of the relation between language and thought *On Thinking and Speaking* (*Ueber Denken und Sprechen*) (1795/6), they argue, develops a 'transcendental semiotics', which anticipates by over one hundred years the claims made in Saussure's *Course*. Humboldt took language to be central to what he called 'reflection'. 'Thinking consists in reflecting, that is, in the act by which the thinking subject differentiates itself from its thought.'[28] Language and linguistic form, in particular, are the transcendental conditions for this reflective activity.

Language, Humboldt writes, consists in:

> arresting the continuous flow of impressions in order to . . . comprehend this something as a separate 'unit' (*Einheit*), and set it as an object over against our thinking activity . . .
>
> [T]he mind can now proceed to compare several of these 'units', divide and combine them in different ways . . . In segmenting its own process, it thereby forms whole units out of certain portions of its activity, and in setting these formations separately in opposition to one another, collectively allows these units to stand in opposition to the thinking subject . . .
>
> No thinking, not even the purest, can occur without the aid from the general forms of our sensibility (*allgemeinen Formen unsrer Sinnlichkeit*) . . . [t]he sensory designations of those units, into which certain portions of our thinking are *united*, in order to be opposed

as parts to other parts of a greater whole as objects to the subject, is called in the broadest sense of the word: language (*Sprache*).[29]

The resonances of this Humboldtian account of language with Saussure's account of linguistic intermediation are unmistakable. In Humboldt's account, in reflection the mind creates 'objects' out of its own activity. Units (*Einheit*) are formed through segmentation, which are then opposed to one another, as parts 'of a greater whole'. This segmentation, however, requires the help of 'the general form of our sensibility'. Thought cannot become an object for itself, unless it first takes the form of sense, and the form of sense it takes is sound. As we saw above, Saussure writes that sound 'is plastic substance divided in turn into distinct parts to furnish the signifiers needed by thought'.[30]

I quoted Humboldt at length, above, because his account makes explicit (in a way that Saussure's does not) the philosophical rationale for the claims that language is radically constitutive of thought, and that speech, or sound, plays a necessary role in producing the units of thought.[31] Derrida's critique of Saussure's phonocentrism refers to the constitutive role that Saussure assigns sound. When Derrida writes of Saussure's phonocentrism, he is referring, not *generically* to Saussure's preference for speech over writing, but *specifically* to the role he assigns sound in his 'transcendental semiotics'. This has not been more apparent, perhaps, because the philosophical tradition in question deviates from the mainstream (Aristotelian) logocentrism, which takes Meaning and thought to be outside and prior to language.[32]

Comparing Saussure's phonocentrism to Hegel's, Derrida argues that this deviation in the philosophical tradition does not amount to much of a challenge to Aristotelian logocentrism; the element of the phoné or sound, which plays the 'sensibilising' role, remains distinct from empirical language, distinct even from the phonic signifier. In this respect, phoné designates not the empirical voice, nor the phonic signifier, and least of all 'the written signifier'. These are all necessarily non-ideal and 'derivative with regard to what would wed the [phoné] indissolubly to the mind or to the thought of the signified sense' (OG, 11). For the same reason 'the *written* signifier ... has no constitutive meaning' (OG, 11). The materiality of both sound and writing excludes either from playing the transcendental role that Saussure assigns to the phoné, which designates sound as a pure (temporal) form of sensibility.

Saussure's signifier, wed indissolubly to the signified or conceptual element, is not, in this sense, a mundane or empirical signifier.

I have suggested that there is something in Saussure's transcendental semiotics – or 'aesthetics' in the Kantian sense – that Derrida believes is indispensable to the grammatologist and to a generalised account of writing. Indeed, the dialectic of the second chapter of *Of Grammatology*, which redesignates 'speech' as 'arche-writing', entails rejecting not the transcendental role of language, but the view that sound uniquely and originally plays this sensibilising role. Substituting arche-writing for sound permits questioning the role that sound or speech plays.

Does Derrida's substitution of arche-writing break with Saussure's phonocentrism but affirm his transcendental semiotics, or does arche-writing imply a modification or break with Saussure's transcendental semiotics? Is arche-writing to be thought according to the conditions that make experience possible – that is, in correlationist terms – or does arche-writing break with Saussure's correlationist understanding of the sign as a form of sensibility? Or again, is Derrida's notion of spacing a modification or break with the notion of an *a priori* form of sensibility? My aim in the last sections of this chapter is to answer these questions.

### Genesis and Structure in Saussure's Semiology

Derrida is clear that Saussure's phonocentrism is problematic and cannot be sustained. The consequences of his critique of phonocentrism for the project of a transcendental semiotics are less clear. What *is* clear is that the philosophical meaning of arche-writing – the sort of transformation or modification of Saussure's phonocentrism that it entails – is legible only in the passage through this transcendental semiotics.

In a section of *The Course* appropriately entitled 'Language as Organized Thought Coupled with Sound', Saussure writes:

> The characteristic role of language with respect to thought is not to create a material phonic means for *expressing* ideas but to serve as a link between thought and sound, under conditions that *of necessity* bring about the reciprocal delimitations of its units.[33]

Here, Saussure refers to the *necessity* of the link between thought and sound. But what are these conditions that 'of necessity' bring about the 'reciprocal delimitation of units' – and why are these units *reciprocally* delimited, rather than just delimited?

The sign articulates and organises sense experience, in a way that is radically constitutive of sense. The articulation, Saussure writes, proceeds by 'decomposition'.

> The linguistic fact can therefore be pictured in its totality – i.e. language – as a series of contiguous subdivisions marked off on both the indefinite plane of jumbled ideas (A) and the equally vague plane of sounds (B). The following diagram gives an idea of it:

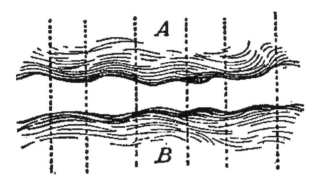

Figure 1.[34]

In Figure 1 – reproduced from the pages of the *Course* – it looks as though linguistic articulation consists in an 'arbitrary' correlation of plane A (undifferentiated, 'jumbled' thoughts) and plane B (undifferentiated, 'vague' sounds). The result of the articulation of these two heterogeneous planes, Saussure supposes, are intervals of thought-sound. If sound is distinct or separate from thought, it can only be because Saussure conceives of sound as something like 'pure' time and thought as a kind of jumbled simultaneity of unformed cross-modal sensations and impressions (which do not include sound). In order for there to be one element 'discriminated', there must be two.

Saussure is asking us to imagine something like the following: a temporal difference or interval of sound (it matters not what) is marked off or discriminated by a spatial interval, of whatever sort, but let us say a visual impression such as 'brightness'. The temporal interval is placed, located or 'spatialised' by its correlation with the spatial interval, and the spatial interval is differentiated and made determinate by its correlation with a temporal interval. Sound as temporal provides for succession, while space provides for duration. Sensibility is produced as the intermediation, 'confusion' or entanglement of space-time, or as the very form of the linguistic sign.

Saussure offers another image for the process of discrimination or decomposition that he has in mind:

> Visualize the air in contact with a sheet of water; if the atmospheric pressure changes, the surface of the water will be broken up into a series of divisions, waves; the waves resemble the union or coupling of thought with phonic substance.[35]

The first analogy presents language as the decomposition of heterogeneous fields of sense; in this second analogy, the sign-form is described as a kind of 'interference pattern'. Saussure struggles for the right analogy to describe a constitutive relation that works by differentiation, an articulation constitutive of differences. Both sound and thought are originally constituted *as such* by their differentiation – prior to their 'interference' there is 'not the least positive term'; the sign-form is produced as the original *différance* of each term.

In both images, the sign is a form that permits sound and thought to appear as such, where 'sound' and 'thought' refer to pure ('unmixed') forms of sensibility. What is perhaps clearer in the second, 'wave' image is that the relation Saussure describes implies the *exchange* of temporal and spatial forms. 'Sound' lends 'thought' its temporal structure and 'thought' lends 'sound' its spatial extension. This interference, according to Saussure, constitutes the form of a present intuition. Yet this account must affirm what it denies, and assume what it claims to account for.

Saussure argues that the differences in question are effects of articulation and, he insists, absolutely indissociable. However, to recur to Saussure's second image, if changes or differences in air pressure produce the 'waves' or differences at the surface of the water, then the 'air' is *already* differentiated. What appears as the spatially differentiated surface of the water are the *temporalised* differences in the 'atmospheric substance'. Of course, one might counter that Saussure only intends the wave as an analogy or illustration, and we should not expect it to perfectly comport with the sign structure that he seeks to elucidate. This is perfectly true. But the problem is that Saussure can provide neither a logical nor analogical account of the constitutive relation he is trying to describe. In each of his attempts, it will turn out that the structure he is trying to account for is not *originally* produced by the linguistic bond, but reproduced. To return to the wave analogy, the spatialising 'inscription' of sound cannot be *radically* constitutive; sound must be always already differentiated or spaced for the differences in sound to be inscribed-spatialised. The 'appearance' or 'sensibilisation' of sound is already its *reinscription*. The differences in sound appear as *traces* in a field of heterogeneous sense or differences; and this trace was always already a trace.

Differences in sound cannot be spatially inscribed if we do not assume them to begin with. Thought cannot be differentiated by its temporalisation, if it were not already internally differentiated. Sense is always already a trace structure, which entails that there is neither a pure temporality nor pure spatiality, but rather *spacing*, their 'originary synthesis' or entanglement.

Derrida writes:

> On the one hand, the phonic element, the term, the plenitude that is called sensible, would not appear as such without the difference or opposition which gives them form ... Here the appearing and functioning of difference presupposes an originary synthesis not preceded by any absolute simplicity. Such would be the originary trace. *Without a retention in the minimal unit of temporal experience, without a trace retaining the other as other in the same, no difference would do its work and no meaning would appear* ... The (pure) trace is *différance*. (OG, 62)

Here, in rewriting the sign as 'originary trace', Derrida 'corrects' Saussure's problematic analogical descriptions. If temporal differences appear 'originally' as spatial differences, while spatial differences appear 'originally' as temporalised, then we should say that spacing produces the *difference* between time and space as *différance*.

> The temporalization of sense is from the very beginning 'spacing'. As soon as we admit spacing at once as an 'interval' or difference and as openness to the outside, there is no absolute interiority. The 'outside' insinuates itself into the movement by means of which the inside of

non-space, which bears the name 'time', appears to itself, constitutes itself, and 'presents' itself. Space is 'in' time.[36]

While Derrida's reading has shown that the sign is an 'originary trace, a synthesis without original simplicity', Saussure interprets it as a *delayed* form of presence. Moreover, if sound can be spaced, or spatially inscribed, it is always already a trace. This is not due to the conditions of possibility of sound's appearance, but the conditions of possibility of the retention of differences that produce sound as a 'text' of differential elements. Sound implies differences, and there can be no differences without spacing.

But Derrida goes further than saying that language – linguistic form – entails the general entanglement of sense. He argues that the trace structure or arche-writing warrants us to say that language is a form or instance of the general entanglement of sense, which, itself, is a form of a still more general entanglement. What the linguistic sign shows is that there is no original entanglement, but an iterative, differantial structure: generalised writing. If the Saussurean sign is an 'originary' trace, then the movement of retention-inscription which accounts for appearance implies the retention of differences in heterogeneous differences, where the differences in question are already traces, already spaced.

Derrida's rewriting of Saussure's transcendental semiotics has the important consequence of establishing the ultra-transcendental status of arche-writing. Arche-writing is more general than consciousness and its forms. The activity of thought or reflection does not constitute differentiated objects, but reconstitutes, rewrites, or respaces. Texts are the condition of linguistic consciousness without being definable by that which they make possible. Consequently, the contrasts in speech or the constituent elements of texts do not depend upon a linguistic consciousness to recognise them. The contrastive structure of texts is rather the condition of linguistic consciousness. Arche-writing defines texts from the start, and if Saussure is right to say that the signified element informs the signifier such that the latter is indissociable from it, this entails that the signified element is not 'in' thought but 'in' the text – that 'thought' is always already a text.

If the materiality or textuality of the signifier implies its irreducibility to consciousness, the entanglement of the signifier and signified implies the materiality of the signified element as well. The deconstructive and grammatological significance of Saussure's phonocentrism can be found here. Despite calling sound the phonic substance, Saussure emphasises that the sound in question is 'ideal' and interiorised – the image or impression that sound makes on the senses. Sound allows for the dematerialisation of the signifier. The refusal of the materiality of the signifier is motivated by the refusal of the materiality of the signified. Yet spacing, as the indissociability of signifier and signified, requires us to affirm that the contrastive elements in speech as in writing are readable, whether or not they are read, whether or not they are enacted or accompanied by 'acts of speech' or 'acts of writing'.

This arche-writing, then, cannot designate the production of sense as interiority in and for a subject. Arche-writing breaks up the interiority of the transcendental subject by demonstrating that this interiority depends upon a non-correlational, textual structure. It is only on this condition that writing can both be generalised and continue to communicate with narrow, empirical writing.

Derrida is clear that spacing radically displaces the transcendental status of Saussure's account. The trace must be understood in terms of what I called, in the second chapter, an extra-correlational instance that cannot, in principle, be correlated with a subject or point of view. This is the meaning of the 'exteriority' or 'space' that always already interrupts subjective interiority.

> [I]t should be recognized that it is in the specific zone of this imprint and this trace, in the temporalization of a lived experience which is neither in the world nor in 'another world,' which is not more sonorous than luminous, not more in time than in space, that differences appear among the elements or rather produce them, make them emerge as such and constitute the texts, the chains, and the systems of traces. These chains and systems cannot be outlined except in the fabric of this trace or imprint. (OG, 65)

Arche-writing or spacing deconstructs the distinction between the real and the ideal. Recognising the necessity that sense must first be inscribed, Saussure ought to have defined the entanglement of sound and sense, signifier and signified, in terms of a generalised spacing. Indeed, linguistic forms are produced not as original inscriptions, but as reinscriptions. Language respaces – or rewrites – sense. Saussure's error was to think the sign both in terms of the transcendental *form* of sensibility and as the *object* of a possible experience. The trace is demonstrably neither. As arche-writing, it names the condition of possibility for the retention of differences. It is describable not in terms of the conditions of experience but in terms of the conditions of retention. Experience must be thought 'in return', according to the possibility of retention, or spacing.

'The pure phonic chain', Derrida writes, 'to the extent that it implies differences, is itself not a pure continuum or flow of time. Difference always already implies the articulation of space and time.'[37] These differences in the phonic chain necessarily reflect and are informed by heterogeneous differences. Each system of writing is ghost-written by another. Or, in the particular spacing of any system of writing, another system of writing is readable.

If phonetic writing can represent the temporal flow of speech, this is because the spaces in graphic writing are the 'becoming-space' of time, and time is itself spaced or the becoming-time of space. Because speech is already spaced, graphic writing can never be purely linear. In the graphic element, the phonic elements become space and the spatial (graphic) elements become time. The relationship or articulation between two chains of writing is itself spacing. This does not mean that time and space wait for phonetic writing; it is rather that the possibility of phonetic writing, of the becoming-space of speech, requires us to think the 'space-time of the trace', which is also 'a priori the space-time that we inhabit' (OG, 316).

Spacing, or the 'space-time of the trace', breaks decisively with Saussure's transcendental semiotics and with the problem of a transcendental aesthetics that would establish the 'unitary and universal ground' for subjectivity and subjective experience in the form of presence. Indeed, any 'new transcendental aesthetic must let itself be guided . . . by the possibility of inscriptions in general, not befalling an already constituted space as a contingent accident but producing the spatiality of space' (OG, 290).

## Encore: What is Arche-writing?

In this chapter, my aim has been to unfold the meaning of arche-writing and its philosophical significance, particularly in Derrida's rewriting of Saussure's 'transcendental semiology'. I began by arguing that the term is not well understood despite its absolute centrality to the grammatological project. Attending to Derrida's 'regulated transformation' of Saussure's Course – in particular, the substitution of 'writing' for Saussure's 'speech' or 'linguistic sign' – reveals the movement by which a narrow conception of writing is generalised. Arche-writing, I have argued, is not limited to questions of signification and meaning but finally to what Derrida calls spacing, or what Barad has called space-time-mattering and differentiation, which 'is no more real than ideal', no more 'material' than psychic, and which 'no concept of metaphysics can describe' (OG, 65).

Now, by way of conclusion, I want to return to the citation from *Of Grammatology* with which we began, and which (I argued) confronted the reader with a number of interpretive challenges: in particular, discerning the logic that links the question of narrow writing to spacing.

> *Arche-writing*, at first the possibility of the spoken word, then of the *'graphie'* in the narrow sense . . . this trace is the opening of the first exteriority in general, the enigmatic relationship of the living to its other and of an inside to an outside: spacing. The outside, 'spatial' and 'objective' exteriority which we believe we know as the most familiar thing in the world . . . would not appear without the gramme, without *différance* as temporalization, without the nonpresence of the other inscribed within the sense of the present. (OG, 71)

In the foregoing pages, I hope to have shown what justifies the transformation of a narrow conception of graphic writing to arche-writing, or spacing. In these last pages, I would like to demonstrate how arche-writing permits us to revise, to think 'in return', some of the familiar concepts that it radically displaces.

1) *Arche-writing as original translatability.* Experience implies structured elements, which appear to us neither as purely spatial, 'convenient' differences, nor as purely temporal sequences of differences. The structure of speech, as Roman Jakobson argued, is neither purely successive (time) nor, more obviously, purely synchronous. For this reason, sound cannot be represented in purely linear terms. Therefore, according to Jakobson, phonetic writing, a purely linear sequence of letters, cannot represent the elements of speech. The musical chord, which represents simultaneity, would better represent the elements of speech (OG, 53–5). Of course, for these same reasons, we might have expected Jakobson to puzzle over how phonetic writing could ever have come – so widely – to 'represent' the elements of speech. The same reasoning, that is, ought to have led him to question the pure linearity of writing.

Phonetic writing 'represents' speech through differential marks and spaces, punctuation, and other graphic markers. 'Represents' is in scare quotes because what is at stake in Derrida's analysis is demonstrating that the relation between speech and writing is not 'representational'. The differences in speech inform and structure phonetic writing. We could not account for the genesis, structure and evolution of systems of writing or other representational notation without accounting for the ways in which, historically and technically, these systems came to be in-formed or out-fitted by another system of marks. Arche-writing is the name for this mutual adaptation and usurpation.

Though phonocentric, Jakobson's descriptions of speech emphasise that the spacing characteristic of speech implies diverse representational possibilities. The spacing of the differential elements in speech will not appear in the same form in systems of writing adapted to signify speech; the differantial form in which these differences will appear in a heterogeneous text cannot be known *a priori*. One can 'represent' speech graphically through phonetic marks or musical notations, but also in another phonic medium – as the tonal drum-writing of the Kele attests (see Chapter 2) – and in other indeterminately varied ways. Arche-writing, or the differantial structure and spacing of differences, entails the 'original' translatability and substitutability of texts. Spaced elements appear each time different; the differences in speech (which came to be represented, for better or worse, through phonetic writing) are themselves not original to speech; speech is rather the translation of heterogeneous differantial patterns.

The sensory substitution device described in the previous chapter exemplifies this principle of sensory spacing and original translatability. With EyeMusic, the *differantial* structures 'spacing' vision 'appear' as spatialised and temporalised aural marks. EyeMusic succeeds if the reader can discern and 'translate' the aural structures in a way that reveals or discloses the visual elements. The EyeMusic interface also exemplifies what any skilled reader of musical notation knows: that musical structures cannot be mapped on to or represented in purely spatial or temporal 'planes'.

2) *Arche-writing as the (non-transcendental) condition of sense experience.* When Saussure broaches the question of the genesis of the sign, he is no longer describing speech or the linguistic sign

per se, but rather addressing the necessity of the entanglement of sound and thought. He speculates that the sign's entangled form – the constitutive indissociability of signifier and signified – should be understood in terms of the conditions for sensibility. As we saw, however, he identified the conditions of sensibility as transcendental conditions of experience, thereby defining the sign in correlational terms.

Derrida's grammatological reading argues that Saussure's transcendental account misinterprets the entanglement or spacing characteristic of the linguistic sign. Saussure was right to think that the form of the sign was related to the condition of experience, but wrong to interpret the sign as a form of sensibility. What a sufficiently rigorous phenomenology of experience will reveal is its 'textual' structure. Textual elements are not self-transparent or given apodictically. Something other than a phenomenological analysis, then, must be used to understand and explain these structures: a *grammatological* analysis.

One of the ways to capture the difference between a grammatological and phenomenological analysis of experience is to consider their respective descriptions of the phenomenology of (everyday) texts. The phenomenologist would enact the phenomenological reduction in order to focus on the mode and manner of the text's appearance or givenness. The phenomenologist is prone to 'aestheticise' the structure of texts, and hence will focus on 'present' forms ('calligraphy') rather than the structure of the text, which does not appear. This will lead the phenomenologist to take the letters and words to be like indicative signs, present givens that the reader has learned to associate with absent meanings.

The grammatologist, by contrast, will be attuned not to the text's manifest but its spaced structure. To get at the structure of the text we would have to recognise its constituents not indicatively but as differential elements; and to understand the relation of these differential elements to the apparently absent (signified elements), we have to understand the way the latter invisibly structure the text.

Spacing ... is always the unperceived, the nonpresent, and the nonconscious. *As such*, if one can still use that expression in a non-phenomenological way; for here we pass the very limits of phenomenology. Arche-writing as spacing cannot occur as such within the phenomenological experience of a *presence*. (OG, 68, emphasis in original)

The case of (everyday) texts is merely exemplary. The aestheticisation problem generalises to all phenomenological description. The phenomenologist will treat all experience aesthetically – as calligraphy rather than text – in terms of the form of appearance; by contrast, the grammatologist is attuned to what does not appear in the form of appearance.

Sense experience sensibilises heterogeneous differences. These differences 'appear' in the texture or the fabric of sense, experienced as a unified sense modality. The constitutively heterogeneous structure of the linguistic sign is continuous with the constitutively heterogeneous structure of sensory perception. What perception gives it does not give *as such*; what is given is not given as itself, but in the guise of the other.

Though decisively breaking with phenomenology and transcendental discourse, arche-writing must still be understood as an *ultra*-phenomenological, *ultra*-transcendental structure. If not, grammatological terms will inherit the problems of naive objectivism and perceptual realism which critical philosophy dispels. The speculative structures that grammatology describes pertain as much to 'objective' written texts as they do to texts as they are heard or read, to experience in the most general sense. However, insofar as these structures pertain, generally, to the structure of experience, grammatology transforms the philosophical meaning of experience, at least the meaning it has had since Descartes. Experience is not inherently first-personal, suffused with subjective presence. Elements of experience are, as David Roden puts it, phenomenologically 'dark'.[38] Their phenomenological description, in other words, will not give us any insight into their underlying or fundamental meaning. Insofar as the meaning of 'our' experience can escape us, experience is, as Derrida puts it, 'no more ideal than real' (OG, 65).

We can better grasp the meaning and implications of what Roden refers to as phenomenologically 'dark' elements if we consider phenomenological descriptions of apparently non-textual, perceptual experience involving indication. Phenomenologically speaking, indication contrasts with whatever is directly given. Indicative elements in perception necessarily involve past experience, depending upon the associational correlation of a present element with a past presence. Classically, seeing smoke as a sign for fire is exemplary of indication. Indication would be used to explain, for example, how it is that we can hear a sound and say, 'You dropped a coin', or even more specifically, 'You dropped a two-euro coin.' How is *that* kind of perception possible?[39]

The phenomenologist might say that the experienced perceiver hears the sound *indicatively*, as a 'sign' representing what is not perceptually present. Just as we can *see* smoke as *indicating* fire, we can *hear* some clinking sound as *indicating* a coin, or some other small metal object, falling. Perceiving indicatively works by bringing to mind absent (possible) perceptions. This sort of perceptual possibility, however, does not alter in the least the sound as it is given in perception. For the phenomenologist, hearing indicatively involves additional associative acts, which bring intuitively absent content to mind on the basis of a present given. Particularly indispensable is the mnemonic and recognitive activity of the perceiver, which takes a given as a sign.

In what sense will the grammatological description differ from the phenomenological accounts of indication – and what does this tell us about the structure of givenness? On the grammatological description, the 'indicated' content is objectively present 'in' the sound of the coin falling; it is always already 'given', whether or not it is heard or recognised. This entails, paradoxically, that there is indefinitely more content/structure informing what we perceive than what we (actually) perceive. Reciprocally, what we do (successfully) perceive is made possible by structures that both condition and exceed our recognitive abilities.

Grammatologically speaking, perceptual indication refers, in the first instance, not to subjective, cognitive activity, but to objective (non-correlational), structural features of the sound heard. We could refer to such recognisable structures as 'signatures'. Here, recognisability does not imply that the signature depends upon or is indissociable from its recognition (as the correlational, phenomenological account assumes). On the contrary, (successful) recognition depends upon there being recognisable structures. Thus, what makes it possible to hear a sound and say 'I think you just dropped a two-euro coin' is that objective features structure the sound. The weight of the coin, its material composition, the hardness (or softness) of the floor have distinctive, isolable sound 'signatures'. Hearing – and perceiving more generally – is a matter of recognising the structural features or signatures *in-forming* sound as heterogeneous differences.

Again, while the formal structure in question is the condition
for hearing, it is not defined by any perceptual or cognitive acts.
Hearing is possible because we can abstract differences or signatures in sound that correspond to visual, haptic or propriocep-
tive signatures in heterogeneous sense modalities. Thus the sonic
signature of weight corresponds to certain visual and propriocep-
tive signatures, none of which are prior, original or more proper.
Instead of any original propriety of sense, we might speak instead
of an original translatability among sense modalities, a translatability in which forms of sensibility are rooted or take place.

3) *Arche-writing is the general form of memory*. Perception, grammatologically speaking, is the recognition and reactivation of what
is present only as a trace. Like all forms of memory, the trace is not
dependent upon being perceived or upon any present perception.
Arche-writing refers the possibility of present experience to the
general mnemonics of the trace, to the generalised retention and
circulation of differences in *modifiable* chains or texts.

'The trace, arche-phenomenon of "memory" ... must be
thought before the opposition of nature and culture, animality
and humanity etc.' (OG, 70). To which we must add that it must
be thought prior to the opposition between materiality and ideality. This is because the form of arche-writing cannot be confused
with graphic form, a mark on a material surface of inscription. It
entails thinking the entanglement of modifiable, differential elements; the preservation of texts in a heterogeneous set of marks.
Hence, arche-writing allows us to describe language and writing
as forms of cultural or human memory or archivisation, but it also
describes the general movement of archivisation, which precedes
any distinctions between forms of memory (genetic or phyloge-
netic, technical or natural, organic or inorganic). Grammatology
demands that each element of these oppositions – culture and
nature, matter and ideality – be thought 'in return', or in terms
of arche-writing. To think, for example, matter in terms of arche-
writing is to describe and investigate the essentially retentive and
modifiable – mnemonic – aspects of *form*.

Arche-writing is both 'the formation of form and the being
imprinted of the imprint' (OG, 63). The form of a written text is
not the structuration of a swarm of amorphous marks; it is the
in-forming of a modifiable structure of marks by a heterogeneous structure. In order for there to be form, there must already

be form. But this means that contrastive elements or marks must afford themselves to modification and restructuration. Arche-writing entails the essential modifiability and retentiveness of the trace. There is no form without modifiability and no modifiability without form. It is the task of a speculative grammatology to think the *a priori* relations of form and memory, retention and inscription, but also of modification and erasure.

## Notes

1. Derrida writes, 'By a substitution which would be anything but verbal, one may replace *semiology* by grammatology in the program of the *Course in General Linguistics*: "I shall call it [grammatology] . . . Since the science does not yet exist, no one can say what it would be; but it has a right to existence, a place staked out in advance. Linguistics is only a part of [that] general science . . . the laws discovered by [grammatology] will be applicable to linguistics"' (OG, 51).

2. Francisco Vitale's recent work on biodeconstruction and the recent publication of Derrida's *La Vie/La Mort* are absolutely central in this regard. While I will not deal here directly with Vitale's work – which was written prior to *La Vie/La Mort*'s publication – it is important to note that the account of arche-writing I present here would be most pertinent to biodeconstruction, or an account of the biological, whether the notion of the biological be that of a code or not.

3. Saussure (2011: 122).

4. 'An arche-writing whose necessity and new concept I wish to indicate and outline here; and which I continue to call writing only because it essentially communicates with the vulgar concept of writing. The latter could not have imposed itself historically except by the dissimulation of the arche-writing, by the desire for a speech displacing its other and its double and working to reduce its difference' (OG, 56).

5. Miller (2011: 47–51).

6. This lack of certainty came out in an interesting admonition by the influential Derrida scholar Geoffrey Bennington, in a *London Review of Books* essay entitled 'Embarrassing Ourselves' (Bennington 2016). Bennington laments that the new translation of *Of Grammatology*, far from dispelling certain interpretive problems arising from translational issues, makes things worse, leaving known errors from Gayatri Spivak's version in place while introducing new

ones. Moreover, Bennington argues that Judith Butler's introduction manages to confuse even the most basic terms. What is presumably embarrassing is that Derrideans ought to know what they are talking about when they are talking about terms such as trace and writing, and when they demonstrate that they do not they also seem to demonstrate what Derrida's detractors have always suspected: that Derrida's texts make no sense, have no determinate or determinable meaning; and that, where sense can be made of them, Derrida's arguments are trivial or easily defeated. I believe, however, that the interpretive problems with respect to grammatology are rooted in a fundamental lack of clarity on the meaning of arche-writing, and that this is due in no small part to difficulties in reading the second chapter, on Saussure. In my view, the main issue is that we, *Of Grammatology*'s contemporary readers, have inherited a very different Saussure than the one Derrida inherited as a student of philosophy in Paris in the 1950s and 1960s. This Saussure, however, is not Derrida's invention. Indeed, his reading is compatible with several recent, innovative readers, including aspects of Beata Stawarska's 'phenomenological Saussure' (Stawarska 2015).

7. We can recall, from the discussion in Chapter 2, that Derrida has already employed a similar strategy with the term iterability. He coins 'iterability', based on a speculative etymology ('iter, again, probably comes from *itara*, other in Sanskrit)', which would name the necessity that binds together repetition and alterity. The 'form' of the trace, in turn, demonstrates the pertinence of this speculative relation.

8. In the preface to *The Order of Things*, Foucault writes,

> This book first arose out of a passage in [Jorge Luis] Borges, out of the laughter that shattered, as I read the passage, all the familiar landmarks of my thought – *our* thought that bears the stamp of our age and our geography – breaking up all the ordered surfaces and all the planes with which we are accustomed to tame the wild profusion of existing things, and continuing long afterwards to disturb and threaten with collapse our age-old distinction between the Same and the Other. This passage quotes a 'certain Chinese encyclopedia' in which it is written that 'animals are divided into: (a) belonging to the Emperor, (b) embalmed, (c) tame, (d) suckling pigs, (e) sirens, (f) fabulous, (g) stray dogs, (h) included in the present classification, (i) frenzied, (j) innumerable, (k) drawn with a very fine camelhair brush, (l) *et cetera*, (m) having just broken the water pitcher, (n) that from a long way off look like flies'. In the wonderment of

this taxonomy, the thing we apprehend in one great leap, the thing that, by means of the fable, is demonstrated as the exotic charm of another system of thought, is the limitation of our own, the stark impossibility of thinking *that*. (Foucault 1970: xv)

9. '[D]ans la langue, on ne saurait isoler ni le son de la pensée, ni la pensée du son; on n'y arriverait que par une abstraction' (Saussure 1967: 158).
10. Malabou (2007a: 432).
11. Malabou (2007a).
12. Kirby (2016: 48).
13. Critics, including me, have argued that Hägglund's account of the generality of the trace departs in critical respects from Derrida's generalisation of the trace structure. See Goldgaber (2017); Johnston (2009); Staten (2009).
14. Saussure (2011: 122).
15. Pavel (1988: 108), as quoted in Maniglier (2007: n.p., my translation).
16. For an excellent account of this sort of typical confusion, which conflates Saussure's account of a system of writing with that of the linguistic sign, see Maniglier (2007) or his magisterial rereading of Saussure, *La Vie énigmatique des signes* (Maniglier 2006).
17. Saussure (2011: 114–15, my emphasis).
18. Maniglier (2007) offers a robust defence of the reading that I have just attributed to Weber. Maniglier argues, correctly in my view, that the inherited readings of Saussure have conflated relations of opposition and contrast from the sort of relations that account for the genesis of the linguistic sign.
19. Weber (1976: 924).
20. Saussure (2011: 112, emphasis added).
21. Maniglier (2007).
22. Saussure (2011: 111–12), as quoted in Weber (1976: 922).
23. Weber (1976: 922).
24. Saussure (2011: 112).
25. Saussure (2011: 111).
26. In *de la Grammatologie*, Derrida uses the expression 'vouloir sensibilisé' to refer to Main de Biran's 'intention'. Spivak translates this as 'wish sensibilized', but this translation is arguably less 'relevant', as Derrida would write, than 'intention', given that Derrida translated Husserlian intentionality as 'vouloir-dire', that is, as Meaning or 'wanting to say'.
27. Forster (2010: 56).

28. Mueller-Vollmer and Messling (2017: n.p.).
29. Mueller-Vollmer and Messling (2017: n.p., translation modified).
30. Saussure (2011: 112).
31. I should point out that while scholars of this period, including those just cited, are aware of the resonances between Humboldt and Saussure, there is considerably less awareness on the Saussurean side. I owe the first suggestion of this connection to Christina Lafont, in private conversation.
32. Interestingly, scholars of German philosophy of language are well aware of the extent to which Humboldt's account anticipates and overlaps with Saussure's. Derrideans and Saussureans, by contrast, seem unaware of the extent to which Saussure is continuous with the German Idealist tradition.
33. Saussure (2011: 111–12, my emphasis).
34. Saussure (2011: 112). Figure found at <http://www2.sims.berkeley.edu/courses/is296a-3/s06/Saussure.pdf> (last accessed 15 July 2018); this reproduces an earlier edition [1959] of the same translation.
35. Saussure (2011: 112).
36. Derrida (1973: 73).
37. Derrida (1978: 248).
38. Roden (2013).
39. It would be perfectly plausible to say that one did not *perceive* a two-euro coin falling, but instead that one *heard* a sound, and then *inferred* that it was a coin, and even a certain kind of coin – based on past perceptual experiences of similar events with similar objects. In this case, one might say that the perception is of a certain sound, and the propositional content the non-perceptual work of inferences (associations, memories) subsequent to hearing the sound. This view can easily explain why experienced hearers will have more success in identifying the sound by, say, comparing it to the memory of the last time they dropped a two-euro coin. The account I develop above defends a non-correlational account where the sound 'signature' is an essentially perceivable, structural feature of the sound.

# 5

# On the Generality of Writing and the Plasticity of the Trace

Différence is therefore the formation of form. But it is on the other hand the being-imprinted of the imprint.

Jacques Derrida, *Of Grammatology*

If I have not very often used the word 'matter', it is not, as you know, because of some idealist or spiritualist kind of reservation. It is that the logic of the phase of overturning this concept has been too often reinvested with 'logocentric' values, values associated with those of thing, reality, presence in general ... This is why I will not say that the concept of matter is in and of itself either metaphysical or non-metaphysical. This depends on the work which it yields.

Jacques Derrida, *Positions*

## The Generality of Writing

Saussure discovered the trace structure, but disavowed it, interpreting it, instead, in terms of the form of the 'minimal *unit* of temporal experience' (OG, 67). Elements, individuated spatially and temporally, appear only by first being retained; their appearance constitutively delayed. But as we saw in the previous chapter, Saussure's analyses should have led him to rather different conclusions.

The entanglement of signifier and signified attests, Derrida argues, to a relation of originary *différance*, and therefore to a form incompatible with present experience or its transcendental conditions. Though he insists that the sign *originally* individuates, Saussure should have concluded that the sign retains what is always already individuated, already a trace. Distinctive temporal and spatial elements appear by first being retained, but their retention depends upon their prior differentiation.

Saussure is trying to specify a relation that constitutes by differentiating, that produces by retaining. Such a relation, which has no name in contemporary metaphysics, is 'spacing'. Spacing names the exchanges of form that produce the spatialised and temporalised elements. These exchanges presuppose the modifiability of form.

Originary *différance* is logically incompatible with an account of a transcendental origin of sense. The trace cannot be explained in terms of the conditions of possibility for experience. If retention is radically constitutive and originary, then, *a priori*, there is no original and no origin. 'The origin is inscribed'; or, the 'origin' of experience implies 'reinscription', the differantial repetition of the trace. What we can isolate as experience presupposes the retention and differential repetition of what is, necessarily, 'older' than experience. Saussure's account, as Derrida reads it, demonstrates that 'the trace is in fact the absolute origin of sense in general' (OG, 69). But this amounts 'to saying, once again, that *there is no absolute origin of sense in general*. The trace is the *différance*, which opens appearance (*l'apparaitre*) and signification' (OG, 69, my emphasis).

The trace is the origin of sense and signification, but it is not a transcendental origin. The trace opens appearance and signification – it names 'the possibility common to all systems of signification' (OG, 69) – but the structure in question is 'absolute' in the sense that it cannot be correlated with an intentional consciousness or its activity. On the contrary, consciousness and its activities must be understood in terms of the (generalised) trace structure and in particular its retentive function.

If the trace structure cannot be identified with the transcendental conditions of experience, nor as an ideal structure, does this mean that it is empirically real? Not if saying so would define it in opposition to (transcendental) ideality. Some precautions must be taken if we are not to 'fall back to a pre-critical discourse' (OG, 61). In this context, Derrida suggests that the trace is 'both/and':

> [A]rticulating the living upon the non-living in general, origin of all repetition, origin of ideality, the trace is not more ideal than real, not more intelligible than sensible, not more a transparent signification than an opaque energy and no concept of metaphysics can describe it. (OG, 65)

We can say that the trace is real (but not in a way that is opposed to ideal) and empirical (but not in a sense that is opposed to transcendental). Indeed, if the trace articulates 'the living upon the non-living', it is a relation that produces the entanglement of materiality and ideality in the real. In this sense, we can say that the trace is ultra-transcendental; it does not fall short of the transcendental critique of naive objectivism and realism; having solicited this critique, the grammatological analysis points to the necessity of going beyond it.

There are at least two other senses in which the trace is ultra-transcendental. In addition to retaining the transcendental critique (of naive realism) even as it moves beyond it, the grammatological trace names what, in the introduction, I referred to as 'speculative structure'. Derrida defines such a structure in phenomenological terms – as one that shows or gives itself as excessive to the *form* of experience (or presence). The sign – or at least, Saussure's description of it – is excessive in this respect. Finally – and this is the sense most difficult to justify – the trace is ultra-transcendental in the sense that it accounts not just for experience, sense and signification, but is *absolutely* general.

*   *   *

*Of Grammatology*'s readers have often kept their distance from what I will refer to below as 'the generality claim' – deflating it or simply bracketing it. Most often, the generality of writing has been taken to signify that experience is structured *like* writing, which, in turn, will mean that the structure of 'writing' – and not phenomenological presence or givenness – will explain or account for experience. While it is understood that writing is meant to disrupt the transcendental account of experience in some way, these deflationary readings, nonetheless, respect the transcendental limits, and interpret grammatology in quasi-transcendental terms.

More recently, as I argued in the first chapter, influential readers have resisted these deflations, arguing that we ought to take the generality claim seriously and consider the ways in which the trace extends beyond experience to account for material processes, down to the quantum level (Barad 2010), the emergence of complex systems (Wolf 2010) and evolutionary processes (Hägglund 2016). Bernard Stiegler, critical of the generality claim, argues that grammatology ought to attend more closely to the specificity of 'phonologic' writing. The generality claim weakens the grammatological project.[1]

Though Derrida quite clearly intends to include, in the sweep of what the trace makes possible, everything from 'the short pro-grammatic chains of the annelids all the way up to the writing of a certain homo sapiens and beyond' (OG, 84), Stiegler argues that grammatology is only plausibly an account of technics, the epochal emergence of a tertiary form of inorganic memory, distinguished from genetics or epigenetics.[2] More recently, Martin Hägglund has attempted to give the ultra-transcendental generality of the trace a robust defence, but he does so by claiming that the form of the trace corresponds to the form of radical finitude, which imposes upon being the absolutely general need to persist and survive.[3] As I will attempt to make clear in what follows, however, the trace structure – the structure of *sur-vivance* – is not finite but indefinite, which is something quite different.[4] *Contra* Hägglund, it pertains, in the first instance, not to singular, finite beings, but rather to forms of memory. The generality claim refers to the generality of mnemonic form.

In *Of Grammatology*, there is no question that the expansion of the gramme from narrow, empirical writing to arche-writing generalises the form of the trace, moving from writing and speech to consciousness and sense, but also to insensate, 'unconscious' material processes of whatever sort. If the trace is 'no more ideal than real', it is also no more dead than alive, no more inorganic than organic.

The speculative generalisation of arche-writing entails that gram-matology is also a deconstructive or ultra-transcendental material-ism. This generalisation required rewriting our conceptions of the sign, just as it imposes the task of rewriting our conceptions of 'matter', which, Derrida emphasises, the metaphysics of presence has always designated as absolute exteriority vis-à-vis the 'inside' of conscious subjectivity.[5] If this task of rewriting materialism has not been taken up – at least until relatively recently – this is arguably because the structure of the trace, along with the passage from empirical to generalised writing, via Saussure's transcenden-tal semiotics, has remained obscure.

### The Trace as Mnemonic Form

Saussure assigned the linguistic sign an essentially retentive func-tion. The sign not only produces experience as a form of (origi-nal) memory, it is an essentially mnemonic form. Derrida often describes the form in question in terms of parasitism.[6] Differences

appear by first being retained ('inscribed' or 'spaced') in heterogeneous differences. Retention entails modification both of the
'hosting' and the 'parasitic' text. As I wrote in Chapter 3, Derrida
introduces 'iterability' to capture the sort of repetition implied by
the structure of the trace; a repetition that always repeats the other
in repeating the same.

Arche-writing, the principle of archivisation, makes recollec-
tion, remembrance and recovery possible. But this understates
the significance of the generality claim. The generality of the trace
entails that everything is or can be described as a form of memory.
If the movement of archivisation is absolutely general, then the
most mundane objects, operations, long described in terms of
and as forms of 'presence', must be susceptible to grammatological redescription. To give but one example, in grammatological
terms, 'reading' is not the restoration of a transcendental signified,
but the recovery of a nested, signifying text, something closer to a
reverse translation than the reduction of the signifier.

It is not just the question of form that must be rethought, but
also that of function. The parasitic structure of the trace makes
signification possible. But it is a mistake to explain the trace structure in terms of the possibility of signification. This sort of explanation would assume – wrongly – that the function of signification
is the (sole) impetus for what makes it possible.

Explaining the level of the constituting in terms of the constituted is, as Derrida puts it, a 'topological confusion', which
obscures the meaning of generalised writing.[7] Since the accepted,
technical sense of topology refers to a mathematical field that
studies deformability, the term Derrida seems to have in mind is
'topographical', which refers to surface morphologies. The trace,
as structural condition, 'does not belong, by definition, by virtue of
its situation, to the field of that which it makes possible'.[8] To get at
what Derrida means by this topographical confusion, I think it is
worth noting the parallels of Derrida's argument, here, to Stephen
Jay Gould's and Richard Lewontin's critique of adaptationalism,
of which it may be a more generalised form.

In 'The Spandrels of San Marco and the Panglossian Paradigm'
(1979), Gould, a palaeontologist, and Lewontin, a biologist, argue
that not all phenotypic features are explicable in terms of the adap-
tive fitness of these features. Adaptivist assumptions miss the fact
that some features – which Gould and Lewontin call 'spandrels'
– are actually unanticipated or opportunistic by-products of other

features, which themselves may or may not have been 'selected' for.[9] Generalising the point, for all spandrels, what makes them possible cannot be deduced from any of their functional features. Grammatologically speaking, signification is a spandrel in the sense that it names a function whose conditions of possibility (the trace structure) cannot be explained with reference to this function. The retentive, memorialising movement of the trace is more original than the functions it makes possible.

Derrida hesitates in using the language of form to describe the trace; he believes it too determined by the system of metaphysical oppositions that he seeks to escape. In the epigraph to this chapter, he expresses the same concern about matter. Whereas the metaphysics of presence installs an opposition between form and matter, form and matter are indissociably entangled in the case of mnemonic form. Demonstrating that an essentially mnemonic *form* is, equally, essentially mnemonic *matter* is relatively straightforward. A form that is essentially retentive retains (heterogeneous) form by modifying 'itself'. Form in-forms (retains) form in its modification. In traditional metaphysics, what is modified or informed by form goes by the name of matter. In the grammatological discourse, matter is already in-formed, no more material form than surface of inscription. By the same logic, the materiality of the trace – its material substrate of inscription – is a heterogeneous trace (form); both the in-forming form and the material substrate are 'textual'.

Beyond the form/matter opposition, the trace structure has still more deconstructive potential. To be legible at all, 'the trace, arche-phenomenon of "memory", must be thought before the oppositions of nature and culture, animality and humanity' (OG, 70); to which, I have just argued, we should also add materiality and ideality. The grammatological point is not that these ontological distinctions do not have their place – that we are powerless to draw distinctions, say, between cultural and natural phenomena – but that these distinctions are not absolute. The trace operates on both sides of these ontological divides and also implies their articulation. 'The possibility of the gramme structures the movement of its history according to rigorously original levels, types, and rhythms. But one cannot think [these levels] without the most general concept of the gramme' (OG, 84). The trace does not erase the topographical emergence of distinctive levels, organisations and 'rhythms' – call these culture or nature, animal and machine; the trace accounts for the evolutionary 'history' of these emergences.

The foregoing was intended to demonstrate that, by right, 'deconstructive materialism' is an expression of the deconstructive potential of the trace. Deconstructive materialism will make explicit the mnemonic dimensions of organic and inorganic material processes. Matter – in grammatological terms – is essentially retentive, and as such, essentially modifiable.

The trace structure has the virtue of making explicit the essential relation between modification and retention. To be sure, according to the standard metaphysical picture, retention analytically presupposes modification. However, modification does not presuppose retention, but rather its opposite. Insofar as something is modified, it 'loses' or 'forgets' the form that it was. Things look very different from the grammatological perspective. The trace structure retains by modifying itself, and therefore any modification implies retention. Because there can be no retention without modification, there is no memory without deformation, loss and 'forgetting'. However, the loss that modification-retention implies does not correspond to any conventional, 'presentist' notion of erasure or forgetting. For the latter, erasure implies the deletion or disappearance of something present or of something formally present. The trace, however, is never, was never, present. Thus, the erasure of the grammatological trace can only refer to its modification. Indeed, as we will see, grammatology as an account of the trace and the structure of sur-vival (more of which below) does not anticipate the conditions of the trace's radical disappearance or annihilation, since this would correspond, in effect, to the erasure of the past *as* past. In the conclusion, I will consider whether this incapacity to factor the trace's own radical disappearance points to the limits of grammatology's deconstructive materialism.

\* \* \*

Before turning to the question of the limits of grammatology as an account of materiality, I want first to give a better sense of the productivity of grammatological descriptions with respect to material form. I will present two distinctive, *non-graphic* instances of the material trace that offer some evidence in favour of the generality claim.

As I argued in the second chapter, Derrida's notion of the trace invites us to think about the nature of evidence and events differently. The trace is not the mark of something left behind, allowing us to infer the past *presence* of an event. Rather, the event (thought 'in return') is 'reduced' to the indefinite dissemination of its traces, to the indefinite modifications and retentions made in the 'fabric' of textual differences. In short, 'events' refer to distinctive modifications of forms, legible and, hence, in principle, recoverable for the future. Perhaps unsurprisingly, given that arche-writing entails originary repetition, the generality of the trace must precisely deny that the essence of an event is its singularity and untranslatability – its sense of being just once.

A recent article on advances in dendrochronology (the study of tree rings) in the *New York Times* will help illustrate how grammatological descriptions modify our understanding of evidence and event, form and materiality. Tree rings offer a compelling image of material form as trace. Noting the amount of information – temperature variation, frequency of fires, jet stream swings – recoverable from ring patterns, the article's author observes: 'trees, it seems, are giant organic recording devices [containing] information about past climate, civilisations, ecosystems and even galactic events, much of it many thousands of years old'.[10] Is the mnemonic capacity of trees exceptional? The author does not speculate about whether this mnemonic capacity is particular to trees or is a general capacity of (organic) matter. It is well known, for instance, that glaciers yield comparable information about the past, to say nothing of rocks, though one does not often hear talk of geo-chronology. In any case, the idea that matter is a 'recording device' is impeccably grammatological. Moreover, this mnemonic capacity of organic or living matter would, in principle, extend to inorganic matter.

Grammatological descriptions of material forms or systems are not incompatible with other sorts of descriptions, but they do have important consequences for descriptions of organic – and inorganic – form. If the author of the *New York Times* article characterised trees as 'recording' information, this image fails to elucidate that, in the case of the tree, 'recording' cannot be distinguished from morphogenesis, memory from morphology, and information from formation. Information about the past – galactic, climatic and civilisational events – is 'stored' or 'recorded' as form: for example, the width of the tree ring *is* the length of the growing season. Indeed, one of the speculative insights of grammatology is that form is always in-formed, that 'form' and 'information' share more than a fortuitous etymological connection.

The second, grammatological description of material form that I would like to consider presents another case of material objects as recording devices. However, unlike the previous instance, which exemplified the absolute solidarity of material form and trace, the material trace in question is not identical with the form of the object recording it. This 'independence' seems to underwrite the distinction between, on the one hand, the form of the trace and the form of the object, and, on the other, the relative impermanence of the trace as compared to the stability of material objects. If this were right, however, rather than confirming the generality of the trace, this case would confirm its decisive limits. The issue is clarified – and potentially resolved – I argue, by a more careful consideration of the 'topographies' of the trace.

Recent research by MIT scientists on the mnemonic properties of everyday objects offers an image of a material trace that is closer to graphic writing than the example of the tree rings. This research demonstrates that everyday physical objects record speech and sound, more generally. The surfaces of objects are visibly – at least machine-visibly – modified in ways that produce a legible, recoverable text. From the vibrating surface of a snack-sized bag of potato crisps, researchers recovered the audible sounds playing in the room.

> A pure-tone version of 'Mary Had a Little Lamb' is played at a chip bag and the motions corresponding to each note are magnified separately. Time slices of the resulting videos, *in which the vertical dimension is space and the horizontal dimension is time*, are used to produce a visual spectrogram, which closely matches the spectrogram of the recovered audio.[11]

When sound 'hits' an object, the object vibrates, and the motion of this vibration creates a visual signal usually invisible to the naked eye.

The researcher notes that 'people did not realize that this *information* was there'.[12] This ignorance, one may assume, is primarily due to the fact that these vibrations are normally imperceptible. But secondarily, it is because it is not obvious that the audible text is, in principle, recoverable from the vibration – that the visual displacements at the surface 'record' sound. Thus, people do not consider the sense in which objects 'hear' – and ambient objects (other than smartphones) may 'eavesdrop'. A grammatologist might say, with greater precision, that what we generally fail to recognise is not the mnemonic capacity of certain material objects, but the general mnemonic capacity of matter. Recognising this as an *essential* capacity demands, in turn, that we rethink what we mean by material objects.

Interestingly, these material traces are not only interesting to researchers because the recorded vibration provides a novel way to recover sound; 'they also gives us a lot of information about the object itself, because different objects and materials . . . respond to sound in different ways'.[13] In other words, from the distinctive spatialisation of sound in the form of visible vibrations at the surface of the crisps packet, researchers (or the algorithms they design) can 'read' heterogeneous material properties of objects – including density and elasticity, which are measures of deformability or modifiability.[14]

The amplitude of the trace, that is, tells us something about intrinsic features of the material object – that is, features that *resist* deformation. Modifiability is the obverse of resistance to modification; both must be thought together. It is, Derrida emphasised in his reading of Freud's proto-grammatological account of memory traces, *differences* in resistance and *differences* in the 'breaching' forces that produce the trace. This means that form must be thought both in terms of essential modifiability and resistance to modification. As I have argued, an essentially modifiable-retentive form is a trace. Hence, we speak imprecisely when we say that an object, form or substance is modifiable. This way of speaking leaves logical space for non-modifiable objects, forms or substances. To think essential modifiability requires recourse to the notions of trace or text.

To make our grammatological description still more precise, we must note that the experiment does not demonstrate that audible sound produces a spatialised vibration. Rather, the audible sound *modifies* the object's (metastable) vibration – in a way that produces a legible text. What is more, the object's vibration can be the surface of 'inscription' only because the vibration is already textual, essentially retentive and modifiable.

It is true that the object is not *reducible* to this vibrational text, but this does not imply that it is not essentially textual. Again, the obverse of modifiability is resistance to modification. Textual structures imply 'layers', or what Derrida calls elsewhere 'reserves'.[15] If vibration or responsiveness to sound can also tell us about the topological features of the object – that is, its 'non-responsiveness' or resistance to modification – this resistance is not absolute. In general, the modifiability of the text produces effects of surface, effects of inscription, and also effects of time, flux and change, while resistance to modification produces effects of substantiality and depth, effects of space, stability and permanence. The apparent independence of object and trace does not, then, indicate the limit to the trace's generality.

The account of the material trace, equally an account of material form, deconstructs any opposition between form and information. While 'form' is usually said of objects, 'information', the more obviously grammatological notion, is said of messages, data and transmissible, quantifiable differences more generally. The trace, by contrast, requires us to speak of in-formed forms. We have seen that the distinction between form and information collapses in the case of graphic texts – the form of differential, graphic mark is explained by what in-forms the text – but also in the case of tree rings, the grooves on a vinyl record, and the vibrational 'text' formed at the surface of a bag of crisps. But these cases, even if they exemplify the structure of the trace, might still seem exceptional rather than general.

Consider, for example, the distinction between the form of a book (a mid-sized, rectangular 'dry good') and the information it contains (text). The exceptionalism of tree rings (and literary texts) seems to be that they exemplify in their structure the indissociability of form and information. The (external) form of the book (and other apparently non-textual items), by contrast, seems qualitatively different. I have argued in the previous section, however, that the distinction between object and trace is not a difference in form but a topographical difference. Objects and their objective features are generally explicable in terms of the trace structure, though this will not always be obvious. Sometimes, objects will appear as apparently trace-like – nowhere is this more obviously the case than with graphic writing – sometimes they will seem to resist grammatological description.

Even if the foregoing analysis has managed to dispel the distinction between form and information, and between textual and objective form, it is still worth considering the extent to which the *apparent* qualitative difference between writing and other sorts of objects first produced the system of metaphysical oppositions and then re-enforced this distinction. That is, the metaphysics of presence would be an effect of factoring the apparent singularity of the writing.

Distinctively, systems of writing – texts, in the narrow sense – Derrida argues, render the trace visible, makes it appear 'as such'. Written marks, as the 'exteriorization of memory', 'enlarge différance and the possibility of putting on reserve' (OG, 91). But historically, writing also produced the illusion of the distinction between ideality and materiality as the difference between ideally repeatable forms and spatio-temporal individuals; between form (as mark) and matter (as substrate); and between (material) token and (ideal) type. Hence, *textual* form is opposed to the form of the *material*, while the opposition functions to obscure both.

An entire system of metaphysical distinctions, in other words, may be grounded on (flawed) intuitions about the radical formal distinctiveness of graphic writing. Derrida writes that the distinctiveness of graphic writing was to 'make the trace visible "as such"' (OG, 69). That is, the trace appears (at least in its most recognisable, phenomenological form) as graphic writing. However, even in the case of graphic writing, the trace appears 'according to a new structure of non presence' (OG, 91). In other words, the structure of the trace – its *in-formed* form – remains invisible. Hence, its emergent phenomenality does not necessarily work in the service of recognition. Indeed, as Derrida demonstrates, the phenomenological analysis of graphic marks and written texts obscures their (in-formed) structure, while the apparent difference between written marks and other sorts of objects obscures the possibility of thinking the generality of the trace.

To describe texts and matter grammatologically is to make explicit the intrinsic modifiability and retentiveness of the trace structure. If, as Claire Colebrook suggests, a deconstructive materialism is 'a materialism without substance and without objects', this is because as traditionally defined neither 'substance' nor 'object' imply the essential plasticity of the trace structure; and, therefore, neither term is conducive for thinking the complex topographies of the trace.[16]

### Plastic Powers

#### *The Non-graphic Trace and its Limits*

The opening pages of *Of Grammatology* testify to the remarkable expansion of writing to cover not only writing in the narrow sense, and all forms of secondary notation, but also the original processes themselves. Nowhere was the theoretical and deconstructive promise of writing more palpable than in the field of cybernetics.[17]

Writing, in the cybernetic *air du temps*, had already expanded to include the ideas of code and information, which seemed to liberate and disentangle it from its phonocentric, linguistic and indeed anthropocentric determinations. One found the code and the program at work everywhere. The human cognitive and sensory apparatus, expanded by its technical supplements, could now be imagined as operating on similar principles to computers. The discovery of the genetic code, of course, allowed us to see a biological 'program' as the basis of life, providing the blueprint and instructions for its constructions. If the notion of a program and a code communicated with narrow empirical writing, it was through a whole network of isomorphisms and analogies primarily related to the notion of a repeatable form, its combination according to grammatical (syntactical) rules, and perhaps most importantly, the image of memory as graphical inscription. As Derrida argued: 'Whether it has essential limits or not, the entire field of the cybernetic program will be the field of writing' (OG, 9). Cybernetics, then, was already a speculative grammatology, but one that was insufficiently critical. It has not submitted its central concepts, those of code and program, to a deconstructive analysis, to ensure that these were not determined by the very system of oppositions they intended to oust. In other words, cybernetics awaited what grammatology promised to provide, the most general, metatheoretic concept of the gramme.

But, as Catherine Malabou has influentially argued, grammatology was 'programmed to fail'.[18] Malabou does not question the historical productivity of writing as a conceptual 'motor schema'; instead, she argues that its productivity was already exhausted by the time *Of Grammatology* appeared. No genuinely deconstructive concept of writing is possible.

The limits of writing and its generalisability – limits that would also account for the ultimate failure of the cybernetic project –

are, on the one hand, its formality, which limited its deconstructive potential, and relatedly, its rigidity. Writing is too formal; it remains opposed to a material substrate for which it cannot account. And the image of writing qua repeatable form is insufficiently *plastic* to be absolutely general. That is, writing precludes the thought of plasticity, as evidenced by the popular idea of a program as deterministic – and which the idea of the genetic code certainly inherited – and the idea of a generalised writing would require such a deformation and reworking of the concept as to make it no longer recognisable.[19] Writing in its 'essence' is not plastic, and the concept of writing is not plastic enough to overcome its limits.

Interestingly, Malabou is concerned to point out that the transformation of a concept cannot itself be thought in terms of writing. No graphic operation – of grafting or crossing out, inscribing or engraving – can account for this sort of transformation. Rather, we must think of the sort of conceptual transformation implied in terms of expansion or inflation, and account for this possibility by pointing to the essential capacity of concepts to expand, contract and modify their relations to each other. In short, Malabou thinks that grammatology relies upon but leaves unexplained the possibility of generalisation. Deconstruction has no adequate philosophical account of the way that it invents (or displaces) concepts, because it thinks only in terms of the production of texts and not about the plasticity of texts, or indeed, the plasticity of the trace itself: namely, the trace's capacity to appear as something other than an inscription.

For Malabou, to think the trace this narrowly (as inscription) leads us to think of memory in terms of the 'engramme', an engraving or permanent record, or as frayage or path-breaking.[20] But this is a very limited, determined mode of memory. We have learned to think human memory otherwise. Similarly, the thought of the genetic code as inscription leads to think of genetic memory as a rigid, unchangeable biological program. Recent advances in epigenetics undermine this account of genetics.[21] In any case, the model of inscription – which determines the meaning of writing – decisively fails to think the plasticity of the code.

The most important aspect of Malabou's critique of grammatology, in my view, is the claim that relates the limitation of writing's generality to what she calls its graphism. Writing, she argues, is necessarily thought as an incision, engraving, graphic mark –

as frayage and path-breaking. It always assumes the marking or breaching of a more or less passive surface of inscription. As a result, writing can never be general precisely because it can never be sufficiently material.

Malabou's argument is not convincing as a critique of arche-writing – at least if the foregoing analyses of the non-graphic trace have served as any kind of demonstration. It does offer, however, a perspicacious diagnosis of problems with many *accounts* of arche-writing. Indeed, the problem with most interpretations of grammatology is that the trace is thought in terms of graphic inscription. But this precludes, as Malabou demonstrates, the generality of writing. The problem with her argument as a critique of grammatology (rather than of its interpreters) lies with the claim that arche-writing, the most general concept of the gramme, is graphic. It is perfectly true that, if grammatology were an attempt to generalise *graphic* writing, its deconstructive potential would be limited, indeed spent, in advance. It is also perfectly true that generalising the trace and *différance* requires the thought of a non-graphic trace. However, this book's aim has been to demonstrate that arche-writing is no more graphic than non-graphic.

Malabou's critique seems particularly apt for diagnosing a problem with Martin Hägglund's account of the trace. In *Radical Atheism* (2008), Hägglund argues that the trace's generality is grounded in its specification of a constitutively finite form. This form is that of survival. Every trace, in order to be, must inscribe itself. This inscription, however, opens the trace to the threat of erasure.

> Given that every temporal moment ceases to be as soon as it comes to be, it must be inscribed as a trace in order to be at all. This is the *becoming-space of time*. The trace is necessarily spatial, since spatiality is characterized by the ability to remain in spite of temporal succession. The spatiality of the trace is thus a condition for the synthesis of time, since it enables the past to be retained for the future . . . In order to remain – even for a moment – a trace cannot have any integrity as such but is already marked by its own becoming past and becoming related to the future. Accordingly, the persistence of the trace cannot be the persistence of something that is exempt from the negativity of time. Rather, the trace is always in relation to an unpredictable future that gives it both the chance to remain and to be effaced.[22]

In Hägglund's account, the materiality of the trace names the conditions both of its 'survival' and its 'finitude'. The 'arche-materiality' of the trace is meant to testify not only to the constitutive materiality of the trace, but also to the pertinence of the form of the trace to material processes.[23] However, if Malabou's critique is correct, Hägglund's account of arche-materiality testifies to the decisive limits of the trace to account for matter.

If matter designates the condition of the trace's persistence or survival, it cannot, logically, be understood in textual terms. If the trace's survival is always dependent, as Hägglund has argued, on its technical or material substrates, its temporality or *séjour* is conditioned by the resilience of the substrate – qualities, in other words, not on the order of the trace. Matter is *a priori* exterior to the logic of the graphic trace, and hence if Hägglund's aim was to justify Derrida's claim about the generality of the trace, he has demonstrated the opposite. To touch matter, what is required is a *non-graphic* notion of *différance*, or a new motor scheme for thinking materiality as *différance*.

Malabou does not claim that it is implausible to think of materiality in deconstructive terms. Indeed, she endorses the project of thinking materiality in terms of *différance* or the trace – that is, in terms of forms of non-identity that would require us to rethink ontological categories of substance and bodies. For Malabou, *plasticity* is integral to the thought of the non-graphic trace; it allows us to think materiality in a way that is neither constrained by the formal properties peculiar to signifying elements on the one hand, nor to what Derrida called forms of presence on the other.

Heir to the deconstructive notion of writing, but capable of thematising what writing has so far obscured, plasticity names the pure possibility of morphogenesis – the original modifiability of matter. Plasticity makes explicit what is implicit in the empirical image of neuronal plasticity: namely, the intrinsic power of matter to take on, lose and give itself form. Neuronal plasticity gives us a non-graphic model through which to think the retention and appearance of difference as a modification of form.

## The Non-graphic Trace and Neuronal Plasticity

The brain does not encode or retain information in the way that a clay tablet retains marks on its surface. Neurons connect by modifying their resistance. Neuronal matter is formed by and defined in terms of a double capacity for retention: 1) synapses retain modifications by lowering or raising their resistance, and 2) these differences (changes in resistance) themselves form chains, 'linkages' or 'assemblies'. As Malabou writes:

> the model of reformation, of recomposition, substitutes itself for the model of frayage: 'it becomes plausible that such assemblies, made up of oscillatory neurons with high spontaneous activity, could recombine among themselves.' 'Linkages,' 'relationships,' 'spider webs,' such are the configurations that the networks of nerve information take. It appears then that the synaptic openings are definitely gaps, *but gaps that are susceptible to taking on form.* The example of neurobiology is only one example of the fecundity of plasticity in the real. *We could surely call together other examples that today show that traces take on form.*[24]

Malabou takes neuronal plasticity to be exemplary of the non-graphic trace. The structure or configuration of nerves and neurons can be described neither in terms of a form of presence nor in terms of frayage, marks or inscriptions. The connections made and unmade by the brain are so many modifications to the strength of resistance. Such modifications sculpt the brain dynamically.

Malabou is right to say that deconstructive materialism requires thinking the non-graphic trace, but, as I argued in the previous chapter, wrong to think that Derridean writing is graphic. As I have already argued, the Derridean trace is essentially retentive rather than inscriptive: 'Without a trace retaining the other as the other in the same no difference would appear or could do its work' (OG, 62). The inscription proper to the trace or to arche-writing is never graphic, at least in the sense that Malabou gives this term. The material substrates of inscription are heterogeneous traces. Factoring the parasitic structure of the trace, we see that the inscription conditioning the trace's appearance demands the plastic modification of heterogeneous elements. The translation of one 'text', 'chain' or 'pattern' by another entails the original modifiability of the elements.

Writing, for Derrida, is not graphic precisely because it is plastic, where plasticity refers to the essential modifiability of the trace, its 'structural' retentiveness and its openness to reinscription. Texts are themselves the matter or substrate 'in' which other texts are inscribed. Texts, thus, are doubly inscribed – informed-forms or patterned-patterns – and hence indissociably form *and* matter.

Malabou writes of the peculiar philosophical hindsight that allowed her to find, secreted in the texts of Hegel and Heidegger, the explosive conceptual power of plasticity. With similar hindsight and interpretive skill, I argue, we can locate in Derrida's early work the notion of a plastic writing. Drawing out the plasticity of the trace is critical for any adequate account of the grammatological project and its future prospects.

Arche-writing functions as an essential supplement to Malabou's conception of the non-graphic trace, insofar as it offers what seems to me a more precise schema for its structure, making evident the essential connection between plasticity and memory, between retention and modifiability. For Derrida, the reciprocal inscription of difference, which Saussure describes as constitutive of the linguistic sign, modifies and transforms traditional notions of form. Derrida selects 'trace' to designate the function that Saussure attributes to the arbitrary sign as a mechanism of original retention. The trace structure, he argues, allows us to account for the necessity which leads Saussure to speak of the sign-form in terms of imprint: 'Différance is therefore the formation of form. But it is on the other hand the being-imprinted of the imprint' (OG, 69).

In Saussure's account of the sign, its two faces are indissociably bonded; the signified and signifier are differences that appear to be reciprocally 'inscribed'. However, if the form that Saussure describes is constituted by the inscription or imprint of one set of differences in another set of differences, such a mechanism of retention necessarily breaks with any model of empirical inscription (e.g. frayage, engraving). Indeed, as Derrida argues, the indissociable bond that Saussure describes is impossible to account for within a metaphysical framework fixed on the traditional distinction between form and matter. This is the very binary in which Malabou claimed that 'writing' remains caught. As Derrida writes:

> it should be recognized that it is in the specific zone of this imprint and this trace . . . that differences appear among the elements or rather produce them, make them emerge as such and constitute the texts, the chains, and the systems of traces. These chains and systems cannot be outlined except in the fabric of this trace or imprint. (OG, 65)

The forms in question are constituted in and through the 'fabric' of what is always already a trace. The text is a system of traces that always already bears (as its form or structure) the imprint or the trace of other traces. This fabric is both the appearance – the spatialisation and temporalisation – of differential elements and the production of these differential elements through a displacement or modification of what was always already imprinted. 'This last concept [that of the imprint] is thus absolutely and by rights "anterior" to all physiological problematics concerning the nature of the engramme [the unit of engraving]' (OG, 65).

The extent to which Malabou's description of neuronal matter resonates with Derrida's account of textuality and what I have called the 'plastic trace' is remarkable. Consider Malabou's gloss of the Italian neuroscientist and cyberneticist Valentino Braitenburg:

'The "things" and "events" of our experience [...] do not correspond within the brain to individual neurons, but to groups of neurons called cell assemblies.' These groups may form in a single area of the brain, but they may also be formed through an overlap of different areas. The assemblies amount to 'units of meaning as "morphemes" appear in linguistics.' Neuronal assemblies would thus form a logic of signification, creating a 'morphematic' distribution of the configurations at the root of our ideas . . . what Braitenberg and so many others since Hebb call a 'trace' is a modification of form that corresponds to a plastic coding of experience.[25]

Malabou, of course, takes this 'plastic coding of experience' to be non-grammatological because it is decidedly non-graphic. Yet Braitenburg's account of how 'events' are encoded in the brain – via a network or assembly of cells which differentially 'wire together, and fire together', and form distinctive patterns – *is* precisely grammatological, or textual in Derrida's sense. Indeed, the structure of the trace enriches and potentially justifies Braitenburg's analogy of neuronal assemblages to linguistic morphemes. These forms can be 'units of signification' insofar as they are in-formed forms – that is, insofar as they transmit and translate in their very patterning another trace structure.

We can state, then, a grammatological principle with respect to what Malabou calls 'plastic coding': any 'morpheme', or in-formed form – any structure or patterning of differential, contrastive elements – can translate another in-formed form. However, this does not mean it can translate any such form. To 'receive' form, there must be the possibility of a mutual affordance between recipient and donor, host and guest. For example, if phonetic writing could come to 'represent' speech, this is because written marks and their spacing were afforded, shaped to receive, the contrastive patternings of speech. The system of phonetic writing is both the effect and the possibility of its 'plastic coding' by speech.

This kind of retroactive 'programming' – in the cybernetic sense of a feedback loop – requires selection and adaptation. Nor should we think of this adaptation as unilateral. The relationality that affords one text or system of writing to another involves the exchange of form. Saussure describes this exchange of form not only in his description of the relation between signifier and signified, but also in the relations between speech and writing. In the latter case, however, he described the 'usurpation' of speech by writing, the aptitude of writing to reform speech as 'pathological'. Arche-writing, on the other hand, would offer a general account of these constitutive exchanges.

\* \* \*

In this section, I have argued that Malabou's critique of grammatology does not recognise the extent to which arche-writing modifies the image of writing as graphic inscription. Nonetheless, her work is perhaps most valuable in the context of deconstructive materialism not principally for bringing this problem of the apparent graphic limitation of the trace into view, but rather for her inquiry into the notion of plasticity. In this respect, it is less interesting to point out the extent to which Derrida's notion of the trace anticipates Malabou's notion of the non-graphic, plastic trace, than to explore the productive encounter of their ideas.

In the remaining pages, I would like to focus on Malabou's more recent critique of what she calls *productive* plasticity, which she argues characterises many of the neuroscientific accounts of plasticity, but which, I argue, would generalise to arche-writing as the account of the non-graphic trace. I want to consider the extent to which arche-writing limits plasticity to what Malabou characterises as productive plasticity and the deconstructive consequences of factoring 'negative' or destructive plasticity.

## Plasticity, Sur-vival, Destruction

With respect to arche-writing, I have argued that plasticity refers to the double movement of retention and modification that constitutes the operation of the trace. The trace, never present as such, undergoes modification with each reinstantiation. This modification is also the modification of a heterogeneous text. Each translation of the trace rematerialises it in/as the 'body' of a heterogeneous trace. The 'hosting' structure undergoes modification with each retention of the 'parasitic' trace. Erasure, forgetting, modification and supplantation characterise the movement of the trace. However, because erasure or deformation is constitutive of the trace, it is *equally* loss and gain. Or, more precisely, each loss appears to be in the service of a gain, and each destruction, regenerative. The history of exchange and modification between systems of writing suggests a similarly productive view of loss. The developmental entanglement of systems of writing disrupts certain possibilities while producing others; the supplantation of a prior organisation creates the space for new possibilities.

As an example of the productivity of erasure, we can consider Derrida's reading of André Leroi-Gourhan's account of anthropogenesis in *Of Grammatology*. Derrida suggests that the French palaeontologist's account of the reorganisation of the human form can be read as an account of the plasticity of the cybernetic 'program' (OG, 84). In the transition to bipedalism, the entangled circuitry of hand and mouth were partially 'liberated' from their older, determined alimentary and motor functions – making possible new adventures, principal among them language and gesture.[26] The liberation in question depends upon the plasticity of the cortical organisation, its aptitude to take on, give and exchange form – an aptitude already evidenced in the becoming-bipedal of the human. Whatever 'reprogramming' (of the cortex) is entailed in becoming bipedal does not disrupt or modify the prior organisation *in toto*. Thus, liberation describes the conscription of 'older', now anachronistic, circuits into new processes that led to the development of language and gesture.

Leroi-Gourhan famously described the subsequent developments and adventures of the human form as a kind of *technical* recoding or reprogramming of organic functions. The 'exteriorisation' of organic functions (for example in tool-making) marks the possibility of further cortical reorganisations, which will also explain the appearance of writing. As Christopher Johnson summarises Leroi-Gourhan's account of 'the program':

> in a circuit of positive feedback, the complexification of the human animal's modifications of its environment – in particular through the

fine coordination of the hand applied to toolmaking – *retroactively* determines the complexification of the neurological and anatomical apparatus that permits such articulations, and lays the foundations of the mental architecture on which human language is built.[27]

Such retroactive reprogramming entails both the preservation and the erasure (modification) of the prior organisation. However, Derrida does not focus on the question of modification in this context, but on a stretch of argument in *Speech and Gesture* where Leroi-Gourhan seems to consider the possibility of its reversibility. Here, what is in question is the possibility of a return of repressed possibilities. In this case, 'liberation' would not simply name a condition for reprogramming, but also the possibility of a return of *human* possibilities repressed by technical means. This possibility would seem to imply the idea of a 'deeper' organisational memory – beyond the reach of technical prosthesis – an elasticity that sanctions the return of a prior organisation. It is, again, not a question of rewriting what has already been rewritten, but of something like an unwriting or deprogramming.[28]

Derrida refers to the possibility of recovery as 'de-sedimenting' the effects of linear writing's hegemonic hold on the body:

> Leroi-Gourhan recalls the unity, within the mythogram, of all the elements of which linear writing marks the disruption: technics (particularly graphics), art, religion, economy. To *recover* the access to this unity, to this other structure of unity, we must 'de-sediment' four thousand years of linear writing . . . Writing in the narrow sense – and phonetic writing above all – is rooted in a past of nonlinear writing. It had to be defeated, and here one can speak, if one wishes, of technical success; it assured a greater security and greater possibilities of capitalization in a dangerous and anguishing world. But that was not done *one single time*. A war was declared, and a suppression of all that resisted linearization was installed. And first of what Leroi-Gourhan calls the 'mythogram,' a writing that spells its symbols pluri-dimensionally; there the meaning is not subjected to successivity, to the order of a logical time, or to the irreversible temporality of sound. (OG, 86–7)

For phonetic writing to be instituted, writing's non-linear elements had to be 'defeated' – adapted or forced into submission. But this 'war' for linearisation is not a struggle that would only affect technical artefacts. Leroi-Gourhan has taught us to think the extent to which our technical practices remake and reorganise the body. In this case, the de-sedimentation in question 'of four thousand years of linear writing' supposes something like the deprogramming of four thousand years of linearising 'code'.

Derrida questions the premise of this recovery in order to affirm the irreversibility of arche-writing. First, linearisation 'could never happen once and for all'. Derrida underscores again that writing is never purely linear, just as phonetic writing is never purely phonetic. The lost kinaesthetic, sensory and cognitive unities evidenced by non-linear writing (for example, by the glyphs in the Lascaux caves) were, therefore, never finally or completely lost. This is not because of the possibility of a restoration or recovery of the mythical past upon 'liberation' from linear writing, but rather because this past was never (entirely) lost. It survives in/ as the very fabric of the present organisation. Modification is, we have seen, equal parts resistance to modification; the sur-vival of the trace is equally the resistance to modification which conditions all modification.

For Derrida, structural usurpation (of speech by writing, for example) is never final, complete or assured. What is adapted or afforded conditions what it receives. However, Leroi-Gourhan's account seems to suggest something like the *arche-memory* of a system, which always makes possible a return. Whereas Derrida points to everything that linear writing puts in 'reserve', Leroi-Gourhan suggests the conservation of the archaic, the possibility of returning to a prior state.

Like the sort of rigidity that would resist modification altogether, such elasticity would assure the possibility of recovering a more archaic past. But this recovery must assume another, more traditional model for memory than the cybernetic model that Leroi-Gourhan elaborates: namely an archaeological or geological model, as if an original form continued to exist under the sedimented layers which obscure it. The point is that the cybernetic account of a program entails a relation that rewrites its initial conditions, and is hence incompatible with the sort of return Leroi-Gourhan suggests.

The point is not that traces do not dissipate or disappear – cede their place – become illegible or submit to supplantation. After all, this sort of erasure is also the very condition of its appearance. But the trace of the trace cannot, in principle, disappear. The modification entailed by the trace cannot itself be modified in such a way as to erase the history of modification. Or, to put the point more directly, the past, as the history of the present, cannot be erased. *Of Grammatology*'s account of arche-writing precludes the possibility of a return of a past; this would amount to annihilating the trace of the trace, the effects of time and the build-up of memory. If the erasure of the trace is nothing but its modification, then it seems that erasure can no longer signify anything like its disappearance or annihilation. Erasure is never radical, in a sense that would be counter to memory. Resistance to modification, we have seen, is also the condition of modification.

* * *

In Malabou's account of destructive plasticity, she does not criticise the Derridean trace for being too productive. As we have seen, she faults Derrida's notion of the trace for failing to factor in plasticity altogether. It is, rather, accounts of neuronal plasticity that she has in mind, accounts that already assume the non-graphic trace. However, insofar as Derrida's trace is non-graphic, the problem she points to bears directly on arche-writing. In this case, the problem with arche-writing would not be that it is the reduction of *différance* to the graphic trace, but that it is the reduction of *différance* to productive plasticity. What productive plasticity fails to think, in fact, is precisely the annihilation or the erasure of the trace – in a radical sense. Or, put another way, the possibility of a negative 'sculpting' or morphogenetic force that works through erasure and death rather than through memory and life.

Under the title of 'destructive plasticity', Malabou presents, I believe, a formidable challenge to the speculative account of arche-writing I have presented here. The challenge hinges on whether arche-writing is a sufficiently deconstructive principle, on whether it relies, as Malabou claims, on an un-deconstructed account of plasticity. Malabou argues that, from Freud's early work to contemporary neuroscience, accounts of psychic life have relied on the 'indestructability' of the trace, or what I have called its structural 'indefinitude'. This indestructability, we have seen, is not a result of its resistance to change and transformation, but precisely a result of its remarkable capacities for transformation, its 'plastic powers'.

Malabou points to a passage from Freud's 'Thoughts for the Times of War and Death' (1915), which captures the trace's plastic development as a temporal succession that implies the coexistence of the past:

The development of the mind shows a peculiarity which is present in no other developmental process ... Here one can describe the state of affairs, *which has nothing to compare with it*, only by saying that in this case every earlier stage of development persists alongside the later stage which has arisen from it; here succession also involves co-existence, although it is to the same materials that the whole series of transformations has applied.[29]

Now, Freud took this peculiar plasticity of the psychic trace to explain the possibility of regression to an earlier state. For Freud, the past persists in the present not as transformed, but as the past. As we saw above, Derrida locates a version of this Freudian idea in Leroi-Gourhan's account of anthropogenesis and liberation, but argues there that such a recovery is incompatible with the latter's cybernetic notion of program or 'retroaction'. Retroaction, or what is known more familiarly as feedback, assumes a transformation (rewriting) of initial conditions. Adequate to the latter idea, the grammatological trace forecloses the possibility of a regression or a return to a prior state. The structure of the grammatological trace establishes that the past *sur-vives*, that it persists in its modification.[30]

For the grammatologist, the past persists in and through its transformation, and in and through what these transformations hold in reserve. Nonetheless, when Malabou turns from the Freudian trace to the trace of contemporary neuroscientific literature, it is clear that the problem she associates with the productivity of the neuronal trace is linked to a 'continuist' prejudice in both discourses: the idea that 'plasticity displaces but does not annihilate'.[31]

The neurological concept of plasticity ... remains attached to the *positive* values of neuronal construction and configuration, of the creation of a style of being. The two types of cerebral plasticity, constructive and destructive, are never related to each other. Both cases, however, entail an elaboration of form. How can these two plasticities coexist?[32]

The crux of the problem that Malabou describes is that grammatological plasticity – which, I have argued, corresponds to what Malabou calls 'neuronal' plasticity – is too often thought as a power always in the service of greater individuation and differentiation. This is so even when both discourses – grammatology and neurology – gesture towards the possibility of the annihilation of form, and the destruction of the trace.

Malabou notes that, in neuroscientific contexts, the possibility of *another* kind of plasticity is recognised but also, curiously, marginalised. This plasticity is destructive not productive, marked by disjunction rather than continuity, the 'wipeout' of the past rather than its mnemonic preservation. It is evidenced, Malabou argues, following closely the work of Antonio Damasio, in what she calls 'the new wounded', sufferers from neurological disease and trauma.[33] In these 'new wounded', what is evidenced, Malabou claims, is a self that has become unrecognisable to itself, a self cut off from its own past, and the counterfactual future that *this* past would have engendered had psychic-neuronal development continued productively and in a 'healthy' fashion.[34]

Malabou argues that 'under the term neural *plasticity* hides, in fact two plasticities'. One is positive:

> It characterizes the formation process of neural connections and the fact that these connections may be transformed during our lifetimes under the influence of experience ... So in the case of the healthy plastic brain, every kind of event is integrated into the general form or pattern of the connections, and the series of events of our lives constitute the *autobiographical* self.[35]

But there also exists a second kind of plasticity, to which we must have recourse if we are to account not only for the 'destructive power of brain damage' but also for the possibility of recovering from these traumas. 'This negative plastic power consists in the transformation of the patient's previous personality and in the emergence of a new individual proceeding from the *explosion* of the former identity.'[36]

If 'good' plasticity appears as a 'balance between the ability to change and the resistance to change ... [it] can be interrupted by what neurobiologists call "disconnection"'.[37] In the case of destructive 'disconnection', traumatised regions of the brain are excised from its organisation. According to Malabou, this sort of disconnection is incompatible with accounts of 'good' or 'productive' plasticity, because these suppose that the modifications in question are in the service of the prior organisation and continuous with it. By contrast, disconnection implies an abrupt caesura, neither anticipated nor accounted for by the productive model of plasticity. The 'plastic power' in question first cuts off the prior organisation – stages a coup, as it were – and then refashions the remnants into an entirely new, unrecognisable form or organisation.

One is tempted to compare this description to what Derrida refers to in 'Structure, Sign and Play' as 'bricolage'.[38] The term is Claude Lévi-Strauss's, and signified for the latter an analogical way to think of the creative activity of myth-making. Like the crafty 'tinkerer' (or bricoleur) who uses devious or indirect means (*des moyens détourné*) – unfitted, heterogeneous elements – as compared to the artisan, to assemble or create, so does mythical thought express itself indirectly, with heterogeneous elements.[39] On the one hand, arche-writing universalises bricolage; all 'expression' occurs through heterogeneous elements. Improper or indirect expression is the grammatological rule – as is the usurping, or turning (*détournement*) of a process or function to new ends. Destructive plasticity and disconnection, however, point to a form of *détournement* more radical than the one grammatology envisions. If plasticity names two kinds of transformation, conservative and explosive, only the latter threatens the trace's *sur-vival*.

Malabou writes that 'destructive plasticity forms what it destroys',[40] though it would be perhaps more perspicuous to say that it destroys what it (then) forms. It is a matter of a 'plastic explosion that erases any trace and every memory and that destroys any archive'.[41] It is important to be clear: the 'explosion' in question is not the traumatic blow or lesion; it is the brain's *regenerative* response to the trauma.[42] Is there, as Malabou suggests, a plastic power, secreted in matter, which would deny the future its own (recognisable) past by somehow exploding form? And is this plastic power unthinkable in terms of the mnemonic trace? I will take these two questions in turn.

Destructive plasticity is no doubt a speculative concept. Much of Malabou's evidence is drawn from other speculative neurological accounts, particularly those of Damasio, that are controversial in the literature.[43] For example, Damasio uses the case of Phineas Gage, the nineteenth-century railway worker whose skull was impaled by an iron spike, as an example of radically discontinuous psychic 'development'.[44] The events causing the radical change were contingent; the force of their trauma could not be assimilated by the 'plastic power of experience upon neural connections'.[45] The response to these events – the radical transformation they precipitated – involved the 'total loss' of the previous personality.

The problem with the Gage example is that there is absolutely no consensus (either among historians of science or scientists) about what sort of cerebral transformations Gage underwent, what their effects were, and whether such changes were lasting. There is ample evidence that Gage's transformation was far less radical and less discontinuous than Malabou's account implies.[46] Moreover, if she recognises that, whatever the particulars of the case, significant parts of the brain's function remained, speech for example, it is hard to see why Malabou also insists that destructive plasticity implies 'total loss'. Malabou's analysis – and the intuitions that guide it – do not, of course, rest on the particulars of the Gage case, but rather with the general problem of accounting for the 'before' and 'after' of traumatic brain injury.

If 'recovery' might mean cutting off – excision, removal, self-cauterising, quasi-suicide – how would this power, internal to life and neuronal matter, *articulate* with that 'plastic power' of the trace to modify itself continuously even as it resists modification – if it *does* articulate with it? In my view, there are any number of phenomena 'closer to home' that would more readily motivate the thought of destructive plasticity (and solicit the latter's deconstructive potential): these include synaptic 'pruning', apoptosis and cellular autophagy (on which, more below).

Malabou writes that 'destructive plasticity is the biological *deconstruction* of subjectivity'.[47] By this she seems to mean that destructive plasticity places strong deconstructive pressure on biological accounts of subjectivity, which assume exclusively productive plasticity. Destructive plasticity is at once radically constitutive and disruptive in a way that neurobiological accounts fail to adequately factor. But the deconstructive potential of destructive plasticity does not lie in deconstructing accounts of subjectivity per se – including the neurobiological 'self' that depends upon the exclusion of destructive plasticity – but rather with deconstructing the opposition between productive and destructive plasticity.

While Malabou takes plasticity to be the deconstructive heir to grammatological writing, she seems to invite us to continue to think of these two 'kinds' of plasticity in terms of opposition rather than in terms of *différance*. The characteristic deconstructive itinerary, by contrast, would demonstrate that where difference is thought as opposition, it is articulable in another (non-oppositional, non-metaphysical) logic (e.g. iterability, *différance*, the trace).

In this case, the question that Malabou's analysis imposes on speculative grammatology is not whether arche-writing is (exclusively) productive as opposed to destructive, but whether arche-writing allows us to think both 'productive' and 'destructive' plasticity in terms of a single differantial logic. Does writing and sur-vival include un-writing; does the trace factor retentive modifications and also what I will call 'autophagic' (that is, self-consuming) modifications? Malabou's account of deconstructive plasticity demands thinking the 'pharmacological' dimensions of plasticity – a plasticity no more 'good' than 'bad', healthy or pathological. The question that speculative grammatology faces is whether arche-writing can factor both.

Let us assume, then, that modification is not always in the name of retention, that modification may also involve disconnection and erasure that is not at the same time a holding in reserve. Can this 'annihilation' of prior form nonetheless be thought as writing? It seems that the questions that Malabou's account raises are not settled by the account of arche-writing that I have presented in these pages. To Malabou's credit – a testament to the powerful contributions that her thought has made to contemporary deconstructive thought – the problem of destructive plasticity is not easily dispensed with. On the contrary, it seems that the full dimensions of the problem are only just now coming into view. In the space remaining, however, I would like to contribute to formalising the issues by presenting a speculative, grammatological description of destructive plasticity in order to consider whether autophagic modifications are *a priori* incompatible with arche-writing.

## Conclusion: Un-writing and the Speculative Limits of Arche-writing

Autophagy, coming from the Greek word for 'self-eating', is most commonly used to describe 'regenerative' intra-cellular processes that work through self-degradation. Like the sort of destructive plasticity that Malabou describes, autophagy is a process of degeneration in the service of regeneration. Instead of productive transformation, it names destructive creation. However, unlike Malabou's account of destructive plasticity, accounts of autophagic processes in the scientific literature assume that these are always already integrated in the very heart of the 'self' and its 'creation', similar, perhaps, to the way that apoptosis is integrated into immunological functions and synaptic pruning is integrated into neuro-morphogenesis.[48]

To propose the name of a part for the whole, let autophagic modifications refer to all such processes of 'negative' morphogenesis or destructive plasticity. The first thing to note is that such processes are often bound to, and in the service of, individuation and development. Malabou recognises this explicitly, writing with reference to biologist Jean-Claude Ameisen's pioneering work on cell suicide that 'the sculpting of the self assumes cellular annihilation or apoptosis, the phenomena of programmed cellular suicide: in order for fingers to form, a separation between the fingers must also form. It is apoptosis that produces the interstitial void that enables fingers to detach themselves from one another.'[49] Thus, far from being distinct from productive plasticity, destructive and productive processes operate in tandem in producing forms of life.

Autophagic modifications would also seem to include classical accounts of synaptic plasticity and pruning, which explains how the brain modifies itself not only in response to the strength of external stimuli (by strengthening synaptic connections) but to the paucity of stimuli as well. While synaptic plasticity usually refers to the differential modification of connections, 'Hebbian' plasticity refers to the differential destruction of connections. Moreover, in certain cases it appears that such destructive activity is behind modifications to the brain's functional organisation. To take one widely cited example, the unused visual cortex of a blind person's brain is (in reading Braille) recruited for tasks typically consigned to the somatosensory cortex. Here the functional connections between the 'visual' cortex and other areas designated for visual processes are 'destroyed' or 'liberated' in order to adopt a new function.[50]

If destructive and productive processes supplement each other in morphogenetic processes, in what sense can these name distinct and opposing principles? It seems that the articulation or entanglement of productive and destructive plasticity must be thought prior to their difference. But this is again to ask whether arche-writing names only the retentive and productive mode of a general arche-plasticity, or whether it is capable of thinking the entanglement of retentive and autophagic modification. Is arche-writing capable of thinking both writing and un-writing, bio-graphy and necro-graphy?

It is certainly true that, in general, the modifiability condition-ing arche-writing has, in these pages, been thought in terms of a radical hospitality, of 'making room' for the other by adjusting the organisation or relations of 'internal' parts. The force implied by arche-writing would therefore be whatever is sufficient to 'force' the alteration, to 'breach' the resistance to modification and main-tain the modification, but not so great as to destroy the host and the possibility of hosting altogether. Nor, *a fortiori*, has 'making room' been thought above in terms of culling, excision, autophagy or other 'suicidal' processes, which Ameisen has characterised as the 'sculpture' of the living by 'creative death' (*mort créatrice*).[51] Autophagic modification requires us to consider that the hosting structure can be 'forced' to accommodate a text not only by modi-fying the spacing and exchanging form, but through its own sub-traction and elimination, self-excision and self-erasure.

The difficulty lies in the fact that un-writing appears incompat-ible and opposed to the modifiability-retentiveness that appeared to condition the trace. Insofar as texts remain parasitically struc-tured, dependent upon the host, modifiability and retentiveness (the conditions of the trace) always seem more productive than destructive. Autophagic modification, or necro-writing, would name, as Malabou suggests, an anarchival principle, working against the archive as continual accumulation of 'experience' in the interest of regeneration. The modification in question retains, but seems to do so by *other* means.

But what if modifiability always already included destruc-tive necro-writing? In this, life–death would name not opposing principles, but the original modifiability of the living. It is true that plasticity thought from the grammatological trace has so far remained, as Malabou argues, too productive. However, rather than marking its limits, I believe the question of necro-writing points to the fecundity of speculative grammatology and its perti-nence to what recent scholars have called biodeconstruction.[52] It is, in other words, the imminent task of speculative grammatology to think of the life that 'writes' with death and also of the death that 'writes' with life.

## Notes

1. 'La grammatologie élabore une *logique du supplément* où l'accidentalité supplémentaire est originaire. Il s'agit de prendre l'*histoire* du supplément en considération *comme* histoire accidentelle gauche dont résulterait un devenir essential de l'accident – mais il faudrait alors parler *aussi* d'un devenir accidentelle de l'essence. En estompant le plus souvent la spécificité de l'écriture phonologique, en suggérant que la plupart du temps *presque* tout ce qui s'y développe était déjà là avant, en ne faisant donc pas de cette spécificité une question centrale (et toute la grammatologie n'en vient-elle pas d'une certaine manière nécessairement à *reléguer* une telle question?), n'affaiblit- on pas par avance le projet grammatologique?' (Stiegler 1996: 43).
2. Beardsworth (1998: 81).
3. Hägglund (2008).
4. Johnston (2009).
5. Derrida (1982: 65).
6. Derrida (1988: 88–90).
7. On 'topological confusion', see Derrida and Steigler (2002: 108).
8. Derrida and Steigler (2002: 108).
9. The term that Gould and Lewontin select, 'spandrel', has an architectural provenance. It refers to the space between the shoulders of adjoining arches, which forms a sort of triangular figure. The architectural feature is the unintended effect or by-product of other functional features of the building, even though these spandrels have come to be appreciated in their own right. In contemporary evolutionary biology, a spandrel is a phenotypical feature which by definition has not been selected for.
10. Robbins (2019: n.p.).
11. Davis et al. (2014: n.p., my emphasis).
12. Davis et al. (2014: n.p.).
13. Davis et al. (2014: n.p.).
14. Identifying these 'tertiary' traces is not unlike what, in the previous chapter, I described as 'hearing' the 'signature' of an object's weight or density in the sound it makes when it falls. It is notable that the signatures or patterns in-forming objects' visible vibrations are, in these and similar experiments, discovered via machine-learning algorithms. The vibrations in question are not usually visible to the human eye, and the signatures in-forming them are even less so. There are, in other words, many more readable texts than human

readers are capable of reading, though grammatological reason permits us to speculate that algorithmic and human readers operate according to the same principle – recovering the in-forming text.

15. Derrida (1995: 7).

16. Colebrook (2011: 19).

17. For an excellent account of the cybernetics movement and particularly its influence on structuralism and 'French theory', see Geoghegan (2011).

18. Malabou (2007a: 432).

19. Moreover, in a kind of metatheoretic twist, Malabou writes that the condition of possibility for the generalisation of writing is not of the order of writing. We would have to think not only the work of opposition and contrast in altering and transforming the meaning of our words, but the modifiability and plasticity that the expansion of writing seems to require.

20. Malabou (2007a: 438).

21. Malabou (2007b).

22. Hägglund (2016: 39).

23. Hägglund (2011: 61–5).

24. Malabou (2007a: 440, my emphasis).

25. Malabou (2010: 59).

26. Leroi-Gourhan (1993).

27. Johnson (2005: 109).

28. Curiously, Leroi-Gourhan also seems to consider the reverse scenario – an 'ironic' liberation of the human via technical prosthesis, where the human is liberated from form itself. The human form undergoes 'blob-isation' as more and more operations are offloaded to technical prostheses. In this sense, the final 'liberation' of the human is also marked by its disappearance. Both possibilities, Derrida suggests, mistake the plasticity of the 'pro-gramme'.

29. Freud as quoted in Malabou and Johnston (2013).

30. To be sure, the whole idea of 'holding in reserve' and its significance for the development of textual structures or mnemonic systems is a central question for speculative grammatology, one that I cannot pretend to have given adequate attention to in this book. To begin to address this question, one might look in the ample Derridean archive for both his account of general economy and his account of putting on reserve. In this context, Derrida's remarkable essay on Bataille in *Writing and Difference* (1978), 'From Restricted to General Economy: A Hegelianism without Reserve', would be indispensable.

31. Malabou (2012: 84).

32. Malabou (2012: 84).
33. Malabou (2012: 84).
34. Like Malabou, Derrida considers the possibility of a radical anni-
    hilation of the trace – not in *Of Grammatology* but in *Archive
    Fever*. In the latter, Derrida speculates about the possibility of an
    'anarchival principle' that destroys its own trace (Derrida 1996: 7).
    But these references to a speculative, destructive counter-party to the
    mnemonics of the trace do not specify whether factoring this spectral
    'un-writing' requires a modification either to the grammatological
    notion of arche-writing or to the deconstructive notion of the trace.
    If un-writing is *possible*, moreover if it is *evidenced* – even if this evi-
    dence is speculative, as Derrida argues is the case with Freud's death
    drive – the question we face is whether speculative grammatology
    and its account of arche-writing has the resources to factor it.
35. Malabou and Johnston (2013: 58).
36. Malabou and Johnston (2013: 58).
37. Malabou and Johnston (2013: 56).
38. Derrida (1978: 351–70).
39. Lévi-Strauss (1996: 16–17), quoted in Johnson (2012: 358).
40. Malabou and Johnston (2013: 58).
41. Malabou and Johnston (2013: 58).
42. Malabou has also described, in an earlier work (2012), another
    form of destructive plasticity, in this case not the destruction of the
    present self's past, but the erasure of the past's future. Some cells
    seem to exhibit the possibility of a de-differentiation, or a return to
    a pluri-potent state from a more developed state which the latter's
    development made possible.
43. Damasio's (1994) depiction of Gage has been roundly criticised, for
    example by Kotowicz:

    > Damasio is the principal perpetrator of the myth of Gage the psychopath
    > ... Damasio changes [Harlow's] narrative, omits facts, and adds freely
    > ... His account of Gage's last months [is] a grotesque fabrication [insinu-
    > ating] that Gage was some riff-raff who in his final days headed for
    > California to drink and brawl himself to death ... It seems that the
    > growing commitment to the frontal lobe doctrine of emotions brought
    > Gage to the limelight and shapes how he is described. (2007: 125)

44. Damasio (1994).
45. Malabou and Johnston (2013: 57).
46. See Macmillan (2000).

47. Malabou and Johnston (2013: 58).
48. For an account of apoptosis and its integration into vital functions, see Amiesen (2003); Malabou (2007b, 2012); Malabou and Johnston (2013); Vitale (2018).
49. Malabou (2012: 4–5).
50. Sadato et al. (1996).
51. Ameisen (2003).
52. For discussion of the term biodeconstruction, see Vitale (2018) and the excellent conversation between Vicki Kirby, Astrid Schrader and Eszter Timar around the term and its contemporary philosophical range in Kirby et al. (2018).

# Bibliography

Amiesen, Jean-Claude (2003). *La Sculpture du vivant. Le suicide cellulaire ou la mort créatrice*. Paris: Editions du Seuil.

Austin, J. L. (1975). *How to Do Things with Words*. Oxford: Clarendon Press.

Barad, Karen (2003). 'Posthumanist Performativity: Toward an Understanding of How Matter Comes to Matter'. *Signs: Journal of Women in Culture and Society* 28.3: 802–31.

— (2007). *Meeting the Universe Halfway: Quantum Physics and the Entanglement of Matter and Meaning*. Durham, NC: Duke University Press.

— (2010). 'Quantum Entanglements and Hauntological Relations of Inheritance: Dis/continuities, SpaceTime Enfoldings, and Justice-to-Come'. *Derrida Today* 3.2: 240–68.

Beardsworth, Richard (1998). 'Thinking Technicity'. *Cultural Values* 2.1: 70–86.

Benjamin, Walter (2012 [1923]). 'The Translator's Task', trans. S. Rendall, in L. Venuti (ed.), *The Translation Studies Reader*, 3rd edn. London: Routledge, 75–83.

Bennington, Geoffrey (2004). 'Saussure and Derrida', in C. Sanders (ed.), *The Cambridge Companion to Saussure*. New York: Cambridge University Press, 186–204.

— (2016). 'Embarrassing Ourselves'. *Los Angeles Review of Books*, 20 March 2016.

Bhaskar, Roy (2008 [1997]). *A Realist Theory of Science*. New York: Routledge.

Borges, Jorge-Luis (1967). *The Book of Imaginary Beings*, trans. Andrew Hurley. New York: Penguin.

Bornedal, Peter (1997). *Speech and System*. Copenhagen: Museum Tusculanum Press.

Bradley, Arthur (2008). *Derrida's Of Grammatology: An Edinburgh*

*Philosophical Guide*. Edinburgh: Edinburgh University Press.

Braidotti, Rosi (2002). *Metamorphoses: Towards a Materialist Theory of Becoming*. Cambridge: Polity Press in Association with Blackwell Publishers.

Braver, Lee (2007). *A Thing of This World: A History of Continental Anti-Realism*. Evanston: Northwestern University Press.

Bryant, Levi (2009). 'Correlationism and the Problem of Ancestrality'. Blog post. <https://larvalsubjects.wordpress.com/2009/04/03/meillassoux-ii-correlationism-and-the-problem-of-ancestrality/> (last accessed 17 May 2020).

Bryant, Levi, Nick Srnicek and Graham Harman (2011). *The Speculative Turn: Continental Materialism and Realism*. Melbourne: re.press.

Buchler, Justus (ed.) (1940). *The Philosophy of Peirce: Selected Writings*. New York/London: Harcourt Brace/K. Paul, Trench, Trubner and Co.

Burroughs, William S. (1986). 'Ten Years and a Billion Dollars', in *The Adding Machine: Selected Essays*. New York: Seaver Books.

Butler, Judith (1993). *Bodies That Matter: On the Discursive Limits of Sex*. New York: Routledge.

— (1999). *Gender Trouble: Feminism and the Subversion of Identity*. New York: Routledge.

Colebrook, Clare (2011). 'Matter Without Bodies'. *Derrida Today* 4.1: 1–20.

Culler, Jonathan (1982). *On Deconstruction: Theory and Criticism after Structuralism*. Ithaca: Cornell University Press.

Damasio, Antonio R. (1994). *Descartes' Error: Emotion, Reason, and the Human Brain*. New York: Avon Books.

Davis, Abe, et al. (2014). 'The Visual Microphone: Passive Recovery of Sound from Video'. SIGGRAPH. <http://people.csail.mit.edu/mrub/VisualMic/> (last accessed 17 May 2020).

DeLanda, Manuel (2012). '"Any materialist philosophy must take as its point of departure the existence of a material world that is independent of our minds": Interview with Manuel DeLanda', in Rick Dolphijm and Iris van der Tuin (eds), *New Materialism: Interviews & Cartographies*. Ann Arbor: Open Humanities Press, 38–47.

Derrida, Jacques (1967). *De la grammatologie*, Paris: Minuit.

— (1973). *Speech and Phenomena. And Other Essays on Husserl's Theory of Signs*, trans. David B. Allison. Evanston: Northwestern University Press.

— (1978). *Writing and Difference*, trans. Alan Bass. Chicago: University of Chicago Press.

— (1981). *Positions*, trans. Alan Bass. Chicago: University of Chicago Press.

— (1982). *Margins of Philosophy*, trans. Alan Bass. Chicago: University of Chicago Press.

— (1985). 'Des Tours de Babel', trans. Joseph F. Graham, in *Difference in Translation*, ed. Joseph F. Graham. Ithaca: Cornell University Press, 165–207.

— (1986). 'But Beyond . . . (Open Letter to Anne McClintock and Rob Nixon)', trans. P. Kamuf. *Critical Inquiry* 13.1: 155–70.

— (1987). 'To Speculate – on "Freud"', in *The Postcard: From Socrates to Freud and Beyond*, trans. Alan Bass. Chicago: University of Chicago Press, 257–410.

— (1988). *Limited Inc.*, trans. Samuel Weber and Jeffrey Mehlman. Evanston: Northwestern University Press.

—(1989 [1978]). *Edmund Husserl's Origin of Geometry: An Introduction*, trans. John P. Leavey, Jr. Lincoln: University of Nebraska Press.

— (1995). 'Deconstruction and the Other', in Richard Kearney (ed.), *States of Mind: Dialogues with Contemporary Thinkers on the European Mind*. Manchester: Manchester University Press, 156–76.

— (1996). *Archive Fever: A Freudian Impression*, trans. Eric Prenowitz. Chicago: University of Chicago Press.

— (1997). *Of Grammatology*, trans. Gayatri Chakravorty Spivak. Baltimore: Johns Hopkins University Press.

— (2002). 'The Animal that Therefore I Am (More to Follow)', trans. David Wills. *Critical Inquiry* 28.2: 369–418.

— (2005). *On Touching – Jean-Luc Nancy*, trans. Christine Irizarry. Stanford: Stanford University Press.

— (2011). 'Living on Border Lines', in Jacques Derrida (ed.), *Parages*. Palo Alto: Stanford University Press, 103–92.

Derrida, Jacques, and Maurizio Ferraris (2001). *A Taste for the Secret*, trans. Giacomo Donis, ed. Giacomo Donis and David Webb. Cambridge: Polity Press.

Derrida, Jacques, and Bernard Stiegler (2002). *Echographies of Television: Filmed Interviews*. Cambridge: Polity Press.

Derrida, Jacques, and Lawrence Venuti (2001). 'What Is a "Relevant" Translation?'. *Critical Inquiry* 27.2: 174–200.

Descombes, Vincent (1979). *Le même et l'autre: Quarante-cinq ans de philosophie française (1933–1978)*. Paris: Minuit, « Critique »

Dolphijn, Rick, and Iris van der Tuin (2012). *New Materialism: Interviews and Cartographies*. Ann Arbor: Open Humanities Press.

Forster, Michael (2010). *After Herder*. Oxford: Oxford University Press.

Foucault, Michel (1970). *The Order of Things: An Archeology of the Human Sciences*. London: Tavistock/Routledge.

Franklin, Seb (2015). *Control: Digitality as Cultural Logic*. Cambridge, MA: MIT Press.

Gasché, Rodolphe (1988). *The Tain of the Mirror: Derrida and the Philosophy of Reflection*. Cambridge, MA: Harvard University Press.

Geoghegan, Bernard Dionysius (2011). 'From Information Theory to French Theory: Jakobson, Levi-Strauss, and the Cybernetic Apparatus'. *Critical Inquiry* 38.1: 96–126.

Gibson, James J. (1986). *The Ecological Approach to Perception*. Hillsdale, NJ: Lawrence Erlbaum Associates.

Gleick, James (2011). *Information: A History, A Theory, A Flood*. New York: Random House.

Glendinning, Simon (2004). 'Derrida and Language', in J. Reynolds and J. Roffe (eds), *Understanding Derrida*. London: Continuum, 5–14.

Goldgaber, Deborah (2017). 'Programmed to Fail? On the Limits of Inscription and the Generality of Writing'. *Journal of Speculative Philosophy* 31.3: 444–57.

— (2018). 'Derrida and Translation', in J. Piers Rawling and Philip Wilson (eds), *The Routledge Handbook of Translation and Philosophy*. New York: Routledge, I, 141–56.

Gould, S. J., R. C. Lewontin et al. (1979). 'The Spandrels of San Marco and the Panglossian Paradigm: A Critique of the Adaptationist Programme', *Proceedings of the Royal Society B* 205.1161. <https://doi.org/10.1098/rspb.1979.0086> (last accessed 17 May 2020).

Grosz, Elizabeth (1990). 'A Note on Essentialism and Difference', in Neja Gunew (ed.), *Feminism as Knowledge Critique and Constructs*. London: Routledge, 332–44.

Hacking, Ian (1999). *The Social Construction of What?* Cambridge, MA: Harvard University Press.

— (2006). 'Making Up People'. *London Review of Books* 28.16: 23–6. <http://www.lrb.co.uk/v28/n16/ian-hacking/making-up-people> (last accessed 17 May 2020).

Hägglund, Martin (2008). *Radical Atheism*. Stanford: Stanford University Press.

— (2011). 'Radical Atheism and "The Arche-Materiality of Time"'. *Journal of Philosophy: A Cross-Disciplinary Inquiry* 6.14: 61–5.

— (2016). 'The Trace of Time'. *Derrida Today* 9: 36–46 doi:10.3366/drt.2016.0118.

Hanna, Robert (2011). 'The Myth of the Given and the Grip of the Given'. *Diametros* 27: 25–46.

Hanna, Robert, and Evan Thompson (2003). 'The Mind-Body-Body Problem'. *Theoria et Historia Scientiarum* 7: 24–44.

Harman, Graham (2007). *Heidegger Explained: From Phenomenon to Thing*. Chicago: Open Court.

— (2009). *Prince of Networks: Bruno Latour and Metaphysics*. Melbourne: re.press.

Haslanger, Sally (2005). 'Social Construction: Who? What? Where? How?', in Elizabeth Hackett and Sally Haslanger (eds), *Theorizing Feminisms*. Oxford: Oxford University Press, 16–23.

Husserl, Edmund (1983). *Ideas Pertaining to a Pure Phenomenology and to a Phenomenological Philosophy*, trans. R. Rojcewicz and A. Schuwer. Boston: Springer Netherlands.

— (1999). *The Essential Husserl*, ed. D. Welton. Bloomington: Indiana University Press.

— (2000 [1970]). *Logical Investigations*. London: Routledge.

Jacob, François (1973). *The Logic of Life: A History of Heredity*, trans. Betty E. Spillmann. New York: Pantheon Books.

Jakobson, Roman (1963). *Essais de linguistique générale*, « Arguments ». Paris: Minuit.

Jakobson, Roman, and Morris Halle (1956). *Fundamentals of Language*. The Hague: Mouton.

Johnson, Christopher (1993). *System and Writing in the Philosophy of Jacques Derrida*. Cambridge: Cambridge University Press.

— (2005). 'Derrida: The Machine and the Animal'. *Paragraph* 28.3: 102–20.

— (2012). 'Bricoleur and Bricolage: From Metaphor to Universal Concept'. *Paragraph* 35.3: 355–72

Johnston, Adrian (2009). 'Life Terminable and Interminable: The Undead and the Afterlife of the Afterlife – A Friendly Disagreement with Martin Hägglund'. *CR: The New Centennial Review* 9.1: 147–89. doi:10.1353/ncr.0.0063.

Kates, Joshua (2005). *Essential History: Jacques Derrida and the Development of Deconstruction*. Evanston: Northwestern University Press.

Keenan, Hagi (2002). 'Language, Philosophy and the Risk of Failure'. *Continental Philosophy Review* 35.2: 117–33.

Kirby, Vicki (1991). 'Corporeal Habits: Addressing Feminism Differently'. *Hypatia* 6.3: 4–24.

— (1997). *Telling Flesh: The Substance of the Corporeal*. London: Routledge.

— (1999). 'Human Nature'. *Australian Feminist Studies* 14.29: 19–29.

— (2005a). 'Just Figures? Forensic Clairvoyance, Mathematics, and the Language Question'. *SubStance* 34.2: 3–26.

— (2005b). 'When All that is Solid Melts into Language', in Margaret S. Breen and Warren J. Blumenfeld (eds), *Butler Matters: Judith Butler's Impact on Feminist and Queer Studies*. Farnham: Ashgate, 41–56.

— (2006). *Judith Butler: Live Theory*. New York: Bloomsbury Academic.

— (2008). 'Subject to Natural Law: A Meditation on the "Two Cultures" Problem'. *Australian Feminist Studies* 23.55: 5–17.

— (2010). 'Original Science: Nature Deconstructing Itself'. *Derrida Today* 3.2: 201–20.

— (2012). 'Initial Conditions'. *Differences: A Journal of Feminist Cultural Studies* 23.3: 197–205.

— (2016). 'Grammatology: A Vital Science'. *Derrida Today* 9.1: 47–67.

Kirby, Vicki, Astrid Schrader and Eszter Timar (2018). 'How Do We Do Biodeconstruction?' *Postmodern Culture* 28.3. doi:10.1353/pmc.2018.0021.

Kotowicz, Z. (2007). 'The Strange Case of Phineas Gage'. *History of the Human Sciences* 20.1: 115–31. doi:10.1177/0952695106075178.

Leroi-Gourhan, André (1993). *Gesture and Speech*, trans. Anna Bostok Berger. Cambridge, MA: MIT Press.

Lévi-Strauss, Claude (1996 [1962]). *The Savage Mind*. Oxford: Oxford University Press.

Macmillan, Malcolm B. (2000). *An Odd Kind of Fame: Stories of Phineas Gage*. Cambridge, MA: MIT Press.

Maidenbaum, S., R. Arbel, G. Buchs, S. Shapira and A. Amedi (2014). 'Vision through Other Senses: Practical Use of Sensory Substitution Devices as Assistive Technology for Visual Rehabilitation', in *22nd Mediterranean Conference on Control and Automation*. Palermo: IEEE, 182–7.

Malabou, Catherine (2007a). 'The End of Writing? Grammatology and Plasticity', trans. Annjeanette Wiese. *The European Legacy* 12.4: 431–41.

— (2007b). *Les nouveaux blessés: de Freud à la neurologie, penser les traumatismes contemporains*. Paris: Bayard.

— (2009). *Changer de différence: le feminine et la question philosophique*. Paris: Galilée.

— (2010). *Plasticity at the Dusk of Writing: Dialectic, Destruction, Deconstruction*, trans. Carolyn Shread. New York: Columbia University Press.

— (2012). *Ontology of the Accident: An Essay on Destructive Plasticity*, trans. Carolyn Shread. Malden, MA: Polity.

— (2016). 'Où va le matérialisme? Althusser/Darwin'. *Lignes* 3.51: 36–51. <https://doi.org/10.3917/lignes.051.0036>.

Malabou, Catherine, and Adrian Johnston (2013). *Self and Emotional Life*. New York: Columbia University Press.

Maniglier, Patrice (2006). *La Vie énigmatique des signes: Saussure et la naissance de structuralisme*. Paris: Léo Scheer.

— (2007). 'L'ontologie du négatif'. *Methodos* 7. doi:10.4000/methodos.674.

Marrati, Paola (2005). *Genesis and Trace: Derrida Reading Husserl and Heidegger*. Palo Alto: Stanford University Press.

Meillassoux, Quentin (2008). *After Finitude: An Essay on the Necessity of Contingency*, trans. Ray Brassier. New York: Continuum.

Miller, J. Hillis (2011). *Reading Derrida's Of Grammatology*, ed. Sean Gaston and Ian Maclachlan. London: Continuum.

Mueller-Vollmer, Kurt, and Markus Messling (2017). 'Wilhelm von Humboldt', in *The Stanford Encyclopedia of Philosophy*, ed. Edward N. Zalta. <https://plato.stanford.edu/archives/spr2017/entries/wilhelm-humboldt/> (last accessed 17 May 2020).

Pavel, Thomas (1992). *The Feud of Language: History of Structuralist Thought*. New York: Blackwell.

— (1998). *Le Mirage linguistique*. Paris: Minuit.

Reynolds, Jack, and Jon Roffe (eds) (2004). *Understanding Derrida*. London: Continuum.

Robbins, Jim (2019). 'Chronicles of the Rings: What the Trees Tell Us'. *New York Times*, 30 April. <https://www.nytimes.com/2019/04/30/science/tree-rings-climate.html> (last accessed 17 May 2020).

Roden, David (2004). 'Radical Quotation and Real Repetition'. *Ratio: An international journal of analytic philosophy* 17.2: 191–206.

— (2006). 'Naturalising Deconstruction'. *Continental Philosophy Review* 38.1–2: 71–88.

— (2013). 'Nature's Dark Domain: An Argument for a Naturalised Phenomenology'. *Royal Institute of Philosophy Supplement* 72: 169–88. doi:10.1017/S135824611300009X

Rorty, Richard (1977). 'Derrida on Language, Being, and Abnormal Philosophy'. *Journal of Philosophy* 74.11: 673–81.

— (1989). *Contingency, Irony, and Solidarity*. Cambridge: Cambridge University Press.

Sadato, N., A. Pascual-Leone, J. Grafman et al. (1996). 'Activation of the

Primary Visual Cortex by Braille Reading in Blind Subjects'. *Nature* 380.6574: 526–8. doi:10.1038/380526a0.

Sanders, Carol (ed.) (2004). *The Cambridge Companion to Saussure*. New York: Cambridge University Press.

Saussure, Ferdinand de (1967). *Cours de linguistique générale*, ed. Rudolf Engler. Wiesbaden: Otto Harrassowitz, I.

— (1993). *Ferdinand de Saussure: Troisième cours de linguistique générale (1910–1911) d'après les cahiers d'Emile Constantin*, ed. E. Komatsu and R. Harris. Oxford: Pergamon.

— (2002). *Ecrits de linguistique générale*. Paris: Gallimard.

— (2006). *Writings in General Linguistics*, ed. S. Bouquet, R. Engler and C. Sanders. New York: Oxford University Press.

— (2011 [1959]). *Course in General Linguistics*, ed. Perry Meisel and Haun Shaussy, trans. Wade Baskin. New York: Columbia University Press.

Schwartz, Jeffrey, and Sharon Begley (2002). *The Mind and the Brain: Neuroplasticity and the Power of Mental Force*. New York: Harper Perennial.

Searle, John R. (1977). 'Reiterating the Differences: A Reply to Derrida'. *Glyph* 2: 198–208.

— (1980). 'Minds, Brains and Programs'. *Behavioral and Brain Sciences* 3: 417–57.

— (1989). 'Artificial Intelligence and the Chinese Room: An Exchange'. *New York Review of Books* 36.2: 4.

— (1994). 'Literary Theory and Its Discontents'. *New Literary History* 25.3: 637–67.

Seebohm, T. M. (1995). 'The Apodicticity of Absence', in W. R. McKenna and J. C. Evans (eds), *Derrida and Phenomenology*. Dordrecht: Springer, 185–200.

Sellars, Wilfrid S. (1956). 'Empiricism and the Philosophy of Mind'. *Minnesota Studies in the Philosophy of Science* 1: 253–329.

Shannon, Claude E., and Warren Weaver (1949). *A Mathematical Model of Communication*. Urbana: University of Illinois Press.

Siewert, Charles (2011). 'Consciousness and Intentionality', in *The Stanford Encyclopedia of Philosophy*, ed. Edward N. Zalta. <http://plato.stanford.edu/archives/fall2011/entries/consciousness-intentionality/> (last accessed 17 May 2020).

Smith, James K. A. (2005). *Derrida: Live Theory*. New York: Continuum.

Spivak, Gayatri (1980). 'Revolutions That as yet Have no Model: *Limited Inc.*'. *Diacritics* 10.4: 29–49.

— (1989). 'In a Word', interview with Eileen Roney. *Differences* 1.2: 124–56.

Staten, Henry (2009). 'Writing: Empirical, Transcendental, Ultratranscendental'. *CR: The New Centennial Review* 9.1: 69–86.

Stawarska, Beata (2015). *Saussure's Philosophy of Language as Phenomenology: Undoing the Doctrine of the Course in General Linguistics*. New York: Oxford University Press.

Stiegler, Bernard (1996). *La Technique et le temps II*. Paris: Galilée.

Tauber, Alfred I., and Scott H. Podolsky (1994). 'Frank Macfarlane Burnet and the Immune Self'. *Journal of the History of Biology* 27.3: 531–73.

Vitale, Francisco (2018). *Biodeconstruction: Derrida and the Life Sciences*. Albany: SUNY Press.

Weber, Samuel (1976). 'Saussure and the Apparition of Language: The Critical Perspective'. *Modern Language Notes* 91.5: 913–38.

— (2001). *Institution and Interpretation*. Stanford: Stanford University Press.

Wheeler, Samuel (2000). *Deconstruction as Analytic Philosophy*. Stanford: Stanford University Press.

Wilson, Elizabeth A. (1998). *Neural Geographies: Feminism and the Microstructure of Cognition*. London: Routledge.

— (1999). 'Introduction: Somatic Compliance – Feminism, Biology and Science'. *Australian Feminist Studies* 14.23: 7–18.

— (2004a). 'Gut Feminism'. *Differences: A Journal of Feminist Cultural Studies* 15.3: 66–94.

— (2004b). *Psychosomatic: Feminism and the Neurological Body*. Durham, NC: Duke University Press.

Wolfe, Cary (2009). 'Meaning as Event-Machine, or Systems Theory and "the Reconstruction of Deconstruction"', in Bruce Clarke and Mark B. N. Hansen (eds), *Emergence and Embodiment: New Essays on Second-Order Systems Theory*. Durham, NC: Duke University Press, 220–45.

— (2010). *What Is Posthumanism?* Minneapolis: University of Minnesota Press.

Young, Iris Marion (2005). *On Female Body Experience: "Throwing Like a Girl" and Other Essays*. Oxford: Oxford University Press.

Zahavi, Dan (2008). 'Internalism, Externalism, and Transcendental Idealism'. *Synthese* 160.3: 355–74.

— (2016). 'The End of What? Phenomenology vs. Speculative Realism'. *International Journal of Philosophical Studies* 24.3: 289–309.

# Index

CPSIA information can be obtained
at www.ICGtesting.com
Printed in the USA
JSHW041550091220
10136JS00004B/16